GREAT PERFORMANCES

A Celebration

A THIRTEEN/WNET SERIES ON PBS

COMMEMORATING TWENTY-FIVE YEARS

GREAT
PERFORMANCES

A Celebration

Preface by Meryl Streep
Foreword by Wendy Wasserstein

JENNIFER DUNNING, JOSEPH McLELLAN, STEVEN WINN

BAY
BOOKS

SAN FRANCISCO

For information, address:
BAY BOOKS & TAPES, INC.
555 DE HARO ST., SUITE 220
SAN FRANCISCO, CA 94107

Publisher: *James Connolly*
Editorial Director: *Pamela Byers*
Art Director: *Jeffrey O'Rourke*
Project Editor: *Mark Brokering*
Editorial Assistant: *Sabrina Rood-Sinker*
Proofreader: *Marianna Cherry*
Copy Editor: *Nancy Palmer Jones*
Book and Cover Design: *Shelly Meadows / Homefire*
Production Assistant: *Kristen Wurz*
WNET Liaison: *Bill O'Donnell*
Editorial Researcher: *Kerry Ashton*
Photo Researcher: *Peter Levy*

Educational and nonprofit groups
wishing to order this book
at attractive quantity discounts may contact:
BAY BOOKS & TAPES, INC.
555 DE HARO ST., SUITE 220
SAN FRANCISCO, CA 94107

Library of Congress Cataloguing-in-Publication Data

Dunning, Jennifer.
    Great performances : a celebration / Jennifer Dunning, Joseph McLellan,
    Steven Winn : foreword by Wendy Wasserstein.
            p.   cm.
    Includes index.
    ISBN 0-912333-55-3 (pbk.)
    1. Great performances (Television program) 2. McLellan, Joseph. 3. Winn, Steven.
    I. Title.
    PN1992.77.G694D86   1997
    791.4572—dc21

Bay Books & Tapes, Inc.

ISBN 0-912333-55-3

Printed in China
10 9 8 7 6 5 4 3 2 1

Right: Director's Board from Big Blonde.

Distributed to the trade by Publishers Group West

"The wonderful thing about PBS's GREAT PERFORMANCES *is that quality is built into every show—a sense of it being special, one of a kind. As a performer, there are few restrictions, and one is given every encouragement to do what one loves to do most. So, whether you are the entertainer, or simply being entertained, it's a 'turn on' either way."* —JULIE ANDREWS

"I love how the program works to choose the best and most representative pieces from each dance company that appears. This is so important in preserving dance in this country as it progresses through the decades and in capturing the unique essence of each company. You feel you are a part of something much larger than your individual performance when dancing on this program—a part of the history of this art form."
—LESLIE CAROTHERS, *Principal Dancer with the Pennsylvania Ballet, formerly with the Joffrey Ballet*

"GREAT PERFORMANCES may be the most tasteful and well crafted performance series on television. It was a joy and an honor to work with the staff and producers and to have our 'Peter, Paul & Mary: Lifelines' be a part of their ongoing efforts." —PETER YARROW

"GREAT PERFORMANCES has been a part of my life from its beginning twenty-five years ago. Dance being my field, I want to single out the great tribute to Antony Tudor, choreographer, at American Ballet Theatre from 1940 until his death in 1987. It was beautifully danced, sensitively filmed, and the great artists who spoke were illuminating. Thank you, Channel Thirteen."
—SALLY BRAYLEY BLISS, TRUSTEE, THE ANTONY TUDOR BALLET TRUST

"My career was bumping its head on the CBS ceiling when Jac Venza called. He invited me to become Series Producer of *Dance in America*, the first television series dedicated to concert dance. I accepted, and years later a friend would tell me, 'Of course you realize that was the single most important decision of your life.' Twenty-two years later, my gratitude continues to Jac and America's dance treasures for my great good fortune." **—MERRILL BROCKWAY, PRODUCER**

*"*DANCE IN AMERICA *had an impossible task—to capture the uncapturable. We, the doubting dancers, moaned constantly about air conditioning, re-choreographing for the camera, endless warmups and endless takes, all for a medium that could never truly understand us. Imagine our horrified delight when they succeeded!"*
—JANET EILBER, **Principal Dancer with the Martha Graham Dance Company**

"In its twenty-five years on PBS, GREAT PERFORMANCES *has made dance on television a way of life, not only for viewers, but also for the dance community. This has often been a herculean task, especially because it had to be accomplished despite ever-shrinking funding. For their success, everyone owes them a great debt."* —MIKHAIL BARYSHNIKOV

"GREAT PERFORMANCES is a national treasure. Every year, it brings the joy of the performing arts to millions of people, building new audiences and inspiring the next generation of performers. I'd hate to imagine television without it." —ITZHAK PERLMAN

"I wrote [the theme music for GREAT PERFORMANCES] in modules, actually, so that it could be adjusted for each individual presentation without having to be re-recorded. There is one amusing note, though: Because my credit at the end of each show always read, 'Music by John Corigliano,' you can't imagine how many times I was congratulated for writing Don Giovanni, Sleeping Beauty, and other famous pieces performed on the series. I must confess, I never denied it!" —JOHN CORIGLIANO, COMPOSER

"Working with the GREAT PERFORMANCES team to create Thomas Hampson: I Hear America Singing has been one of the most fulfilling projects in my artistic life. WNET/Thirteen and GREAT PERFORMANCES remain singular in their courage, creative vision, and commitment to preserving public access to the wonderful world of the humanities. Their partnership helped me to realize my dream of sharing with a wide spectrum of Americans my passion for our nation's poetry, visual art, and song in a form that was entertaining as well as educational. I was energized and inspired by the collaboration!" —THOMAS HAMPSON

"PBS's GREAT PERFORMANCES series has brought the finest jewels from the world of the performing arts to the lives of millions. What an honor for me to have played a small role in several of their outstanding productions. And I look forward to many more glorious moments captured by GREAT PERFORMANCES."
—JULIE KENT, DANCER WITH THE AMERICAN BALLET THEATRE

"AT A TIME WHEN BUDGET CUTS ARE THREATENING THE VERY EXISTENCE OF THE ARTS, IT'S IMPORTANT TO RECOGNIZE HOW A SERIES LIKE **GREAT PERFORMANCES** ENRICHES THE LIVES OF SO MANY. WHETHER THROUGH CONCERTS, PLAYS, EVENINGS OF DANCE, OR RETROSPECTIVES, IT EMBODIES THE VERY IDEAL OF TELEVISION—TO EDUCATE NOT ONLY THE MIND, BUT THE SPIRIT." —JESSYE NORMAN

"What a privilege to have shared the vision that values excellence over expedience, merit over mediocrity, and culture over commerce. Happy anniversary, GREAT PERFORMANCES." —Kirk Browning, Director

"A standard of vision, excellence and taste was established and maintained by GREAT PERFORMANCES decades ago. It helped set the tone for my own ambitions in television. Being part of the team that brings that to life has provided me with some extraordinary artistic opportunities. It has enriched my soul." —*Matthew Diamond, Director*

"There's nothing like a 'live' performance while it's happening. But unlike a movie, when it's over it's gone for good, and sometimes that's heartbreaking. Fortunately GREAT PERFORMANCES has helped record and save forever a variety of American cultural experiences. As an artist and an audience they have my thanks." —ROBERT ALTMAN

GREAT PERFORMANCES
Table of Contents

THIS PAGE, TOP TO BOTTOM: Jason Robards and Colleen Dewhurst in *You Can't Take It with You*; Ken Page in Duke Ellington's *The Music Lives On*; The New York City Ballet in Balanchine's *Serenade*; Sally Kellerman as Hazel Morse in *Big Blonde*, adapted from a Dorothy Parker story; Tommy Tune and Drew Barrymore in "Celebrating Gershwin"; The Mark Morris Dance Group performs *Prelude*. PREVIOUS PAGES: Mark Rylance stars in *Henry V* at Shakespeare's Globe opening season.

THIS PAGE, TOP TO BOTTOM: Danitra Vance welcomes slaves to *The Colored Museum*; Michael Feinstein and Liza Minnelli in "Celebrating Gershwin"; Monteverdi's *The Coronation of Poppea*; Ralph Fiennes in "A Dangerous Man: Lawrence After Arabia"; Linda Ronstadt and the mariachi band in "Canciones de Mi Padre"; Diane Venora and Kevin Kline in *Hamlet*.

FOREWORD

∽

WHILE I WAS LOBBYING IN CONGRESS FOR THE NATIONAL ENDOWMENT FOR THE ARTS, A well-informed senator remarked to me, "You know my wife and I love the ballet and our daughter takes lessons, but the arts are elitist." The triumph of twenty-five years of GREAT PERFORMANCES is the total negation of that statement. GREAT PERFORMANCES has provided a stage on which the best American artists have helped define our national culture. The opera, dance, and theater shown on GREAT PERFORMANCES, far from being elitist, are the soul of the nation.

The artists in this book have performed the world's greatest hits. Just flipping through, you can find Kevin Kline playing Hamlet, Lena Horne singing Rodgers and Hart, Stephen Sondheim's *Sweeney Todd,* Wagner's complete *Ring* cycle, and Mikhail Baryshnikov demonstrating George Balanchine's choreography. If it had not been for public television, most of these great performances would live today only in the memories of those few lucky enough to have seen them in the theater. After all, there's nothing quite so tantalizing as hearing, "You should have seen Suzanne Farrell dance Balanchine, or Blythe Danner in *Eccentricities of a Nightingale.*" And there's nothing quite so frustrating as the inevitable follow-up: "It's a pity you weren't there because no one will ever be quite that great again." But because these evenings have been captured on film and video and broadcast on GREAT PERFORMANCES, they will live in the memories of the many thousands who have "been there," as some of American culture's most memorable moments during the past twenty-five years have made their way into our homes.

My connection to GREAT PERFORMANCES is a very personal one. To this day, I believe I am a playwright because Jac Venza chose to produce my first play, *Uncommon Women and Others,* for GREAT PERFORMANCES. Of course, I'm also a playwright because I enjoy organizing action in small dark places and inviting a few people in to laugh, listen, and, hopefully, be moved. Most playwrights have a similar history. Mine differs in my connection to a man to whom I once gave a "K" for Christmas (since his name is spelled Jac without a "K").

In 1977 Jac Venza, executive producer of GREAT PERFORMANCES, saw my off-Broadway play, an all-female reminiscence of my years at Mount Holyoke College. It starred, among others, Swoosie Kurtz, Jill Eikenberry, Glenn Close, Alma Cuervo, Ann Levine Thompson, and Ellen Parker. We were mostly in our late twenties and at the beginning of our lives in the theater. The play had received very favorable notices but was on just a two-week run at New York's Phoenix Theater. Jac believed that the play represented a new generation

LEFT: Blythe Danner, Nancy Marchand, and Cynthia Nixon from *Kiss, Kiss Dahlings,* seen on "GREAT PERFORMANCES 20th Anniversary Special," are flanked by director Gerald Gutierrez and playwright Wendy Wasserstein

of voices in American theater and that these young actors were of a caliber worthy of record. One of Jac's many gifts, which becomes apparent as you look through this book, is his ability to match his contagious enthusiasm for the classics with an unrelenting support for the future.

Glenn Close was unable to remain in the cast of *Uncommon Women and Others,* so her part was taken by my drama school classmate Meryl Streep. We shot the play over the course of a week at Trinity College, Hartford, using the Connecticut Public Television studios on the campus. For all of us, it was a seminal experience, almost a point of debarkation for our careers. Whether we continued in theater, film, or television, our purpose as artists became to continue to create work of the standard set for us by that production. The kind of respect for potential and craft demonstrated by the GREAT PERFORMANCES team is unforgettable in the life of an artist.

One of my greatest joys now is to meet young playwrights who became interested in the theater because they saw my play on GREAT PERFORMANCES. "I didn't know there were plays about people like me," one aspiring writer said. "And then I started watching all these Shakespeare plays and Shaw and thought, like, they were great!"

That's the point, isn't it! These television shows are, "like, great." There's no false advertising here. Moreover, I'm sure that this story about the young writer and my play can be repeated by a young dancer in Texas who saw a Paul Taylor dance for the first time on GREAT PERFORMANCES or by the musician who saw Itzhak Perlman play. These television programs have engendered a future generation of American artists and audiences. No other television station, even among the new world of five-hundred-channel satellite dishes, has shown this kind of commitment to the arts.

Looking through this gathering of artists and their works, one wishes GREAT PERFORMANCES could bring them all together for the most gala of galas. Each offering brings a little gasp of anticipation and awe. This book, in fact, is a great celebration of its own, gathering together all the world's finest performing artists to prove that the performing arts are not only central to American life but also among our greatest achievements. Over the past twenty-five years, Jac Venza and GREAT PERFORMANCES have made these landmark ballets, operas, and plays accessible to the greatest number of viewers through public television. It is the perfect confluence of the artist, the electronic medium, and the audience.

I look forward to leafing through this book again and again. If I can never leap like Baryshnikov, conduct like Bernstein, or write like Tennessee, at least I know where I can see their greatest work—and I am eternally grateful.

—WENDY WASSERSTEIN
September, 1997

PREFACE

WHEN I BEGAN AS A STUDENT AT THE YALE SCHOOL OF DRAMA, A NEW SERIES WAS BEGINNING on public television—one that would become the longest-running dance, music, and drama series in the country. That series was, and is, GREAT PERFORMANCES, and we're here to celebrate its 25th anniversary.

GREAT PERFORMANCES played an important role at the beginning of my career. Just after I graduated, one of the first plays I did in New York—a Civil War melodrama called Secret Service—was taped for the series in 1976. It was the first time I ever appeared in front of a camera—and got paid for it.

A year later, I appeared again on the series in Wendy Wasserstein's *Uncommon Women and Others,* one of her first plays. That's the magic of GREAT PERFORMANCES. It's a record of all those "great performances" that would have just floated off into the air.

GREAT PERFORMANCES has pulled that magic from the air and made it permanent, giving us a record of artists doing what they do best. And in honor of the series' 25th anniversary, what you will find in the following pages of *GREAT PERFORMANCES: A Celebration* is a look back at the highlights, including hundreds of breathtaking photos as well as memories and anecdotes from the people who were involved in the programs—stories about their lives in art that show us the art in life.

That's what GREAT PERFORMANCES has been doing for the last 25 years, and what we hope they will be doing for the next 25. Happy anniversary, GREAT PERFORMANCES!

—MERYL STREEP
September, 1997

INTRODUCTION

How It Began, What We Intended, What We Accomplished, What We've Learned

—⚭—

THROUGHOUT ITS EARLY YEARS, AMERICAN TELEVISION WAS AN UNLIKELY PLACE FOR THE fine arts to flourish. In fact, it would take a complete reexamination of television's potential before the arts could find a home in the American mass media. When I began my career in commercial television in the early 1950s—first as a designer and then as a director and producer at CBS—I worked mainly with prime-time entertainment programs, but I was also drawn to such atypical projects as Bernstein's children's concerts, the *Omnibus* series, and the minimal arts programming produced for Sunday mornings. These offerings were the rare exceptions in the overall schedule, and a television appearance by a classical musician, opera singer, or dancer (usually on a variety show) often required that the artist adapt or abridge his or her performance in order to make it palatable for the largest possible audience.

Yet by 1972, two key elements had moved into alignment, allowing the creation of the first season of what would eventually evolve into the public television series called GREAT PERFORMANCES. The first factor was the establishment of a noncommercial television broadcast system, and the second was postwar America's dazzling preeminence in theater, music, and dance, with American artists and arts organizations acclaimed not only at home but the world over. New York City, where GREAT PERFORMANCES is produced, had evolved into an arts capital on an equal footing with any of the legendary international cultural centers.

Despite this acclaim, it was still true that even the longest run at the largest theater could reach only a comparatively small audience, and there was no national platform for showcasing this dynamic explosion of performing arts activity. An experimental solution finally arrived in the form of the Ford Foundation's visionary commitment to National Educational Television (NET). I joined the television professionals who had been engaged to lay the necessary groundwork for NET, and my goal was to persuade artists (and the related unions and guilds) to re-envision television not simply as a vehicle for lowest-common-denominator entertainment but as a legitimate venue for unencumbered expression. And with the Johnson administration's creation of the National Endowment for the Arts, a federal agency was at last endorsing and supporting this quest to extend the impact of the arts in America.

LEFT: Jac Venza, Executive Producer of GREAT PERFORMANCES.

So when people ask about the secret to GREAT PERFORMANCES' longevity, it is really quite simple: for the first time, this series asked artists to appear on prime-time television to do what they had spent their lives excelling in, performing classics as well as new works from new voices. Our primary achievement as a fresh breed of producer-directors working in public television was to dispel the unhappy memories of artists' abbreviated appearances as novelty acts wedged among jugglers and acrobats.

Since live performance is the most ephemeral of the arts, the focus of GREAT PERFORMANCES has ultimately been to extend (but not replace) the experience of live theater, live dance, live concert music, and live opera. And in the process of experimenting with the many ways of translating live performance for television, the series' extraordinary team of producers has created the most valuable performing arts archive of the twentieth century. Looking back, my staff producers and I are proud of the number of major choreographers, dancers, directors, playwrights, actors, composers, musicians, singers, and conductors who at the conclusion of their first experience with GREAT PERFORMANCES have immediately begun discussing plans for their next collaboration.

In the series' early years, the positive word of mouth was especially important in opening doors to the world's leading performing artists and arts organizations. It is impossible to measure the contributions of all of these artists over twenty-five years, especially since everyone has been willing to put monetary considerations aside. The series has become a primary place where new audiences for the performing arts are nurtured, and it is especially gratifying for me to encounter young talents who confess that their first exposure to theater, music, or dance was at home watching GREAT PERFORMANCES on PBS.

The belief that unified all the funders during public television's early years was that the performing arts provided both enrichment and education for American society. The profit motive was set aside—something that was impossible for commercial television even to consider—and the quality and uniqueness of the artist's voice took precedence over the size of the viewing audience. Fortunately,

through the intervening years, we have not been alone in upholding these beliefs, for GREAT PERFORMANCES would never have been able to survive for as long as it has without the enduring support of PBS, the Corporation for Public Broadcasting, the National Endowment for the Arts, and a dedicated group of foundations and private individuals. In addition, the series has found partners in some of America's leading corporations, who took the initiative to expand their customary support of the arts to include television.

H. L. Mencken once said that no one ever went broke underestimating the intelligence of the American people. I believe that GREAT PERFORMANCES is celebrating twenty-five years on public television precisely because we have respected that intelligence. In 1972, we put our faith in America's high regard for imagination, creativity, and innovation. And now, looking back to our beginnings as 1997 draws to a close, I think it is safe to say that this faith has been amply rewarded.

—JAC VENZA
Executive Producer

GREAT PERFORMANCES
Awards

DIA = DANCE IN AMERICA
LFLC = LIVE FROM LINCOLN CENTER

1975–1976

AMERICAN BALLET THEATRE, LFLC
Swan Lake
EMMY (CLASSICAL PROGRAM)

JENNIE: LADY RANDOLPH CHURCHILL
EMMY (COSTUME DESIGN—JANE ROBINSON,
JILL SILVERSIDE)

MARTHA GRAHAM DANCE COMPANY, DIA
CHICAGO INTERNATIONAL FILM FESTIVAL

NEW YORK PHILHARMONIC
Bernstein
EMMY (CLASSICAL MUSIC PROGRAM)

1976–1977

AMERICAN BALLET THEATRE, LFLC
Giselle
EMMY (CLASSICAL PROGRAM)

DANCE THEATRE OF HARLEM, DIA
CHICAGO INTERNATIONAL FILM FESTIVAL
(AWARD PRESENTED IN 1980),
9TH ANNUAL DANCE, FILM AND VIDEO
FESTIVAL (AWARD PRESENTED IN 1980)

TRAILBLAZERS OF MODERN DANCE, DIA
Documentary
9TH ANNUAL DANCE, FILM AND VIDEO
FESTIVAL (AWARD PRESENTED IN 1980)

1977–1978

THE ROYAL FAMILY
EMMY (SUPPORTING ACTRESS—EVA
LE GALLIENNE)

SAN FRANCISCO BALLET: *ROMEO AND JULIET*, DIA
EMMY (SET DESIGN/COSTUMES—WILLIAM
PITKIN)

VERNA: USO GIRL
EMMY (SUPPORTING ACTOR—HOWARD
DA SILVA)

1978–1979

**CHOREOGRAPHY BY BALANCHINE—PART 3
WITH THE NEW YORK CITY BALLET,** DIA
CHICAGO INTERNATIONAL FILM FESTIVAL,
DIRECTOR'S GUILD OF AMERICA

**CHOREOGRAPHY BY BALANCHINE—PART 4
WITH THE NEW YORK CITY BALLET,** DIA
EMMY (CLASSICAL PROGRAM)

**MARTHA GRAHAM DANCE COMPANY:
CLYTEMNESTRA,** DIA
CHICAGO INTERNATIONAL FILM FESTIVAL

1979–1980

PAVAROTTI IN CONCERT, LFLC
New York Philharmonic
EMMY (INDIVIDUAL ACHIEVEMENT:
CREATIVE TECHNICAL CRAFTS)

1980–1981

**NUREYEV AND THE JOFFREY BALLET:
IN TRIBUTE TO NIJINSKY,** DIA
EMMY (LIGHTING DIRECTION—RALPH HOLMES)

**THE SPELLBOUND CHILD
WITH THE NEW YORK CITY BALLET,** DIA
DIRECTOR'S GUILD OF AMERICA

**THE TEMPEST:
LIVE WITH THE SAN FRANCISCO BALLET,** DIA
EMMY (COSTUME DESIGN—WILLA KIM)

1981–1982

DANCE IN AMERICA SERIES
PEABODY AWARD BROADCASTING AWARD

**THE MAGIC FLUTE WITH THE NEW YORK CITY
BALLET,** DIA
EMMY (TAPE SOUND MIXING)

1982–1983

NEW YORK PHILHARMONIC, LFLC
Mehta
EMMY (INDIVIDUAL PERFORMANCE—
LEONTYNE PRICE)

1983–1984

BALANCHINE: PARTS I AND II, DIA
Documentary
CHICAGO INTERNATIONAL FILM FESTIVAL,
27TH ANNUAL INTERNATIONAL FILM AND
TELEVISION AWARDS OF NEW YORK,
MONITOR AWARDS (5)

PLÁCIDO DOMINGO CELEBRATES SEVILLE
Levine, Vienna Symphony
EMMY (CLASSICAL PROGRAM)

**SAN FRANCISCO BALLET:
A SONG FOR DEAD WARRIORS,** DIA
EMMY (CHOREOGRAPHY—MICHAEL SMUIN),
EMMY (CLASSICAL MUSIC/DANCE
PROGRAMMING-DIRECTING—MERRILL
BROCKWAY), MONITOR AWARD

1984–1985

**BARYSHNIKOV BY THARP
WITH AMERICAN BALLET THEATRE,** DIA
EMMY (CHOREOGRAPHY—TWYLA THARP), EMMY
(DIRECTING), EMMY (LIGHTING DIRECTION)

RIGOLETTO
Chailly, Vienna Philharmonic
EMMY (CLASSICAL MUSIC/DANCE
PROGRAMMING-PERFORMING—LUCIANO
PAVAROTTI AS DUKE OF MANTUA)

**SWEENEY TODD:
THE DEMON BARBER OF FLEET STREET**
EMMY (DIRECTING—TERRY HUGHES), EMMY
(PERFORMANCE—GEORGE HEARN), EMMY
(VIDEOTAPE EDITING—JIMMY B. FRAZIER)

1985–1986

CAVALLERIA RUSTICANA
EMMY (CLASSICAL MUSIC/DANCE
PROGRAMMING-DIRECTING—FRANCO ZEFFIRELLI)

**CHOREOGRAPHY BY JEROME ROBBINS
WITH THE NEW YORK CITY BALLET,** DIA
CHICAGO INTERNATIONAL FILM FESTIVAL,
CINE AWARD, INTERNATIONAL FILM & TV
FESTIVAL OF NEW YORK

**DANCE THEATRE OF HARLEM
IN *A STREETCAR NAMED DESIRE*,** DIA
CHICAGO INTERNATIONAL FILM FESTIVAL,
GOLDEN PRAGUE FESTIVAL

THE GOSPEL AT COLONUS
INTERNATIONAL FILM & TV FESTIVAL
OF NEW YORK

LAURENCE OLIVIER: A LIFE
Documentary
EMMY (INFORMATION SERIES),
ACAPULCO WORLD FESTIVAL

SAN FRANCISCO BALLET IN *CINDERELLA*, DIA
CINE AWARD, INTERNATIONAL FILM &
TV FESTIVAL OF NEW YORK,
PARENTS' CHOICE AWARD

SYLVIA FINE KAYE'S MUSICAL COMEDY TONIGHT
EMMY (CHOREOGRAPHY—WALTER PAINTER),
EMMY (COSTUME DESIGN)

1986–1987

AGNES, THE INDOMITABLE DE MILLE, DIA
Documentary
EMMY (INFORMATIONAL SPECIAL),
CHICAGO INTERNATIONAL FILM FESTIVAL,
CINE'S GOLDEN EAGLE CERTIFICATE

BROADWAY SINGS: THE MUSIC OF JULE STYNE
EMMY (MUSIC DIRECTION—DAN PIPPEN)

THE GOLDEN YEARS
3-part series
December Flower
CHRISTOPHER AWARD
Monsignor Quixote
CHRISTOPHER AWARD

GOYA
Washington Opera
EMMY (CLASSICAL MUSIC/DANCE
PROGRAMMING-DIRECTING—KIRK BROWNING)

IN MEMORY OF . . .
A BALLET BY JEROME ROBBINS, DIA
New York City Ballet
CHICAGO INTERNATIONAL FILM FESTIVAL,
CINE'S GOLDEN EAGLE CERTIFICATE

JAMES STEWART: A WONDERFUL LIFE
CINE'S GOLDEN EAGLE CERTIFICATE,
INTERNATIONAL FILM & TV FESTIVAL
OF NEW YORK

MARK MORRIS, DIA
Mark Morris Dance Co.
ACAPULCO WORLD FESTIVAL, AMERICAN FILM
AND VIDEO FESTIVAL, CHRISTOPHER AWARD,
CINE'S GOLDEN EAGLE CERTIFICATE, INTER-
NATIONAL FILM & TV FESTIVAL OF NEW YORK

VLADIMIR HOROWITZ: THE LAST ROMANTIC
EMMY (CLASSICAL MUSIC/DANCE
PROGRAMMING-DIRECTING—ALBERT MAYSLES,
DAVID MAYSLES)

1987–1988

BACALL ON BOGART
Documentary
CHICAGO INTERNATIONAL FILM FESTIVAL

**BALANCHINE AND CUNNINGHAM: AN EVENING
AT AMERICAN BALLET THEATRE,** DIA
INTERNATIONAL FILM & TV FESTIVAL
OF NEW YORK

CELEBRATING GERSHWIN
in 2 parts:
The Jazz Age, 'S Wonderful!
EMMY (DIRECTING—PATRICIA BIRCH,
HUMPHREY BURTON)

NIXON IN CHINA
Houston Grand Opera
EMMY (CLASSICAL PROGRAM)

PAUL TAYLOR: *ROSES* AND *LAST LOOK*, DIA
Paul Taylor Dance Co.
CHICAGO INTERNATIONAL FILM FESTIVAL

1988–1989

BARYSHNIKOV DANCES BALANCHINE, DIA
American Ballet Theatre
EMMY (PERFORMANCE IN CLASSICAL
MUSIC/DANCE—MIKHAIL BARYSHNIKOV),
CHICAGO INTERNATIONAL FILM FESTIVAL

BERNSTEIN AT 70
EMMY (CLASSICAL PROGRAM)

**GREGORY HINES:
TAP DANCE IN AMERICA,** DIA
EMMY (EDITING), DIRECTOR'S GUILD
OF AMERICA

***LA SYLPHIDE* WITH THE PENNSYLVANIA/
MILWAUKEE BALLET,** DIA
CHICAGO INTERNATIONAL FILM FESTIVAL,
MONITOR AWARD

LINDA RONSTADT: CANCIONES DE MI PADRE
EMMY (INDIVIDUAL PERFORMANCE—LINDA
RONSTADT)

A NIGHT AT THE JOFFREY, DIA
Joffrey Ballet
CHICAGO INTERNATIONAL FILM FESTIVAL,
IMZ GRAND PRIX VIDEO-DANSE,
INTERNATIONAL FILM & TV FESTIVAL OF
NEW YORK, MONITOR AWARD

1989–1990

BOB FOSSE—STEAM HEAT, DIA
Documentary
EMMY (INFORMATIONAL SPECIAL), CHICAGO
INTERNATIONAL FILM FESTIVAL, GOLDEN ROSE
INTERNATIONAL COMPETITION-MONTREAUX,
OHIO STATE AWARD

JULIE ANDREWS IN CONCERT
EMMY (MUSIC DIRECTION—IAN FRASER)

THE ORCHESTRA
EMMY (VISUAL EFFECTS—CONCEIVED
AND DIRECTED BY ZBIG RYBCZYNSKI;
JOHN O'CONNOR, VISUAL EFFECTS EDITOR),
PRIX ITALIA

***THE SEARCH FOR NIJINSKY'S RITE
OF SPRING,*** DIA
Documentary
IMZ GRAND PRIX VIDEO-DANSE, INTERNATIONAL
FILM & TV FESTIVAL OF NEW YORK

1990–1991

BALANCHINE IN AMERICA, DIA
New York City Ballet
INTERNATIONAL FILM & TV FESTIVAL
OF NEW YORK

THE MAHABHARATA
3-part series:
Game of Dice, Exile in the Forest, The War
INTERNATIONAL EMMY

1991–1992

A DANGEROUS MAN: LAWRENCE AFTER ARABIA
INTERNATIONAL EMMY

EVERYBODY DANCE NOW, DIA
Documentary
(Choreography in music videos), CHICAGO
INTERNATIONAL FILM FESTIVAL, GOLDEN ROSE
INTERNATIONAL COMPETITION-MONTREAUX,
GRAND PRIX INTERNATIONAL VIDEO-DANSE
AWARD, INTERNATIONAL FILM & TV FESTIVAL
OF NEW YORK, PEABODY AWARD

**LAR LUBOVITCH DANCE CO. AND MOMIX:
PICTURES ON THE EDGE,** DIA
CHICAGO INTERNATIONAL FILM FESTIVAL,
INTERNATIONAL EMMY

PAUL TAYLOR'S *SPEAKING IN TONGUES*, DIA
Paul Taylor Dance Co.
EMMY (CHOREOGRAPHY—PAUL TAYLOR),
CHICAGO INTERNATIONAL FILM FESTIVAL,
INTERNATIONAL EMMY, INTERNATIONAL FILM
& TV FESTIVAL OF NEW YORK

**UNFORGETTABLE WITH LOVE: NATALIE COLE
SINGS THE SONGS OF NAT KING COLE**
EMMY (DIRECTING—PATRICIA BIRCH), NAACP
IMAGE AWARD

1992–1993

**GREAT PERFORMANCES
20TH ANNIVERSARY SPECIAL: CELEBRATING
CREATIVITY, AMERICAN STYLE**
THE NEW YORK FESTIVALS

***THE HARD NUT* WITH
THE MARK MORRIS DANCE GROUP,** DIA
THE NEW YORK FESTIVALS

OEDIPUS REX
Ozawa
EMMY (COSTUME DESIGN—EMI WADA,
JULIE TAYMOR)

***TOSCA* FROM ROME**
EMMY (CLASSICAL PROGRAM), EMMY
(CLASSICAL MUSIC/DANCE PROGRAMMING-
DIRECTION—GIUSEPPE PATRONI GRIFFI,
BRIAN LARGE), EMMY (CLASSICAL MUSIC/DANCE
PROGRAMMING-PERFORMANCE—CATHERINE
MALFITANO AS FLORIA TOSCA)

1994–1995

TWO BY DOVE, DIA
Alvin Ailey Dance Co., Royal Swedish Ballet
EMMY (CHOREOGRAPHY—ULYSSES DOVE),
EMMY (DIRECTION—DAVID HINTON)

THE WORLD OF JIM HENSON
Documentary
PARENTS' CHOICE HONOR

1995–1996

A RENAISSANCE REVISITED, DIA
THE NEW YORK FESTIVALS

ITZHAK PERLMAN: IN THE FIDDLER'S HOUSE
EMMY (CULTURAL MUSIC-DANCE PROGRAM),
GOLDEN ROSE INTERNATIONAL COMPETITION-
MONTREAUX

Drama

BY STEVEN WINN

A Promise Fulfilled

Televised Drama's New Golden Age

———— ✌ ————

In television's original Golden Age, plays were the precious metal. Lost in memory's mists now, the thriving drama anthology series of the 1940s and 1950s transformed America's living rooms into prime theater seating. Week after week brought new works by the finest writers of the time—Paddy Chayefsky, Horton Foote, Tad Mosel, Gore Vidal—as well as classics by William Shakespeare and George Bernard Shaw.

The roster of actors who appeared on the *Alcoa Hour, Kraft Television Theatre, Playhouse 90,* and others was a roll call of the famous and the destined to be: Charles Boyer, Julie Harris, Grace Kelly, Sidney Poitier, Robert Redford, Rod Steiger. George Roy Hill (whose credits include *Butch Cassidy and the Sundance Kid, Slaughterhouse Five,* and *The Sting*) directed teleplays, as did Sidney Lumet. A modern-dress *Julius Caesar* and the musical *Peter Pan,* starring Mary Martin, played to a national audience. There were productions of Noël Coward and Robert Sherwood, adaptations of Joseph Conrad and Ernest Hemingway. Those Golden Age anthologies, doomed as they were by the migration of talent to Hollywood and the thundering onset of Westerns and other continuing-character series in the 1960s, offered the hope of a second gilded era in televised drama.

It would be another lifetime, in quicksilvery television terms, before Great Performances came to the airways in 1972. When it did, the promise of that bygone age would be fulfilled beyond any TV pioneer's imaginings. Where intimately scaled teleplays had once seemed the medium's defining genre, Great Performances has expanded the borders of time, space, and literary imagination in every conceivable direction.

ADDING BREADTH AND DEPTH TO DRAMA ON THE SMALL SCREEN

With a stately *Brideshead Revisited* that took eleven hours to tell, as well as with Peter Brook's patient exploration of the Sanskrit classic *The Mahabharata,* the series has opened fresh vistas of narrative amplitude and cultural breadth to the home audience. Works as old as the *Chester Mystery Plays* and Richard Brinsley Sheridan's *The School for Scandal* have taken their turn in the series alongside the newest plays by A. R. Gurney, Vinnette Carroll, and the Chicano comedy trio Culture Clash. Jean Anouilh, Samuel Beckett, Athol Fugard, Harold Pinter, Luigi Pirandello, and Heinrich Von Kleist have spoken from around the globe, while plays by Frank Chin, Clifford Odets, Eugene O'Neill, Lanford Wilson, and George C. Wolfe, among many others, have chronicled the variety of American experience.

"[Since 1972] Great Performances *has been (alas too many times single-handedly) fighting the good fight for all the performing arts that television has ever had to offer—dance, drama, opera, classical and jazz music, every blessed thing that graces our culture. Ah, but we remember with sorrow the arrogant head of one commercial network who, during one of the first press tours we ever attended, was asked why his network and/or the competition didn't present such superior fare on any kind of a regular basis. 'Look,' he explained, 'we're not in the business of improving your tastes. If you wanna have culture, tune in to PBS.'"*

— Jerry Krupnick
STAR-LEDGER

LEFT: Cast members of *Hamlet* receiving direction from Kirk Browning; PREVIOUS PAGES: Kevin Kline as Hamlet watches Gertrude, played by Dana Ivey, die.

In adaptations of literature from here and abroad, GREAT PERFORMANCES has fashioned a library of dramatized novels and short stories. Works as sprawling as Thomas Mann's *Buddenbrooks* or as light-fingered as an Irwin Shaw short story have been presented. Original teleplays form another wing of the collection, and biographies yet another, where the life stories of Sarah Bernhardt, Lorraine Hansberry, and Molière reside.

As the series has progressed, the programming has taken on a choreographic richness. One sequence of shows was organized around the theme of tyranny; another presented different views of people in the theater. A 1985 celebration of the American musical put *Sweeney Todd, The Gospel at Colonus,* and a Leonard Bernstein–conducted recording session of *West Side Story* in the spotlight. Viewers could make their own connections, too, between the Kevin Kline *Hamlet* and Tom Stoppard's *Rosencrantz and Guildenstern Are Dead,* or among Anton Chekhov's *The Seagull* and *Uncle Vanya* and Neil Simon's *The Good Doctor,* based on Chekhov short stories.

GREAT PERFORMERS IN GREAT ROLES

Like the anthology series of the 1940s and 1950s, GREAT PERFORMANCES boasts a distinguished honor roll of great performers. An arbitrary sampling includes Alan Bates, Faye Dunaway, Ralph Fiennes, Rosemary Harris, Rex Harrison, Jeremy Irons, James Earl Jones, Kevin Kline, Angela Lansbury, Laurence Olivier, Eva Le Gallienne, John Lithgow, Natasha Richardson, Ralph Richardson, Jason Robards, Meryl Streep, and Emma Thompson.

While many actors have made important early showings on GREAT PERFORMANCESS—an unknown William Hurt in *Verna: USO Girl,* for example, or Streep and Swoosie Kurtz in Wendy Wasserstein's *Uncommon Women and Others*—many others were already established stars on Broadway and in Hollywood. They have worked for GREAT PERFORMANCES, often for fees well beneath their accustomed levels, because so many productions in the series have offered roles, a respect for theater artists, and the sort of eager national audience they could find nowhere else. "GREAT PERFORMANCES gave us the chance to do something we all longed to do," says Blythe Danner, who appeared in *The Seagull* and *Eccentricities of a Nightingale.* "We were getting to do the classics on television."

A PROCESS OF DISCOVERY

In tapping the theater's rich traditions for a new group of actors and audiences, GREAT PERFORMANCES fulfilled the hope that *Playhouse 90, Studio One,* and other series had raised a generation before. It did so, fittingly enough, on the conviction and moxie of an executive producer who had begun his career designing sets for television drama and musical productions in the 1950s. In 1964, Jac Venza launched the early performing arts programming at National Educational Television. Venza recalls the pioneer days of *NET Playhouse* with a mixture of pride and amazement. Soon after his appointment as head of drama for NET, he scouted a new actor in an Off-Broadway play. "A week later," Venza remembers, "we were in

"We do want to dispel the myth that only British actors can perform successfully in classics like King Lear *or* Cyrano de Bergerac. *But I also want to do some great American plays. The regional theaters have to emphasize the classics in order to get an audience, just the way an opera company . . . has to do the staples, like* La Traviata *and* La Bohème. *There'd be nothing but empty seats for a season of new American plays."*

—JAC VENZA

RIGHT: James Earl Jones as King Lear.

the studio recording *The Journey of the Fifth Horse,* Dustin Hoffman's theater debut as a tortured Turgenev character."

Distribution was a process of discovery as well. From a base in Ann Arbor, NET shipped out ten copies of each tape, routing them first to major market stations and then to smaller cities. A program that played in Los Angeles and Chicago one week might not reach Boise or Little Rock for another month.

Bolstered by key Ford Foundation grants and the emergence of the National Endowment for the Arts, a national network focusing on serious arts programming was inevitable. Congressional approval of the Public Broadcasting Act in 1967 made the Public Broadcasting System (PBS) a reality. With PBS as a powerful new tool, Venza was determined to restore the special vitality to television that only the theater could provide. "Our idea was to tap the talent, substance, and sensibility of the writer," he recalls, "as opposed to a television production office." Venza turned simultaneously to the burgeoning new writing scene centered in New York and to the vibrant and artistically diverse regional theaters around the country to program *Theater in America,* the Exxon-funded series that was later incorporated into GREAT PERFORMANCES.

ABOVE: Christopher Foster, Alice Drummond, Elizabeth Wilson, Arthur French, Jason Robards, Jack Dodson, George Rose, and Carol Ambrothy in *You Can't Take It with You.*

Contemplating an initial repertoire of Maxim Gorky's *Enemies,* George S. Kaufman and Ring Lardner's *June Moon,* Edmond Rostand's *Cyrano de Bergerac,* William Shakespeare's *King Lear* (starring James Earl Jones), and Eugene O'Neill's *A Touch of the Poet* (with Fritz Weaver), the

Wall Street Journal's Michael J. Connor foresaw that "Wednesday evenings for the next several months may turn out to be good nights to stay home and go to the theater."

This was just the beginning. The new series caught the heat and light from the Actors Theatre of Louisville, San Francisco's American Conservatory Theater, the Guthrie Theater in Minneapolis, Princeton's McCarter Theatre, the Old Globe Theater in San Diego, and many others. Contemporary writers like Peter Nichols, Ronald Ribman, David Storey, and Lanford Wilson now had a new forum.

Venza believed strongly in the merit of original teleplays, adding works by Tom Stoppard, Paddy Chayefsky, Terrence McNally, and others. Literary adaptations and dramatic biographies have given the programming breadth, its single biggest hit (in *Brideshead Revisited*), and a certain classy legitimacy. While *Masterpiece Theatre* has come to be most strongly identified with the serial adaptations of literary works, Venza has always known that their presence on GREAT PERFORMANCES is important.

"You couldn't expect people to make the kind of concessions we were asking them to make, in wages and working conditions, if things looked threadbare," explains Venza. "Importing those beautiful and at the time inexpensive series from England was one way of signaling that."

MASTERING THE BOTTOM LINE

Venza's skills as a negotiator and subliminal persuader underlie everything GREAT PERFORMANCES has done. With live theater productions, Venza has insisted that the blocking, costumes, and makeup be redone to make the best use of television's sometimes unforgiving eye. He has lobbied hard for multiple broadcast rights and wage breaks from the unions. The partnerships he has forged between WNET and the BBC—on *The Miser* and *Once in a Lifetime*—and Granada TV on *Brideshead* were feats of producing skill that have made those and many other ventures possible.

Money is the perennial backstory. Faced with uncertain government and corporate support and spiraling costs, drama programming has declined. Some of it moved to *American Playhouse*, conceived by Venza in 1982. But in the crucial area of corporate sponsorship, Venza and GREAT PERFORMANCES have endured periods of both crisis and calm. Venza recalls, with a wry smile, meeting a new executive from one longtime sponsor. "Shouldn't we be sponsoring tennis?" the executive ingenuously asked.

Tennis will always have its advocates. The arts need people like Jac Venza. Trained in the golden age of televised drama, he has created the wider, grander setting in which GREAT PERFORMANCES now shines, and in the process he has mastered the subtle theater of the boardroom—all in the service of the performances that matter most, the ones that make the graceful leap from stage to screen.

It has been twenty-three years since Venza helped *Feasting with Panthers*, Adrian Hall and Eugene Lee's nightmarish evocation of Oscar Wilde in prison, make such a leap. He still relishes the memory. "The prisoners were doing scenes from *Salomé* and *Lady Windermere's Fan*," Venza says. "It was an extraordinary idea theatrically, and I don't know why we even thought it would work. But it did. It all worked brilliantly."

Great Productions of Great Plays

—⟨♫⟩—

OVER THE PAST QUARTER CENTURY OF TELEVISING DRAMA, GREAT PERFORMANCES HAS drafted a sizable army of artistic recruits. Led by veteran generals like television director Kirk Browning, stage actors, directors, playwrights, and designers have braved a new medium. In these pages, they discuss their strategies, decisions, doubts, and debuts.

DARING TO MAKE THE BIG GESTURE
HOGAN'S GOAT

Hogan's Goat wasn't merely two hours of powerful televised drama. In the inaugural season of GREAT PERFORMANCES, it served bracing notice of what this series could become.

A drama set in 1890 and written in blank verse by a Harvard scholar scared off some critics as gloomy and humorless. Others recognized the potency of translating an intense and uncompromising piece of theater to the screen. "The most moving dramatic work we've experienced on television," wrote the *Los Angeles Herald Examiner's* Morton Moss. Compact, unsparing, and sparked by a fervent figurative language, William Alfred's 1965 Off-Broadway play tracks the ambitions of a Brooklyn Irish immigrant to a grim end. Robert Foxworth plays Matt Stanton, a self-made businessman who has clawed his way to the brink of his party's mayoral nomination. George Rose is the incumbent Mayor Quinn, a corrupt ward politician who knows he's nothing without his office.

Quinn has two bare-knuckle blows to deliver. First is the threat to expose Stanton's three-year love affair with Agnes Hogan, a woman Quinn himself loved. Second is the fact that Matt's present marriage to the English beauty Kathleen (Faye Dunaway) took place in a city hall, not a Catholic church. And then Quinn has a knockout punch: Stanton's secret marriage to Agnes, the woman who has made Matt her fancy boy, her "goat"; although she never appears on-screen, Agnes is an important presence in the story.

In the GREAT PERFORMANCES production, Faye Dunaway, her eyes watchfully bright and her hair fixed in a luscious thick chignon, returned to the role that launched her career in 1965. "Emotionally, I'm very close to Kathleen Stanton," she said, "this sensual and spiritual struggle of a woman of good birth, convent bred, yet dominated by her senses."

Passion runs deep in *Hogan's Goat* but does not always follow a predictable course. In one quietly remarkable scene, after Matt confesses his affair with Agnes to Kathleen, he beguiles his wife with a rhapsodic description of his lover. "Her skin was like new milk," he says, "and her blue veins trembled in the shimmer of her full straight neck like threads of violets fallen from her hair and filliped by the breeze." Alfred uses language to enchant and wound, to exalt and scorn. When Matt seeks absolution for his and Agnes's sins on the night of her death, a parish priest issues a wither-

LEFT: Faye Dunaway as the doomed Kathleen Stanton in *Hogan's Goat.*

ing refusal through the confessional screen. Matt shoots back, "Pride steams off you like the stink of cancer. Who can absolve us but ourselves?"

Heresy and shame are old-fashioned issues for late-twentieth-century viewers. As Matt Stanton hurtles from the confession box toward the ruins of his political career and marriage, *Hogan's Goat* makes these themes gripping and immediate.

The cast shines from top to bottom. Foxworth and Dunaway look fatefully matched, the secrets flickering behind their confident bearings and evident physical craving for one another. George Rose, his doleful moon face enlarged by thick mutton-chop whiskers, finds the hollow core of a ruthless career politician. A lean Philip Bosco plays a stern and quick-tempered priest.

Rue McClanahan is the parish gossip Jo Finn, miserably triumphant as she blurts out the truth about Matt's past to the prim Kathleen. Margaret Linn's blubbering tart Bessie is perfectly observed. Director Glenn Jordan sets off the scenes with sepia-toned freeze-frames that enhance the production's period texture and subtly tighten the story's tension.

"Cry for us all while you're at it," Bosco intones in the final scene, as Dunaway lies with her neck broken at the bottom of a flight of stairs. "Cry for us all."

Hogan's Goat dares to make the big gesture, to submit its striving characters to the gnashing wheels of church and state. In the tiny world of a Brooklyn parish, Matt Stanton's ambition brings down a thundering destruction.

WEARING THE TRIPLE CROWN

WENDY WASSERSTEIN, UNCOMMON WOMEN, AND OTHERS

"Ms. Wasserstein treats her characters with intelligence, great good humor, and respect. She offers insights into the challenges and crises confronting modern women, but there are no polemics, no facile rules."

—John J. O'Connor
NEW YORK TIMES

RIGHT: Josephine Nichols, Jill Eikenberry, and Meryl Streep in *Uncommon Women and Others*.

Wendy Wasserstein takes the triple crown for writers in the Great Performances league, with a play, short-story adaptation, and teleplay to her credit. Her first hit came in 1978, with the airing of *Uncommon Women and Others*. Wasserstein's precocious and comically blunt early play profiles a group of friends looking back on their college years at Mount Holyoke and mulling the choices they have made about careers, sex, and marriage. The casting was precocious, too, with then unknowns Jill Eikenberry and Swoosie Kurtz transferring to television from the stellar Phoenix Theatre cast and Meryl Streep joining them for the televised production. *Uncommon Women,* uncommonly popular the first time around, was rebroadcast in 1989.

In 1979, Wasserstein's version of John Cheever's "The Sorrows of Gin," a short story about a lonely young girl who secretly pours her father's Tanqueray down the drain, inaugurated a three-part series of Cheever adaptations. ("O Youth and Beauty!" adapted by A. R. Gurney, and "The Five Forty-eight," adapted by Terrence McNally, followed.) Then, in 1992, Wasserstein's gift to GREAT PERFORMANCES' twentieth anniversary special was *Kiss, Kiss Dahlings,* a brief comic celebration of the theater. Nancy Marchand, Blythe Danner, and Cynthia Nixon play three generations of an acting family in three different eras, from the age of Chekhov to the dawn of Charlie Rose.

WENDY WASSERSTEIN

MEMORIES OF THE MOMENT

Wasserstein began her recollections with a little shiver of what might have been. "Someone wanted to buy *Uncommon Women* for one of the networks and put Charlie's Angels in it," she recalled. "No one had ever heard of the actors we had. Fortunately we were able to preserve that original production."

Q: *The play has some pretty frank language. What could you get away with in 1979?*

A: Oh, the text is just filthy! Swoosie couldn't say "fucking amazing," but we fought hard for the menstrual blood scene and won. There was also some pressure—which we resisted—to trim the long monologue Alma Cuervo does when she telephones the doctor in Minneapolis. You just didn't have speeches that long on television.

Q: *And playwrights didn't write about women in this way, either.*

A: I think the play did raise some issues for contemporary women—about the price of success and whether it's professional or personal or emotional and how it may differ from a man's idea of success. Until then there hadn't been very many plays on television about women. The ones that were tended to be on "women's issues"—breast cancer or divorce or battered women.

My most recent play, *An American Daughter,* reminds me of *Uncommon Women.* It's very deliberately about a woman undergoing some of the same pressures in a different place and time, and it's got a similar sort of earnestness.

Q: *How autobiographical is* Uncommon Women?

A: I was this trippy Jewish girl from New York, like Holly Kaplan in the play, so Mount Holyoke was a very peculiar place to me when I started there in 1967. There were still teas and this gracious-living tradition that I talk about in the play.

Q: *Is the play dated?*

A: Whenever it gets done now, I keep thinking audiences will say, "We never experienced any of this. This is nonsense." But that's not what happens. "What should I do with my life?" is still a current question. A lot of young women now believe they can do everything by age thirty, plus exercise, and they'll have a happy life. What's interesting to me about the characters in *Uncommon Women* is that in some ways they already don't believe that.

Q: *How did you connect to the Cheever story?*

A: It's a distant world for me. Those commuters in raincoats on the train to Darien or New Canaan—they're the people I always wondered about. I knew more about fathers and daughters than I did about the sorrows of gin.

Being an outsider helped, in a way. There's a wistfulness in Cheever that reminds me of Chekhov, who's my favorite playwright.

Q: *So it's no accident that Nancy Marchand, in the first scene of* Kiss, Kiss Dahlings, *is a Chekhov actress at the Moscow Art Theatre?*

A: I'd never done any costume drama, so that was fun. I also wanted to pay tribute to the theater itself. I'm someone who probably could have written for television, but there's always been this pull to the stage. It's still an art form, a place of ideas, and not about how is this going to play in Missouri or what are the numbers. It may sound old-fashioned, but I happen to think it's a real privilege to write for the theater.

ECCENTRICITIES OF A NIGHTINGALE

Artists are never satisfied. Four years after *Summer and Smoke* opened in 1947, Tennessee Williams radically reworked his tale of a love-struck young woman pining away for a doctor's son in a small Mississippi town. Trimmed of the original version's implausible subplot and extraneous characters, *Eccentricities of a Nightingale* is, as Williams himself said, "less conventional and melodramatic." It is also less well known. *Eccentricities* was not produced until 1964, finally reaching Broadway in 1976.

The play arrived on GREAT PERFORMANCES that same year, in a production that stars Blythe Danner as the unhappy but vibrant Alma Winemiller. In a beautifully shaped and detailed performance, Danner unfolds the character's progression from timid wallflower to flagrant seductress, exhibiting a powerful drive beneath a fluttering surface. But don't expect the actress to agree.

"I thought I was too busy and over the top," says Danner. "I remember I was nursing my son on the set, and it was a frantic time. I'm afraid some of that came through."

Whatever the source or process, Danner got hold of the fitful, elusive spirit that makes Alma one of the playwright's most fascinating heroines. Part tenuous Laura Wingfield and part self-dramatizing Blanche DuBois, Alma is finally a distinctively sympathetic creation. Williams thought she "may very well be the best female portrait I've ever drawn in a play."

Alma is a caged songbird in the first scene, where she performs in the Glorious Hill, Mississippi, gazebo on the Fourth of July. Her real captivity comes at home where her father, a frowning Episcopal priest played by Tim O'Connor, harangues Alma for her eccentric, arty habits. This was just the way her mother (Louise Latham as the delusional Mrs. Winemiller) got started, he warns.

Danner cringes and wilts under the scorn, but she's never shaken from her hopeless devotion to the boy who has grown up across the street and now gone off to medical school. Frank Langella, looking poised and freshly scrubbed on his social calls to Alma, is John Buchanan.

In the play's best scene, Alma comes down with a fit of palpitations and pounds on the Buchanans' door in the middle of the night. John's sober bedside manner proves powerless against her pinwheeling emotions. She's desperate, seductive, abusive, and finally proud, her quivering features and flyaway hands now defiantly still. "How few people in this world," the young doctor responds, "dare to say what's in their hearts."

Danner remembers the magic of catching the scene on one take during the taping. "It's so wonderfully written, so quicksilvery. Most of us don't get to play anything at that level very often."

A SOUTHERNER IN SPIRIT

The Philadelphia-born Danner is at somewhat of a loss to explain her apparent affinity for Southern

"Eccentricities of a Nightingale is fortunate in having a powerful actress in this first national production. Blythe Danner plays Alma for full value in every tremolo of her confused sensitivities, now hoping against hope, now angry, now despairing, now exultant. She flutters, she chirps, she sings, she never does spread her wings in flight; finally she bleeds and dies. It's a remarkable performance."

—Frank Getlein
WASHINGTON STAR

"The production to catch is the one on PBS tonight. Blythe Danner's Alma is as much of a television event as Katharine Hepburn's Amanda in The Glass Menagerie *several seasons back. Her body and her speech flutter, but her mind never does. Frank Langella is such a warm, dreamy-eyed Dr. Buchanan that the role is reimbursed for the loss of its cynical edge with a smooth romanticism that complements Danner's determined honesty splendidly. Lindsay Law and Glenn Jordan have set their stars in a flawlessly cast, nicely fluid production."*

—Don Shirley
WASHINGTON POST

RIGHT: Blythe Danner as Alma Winemiller greets a stranger in *Eccentricities of a Nightingale.*

characters. Williams paid steady court to her after *Eccentricities,* offering one new role after another. "I think in another life I must have been Southern," she says. "There's something about the gentility, something that's genuine and full of heart and extremely funny."

Danner keeps all that in fluid motion in Alma. In the one-night stand she persuades John to give her in the last act, Alma has a kind of shameless dignity. "You give the hour and I'll make a lifetime of it," she tells him, and her radiant gratitude makes that seem true, if only for the moment. In the epilogue, Alma has become a curdled tart, cruising the town square for traveling salesmen.

Is Danner routinely self-critical about her work on the screen? "I've always had a hard time with the camera," she admits. "It's only now that I'm becoming older that I've started to relax with it more and forget it's there. Back then it was still very intimidating."

If Danner suffered through GREAT PERFORMANCES' *Eccentricities of a Nightingale*, the camera never gives her secret away.

AN IRRESISTIBLE *ROYAL FAMILY*

No one ever makes a straightforward entrance in *The Royal Family*. Instead, they swoop and flutter, storm down the set's curved staircase, or pour through the front door on a flood tide of crisis, steamer trunks, and live parrots. George S. Kaufman and Edna Ferber's 1927 satire pays affectionate tribute to a clan of extravagant stage actors, modeled on the Barrymores. The action never strays from the lavish duplex apartment the Cavendish family occupies on Manhattan's East Side. Ellis Rabb's exuberant Broadway production, codirected for television with Kirk Browning, makes that setting glow with a burnished theatrical warmth.

Before a single late-rising Cavendish appears in the first act, the camera wanders from room to room, admiring furnishings, cut flowers, a grand piano draped with a fringed runner, and acres of theater photographs that crowd the walls and side tables. There's the matriarch Fanny Cavendish (Eva Le Gallienne), beaming in triumph, and there she is again in valiant profile, along with her stage actress daughter Julie (Rosemary Harris) and movie matinee idol son Tony (Ellis Rabb). A portrait of Fanny's late husband Aubrey hangs over the fireplace. In one sweetly comic moment, Fanny boasts that her husband not only died in the theater but also managed to take four curtain calls before expiring.

Their granddaughter Gwen (Mary Layne) is an actor, too, an ingenue who's torn between the theater and motherhood. Her baby son will be a performer as well, if the family has anything to say about it. The Cavendishes are grand creatures of the stage, in photographs or in infancy, before they've ever said a word.

When they do start swarming onto the scene, *The Royal Family* unfolds in a featherweight plot pinned to various theatrical enterprises. Fanny yearns to go back on the road again. The family's business manager (an endearingly tender Sam Levene) offers a brilliant new play to Julie and Gwen. Even pampered Tony, fleeing the sunshine and a breach-of-promise scandal in Hollywood,

"The Royal Family . . . has been filmed with loving restraint by producer Ken Campbell and director Ellis Rabb. In the final act, Eva Le Gallienne is alone onstage, in a rapture of private recollection about her long years as an actress. Her hands seem to dance, and her eyes and face are transfigured—it is indeed a magical moment, and we are lucky to have it on film. I pity the impatient viewer who has switched channels to Charlie's Angels. *"*

—Karl E. Meyer
SATURDAY REVIEW

decides to take to the boards again in a wild new Constructivist drama about Christ that he has discovered in Europe. Naturally, he'll play the lead.

THE SOUL OF A THEATER LIFE

Le Gallienne, in one of her great career's crowning roles, is the play's shining soul, a life in the theater incarnate. Tossed off with a benign smile, Fanny's wit turns devastatingly efficient. "Marriage isn't a career," she pronounces. "It's an incident." When her daughter's unimaginative suitor sends roses every day, Fanny compares them to a milkman's mundane delivery.

Fanny's longing for the theater is an almost physical hunger. She remembers greasepaint, rouge, mascara, the stage doorman's keys, and a lucky rabbit's foot she kept in her dressing room, her face all dreamy at the thought. Left alone at the end of the third act, she picks up a script and rehearses some lines and graceful moves. The dog-eared script is the last thing Fanny touches before she collapses in a chair and dies.

The camera keeps finding mementos of the Cavendish legacy. A Yorick's skull waits on a bookshelf. Masks cluster over a doorway. The camera's roving eye returns most often to the photographs, drawn by those Cavendish faces that seem, in their carefully struck poses, exalted, a little ridiculous, and altogether irresistible.

EMBRACING THE COMPLEXITIES
THE COLORED MUSEUM

In his 1986 play *The Colored Museum*, George C. Wolfe sketches a series of bitingly funny send-ups of black stereotypes and sacred cows. In each "exhibit," as he calls them, Wolfe zings his targets—Aunt Jemima, *Ebony* magazine, revered "Mama-on-the-couch" plays like *A Raisin in the Sun*—and in the process sounds their complex cultural resonances.

Wolfe doesn't preach to the choir about racism. He delivers a warning, as hilarious as it is grave, about the dangers of people ignoring history and forgetting who they are. In the opening number, "Git on Board," a smiling black stewardess (played by the astonishing Danitra Vance) welcomes a cabinful of slaves to a transatlantic flight through history. "Shackles must be worn at all times," she chirps. The black businessman (Tommy Hollis) in "Symbiosis" is confronted by a younger version of himself (Victor Mack) when he tries to pitch into a dumpster such emblems of his past as an Afro comb, *Soul on Ice,* and Motown albums. "Man kills his own rage," the older man remarks balefully. "Film at eleven."

The Colored Museum opened in New York at Joseph Papp's Public Theatre and aired on GREAT PERFORMANCES in 1991, in a production smartly codirected with Andrew Carl Wilk; it has circulated to theaters around the world. Wolfe's other works include *Spunk, Jelly's Last Jam* (the making of which was profiled in GREAT PERFORMANCES' *Jammin': Jelly Roll Morton on Broadway*) and *Bring in 'da Noise, Bring in 'da Funk,* a tap-dance chronicle of twentieth-century black America.

"Theater, because it's a less public and thus safer haven for dramatic experiment, is more free than television to explore daring, unsettling, potentially offensive and controversial material. The fact that television has caught up to The Colored Museum *is good news, because a lot of unsuspecting viewers—blacks and others—are going to have stereotypes turned upside down with the ten 'exhibits' unfurled in this museum."*

—Ray Loynd
LOS ANGELES TIMES

GEORGE C. WOLFE

SPEAKING DIRECTLY

Q: *How did you come to write* The Colored Museum?

A: It was the strangest thing. I was in the dramatic writing program at New York University at the time, and there were three or four other writers in the program, all white, who were writing plays about old black tap dancers. It triggered this thought process in me about the kind of assumptions people can make in a racist society.

Q: *What's under those assumptions?*

A: The thing that's so fascinating about black culture is how complicated and contradictory it is. It's African; it's American; it's European; it's a subculture that dominates the dominant culture. I wanted to shatter people's predetermined notions about something that just isn't as simple as it looks.

And I mean black people's notions, too. A lot of people thought the stewardess in "Git on Board" should have been white. The fact that she's black and addresses the slaves the way she does makes it less easy to categorize and dismiss.

Besides, I said right from the start that the only thing that was going to be white in this play were the walls.

Q: *Like a museum.*

A: I originally thought of doing this as an installation piece, where the audience would walk through and visit the various exhibits face-to-face. There's still a lot of direct engagement between the audience and the performers.

Q: *How do you think that works in the television version?*

A: Some of the intensity is missing. But TV does something else. Even when it's distant, when it's mediated by the camera, there's a real intimate charge in the way you can speak directly to an audience at home.

Q: *The man in "Symbiosis" says, "Being black is too emotionally taxing." Would you talk about that?*

A: Topsy has a line in the last exhibit that goes, "I can't live inside of yesterday's pain, but I can't live without it." If you disconnect from the pain, then you're like every other bland person in America.

LEFT: Linda Hopkins stirs up "a batch of Negroes" in the "Cookin' with Aunt Ethel" exhibit of *The Colored Museum.*

On the other hand, if you live completely inside that pain all the time, it produces rage, and too much rage produces immobility. The resolution, the only way to go forward, comes when you embrace the complexities.

Photographing the Subtext in *Our Town*

"You want to know the secret of television?" Kirk Browning asks. "Television is photographing subtext."

At age seventy-seven, with a roster of GREAT PERFORMANCES directing credits that ranges from *Enemies* and *A Touch of the Poet* to *Tartuffe* and *Our Town*, Browning has earned the right to be epigrammatic. "The trick," he adds, "is that you may have to do that a different way every time."

For *You Can't Take It with You*, Browning and stage director Ellis Rabb chose to shoot the bohemian chaos of Moss Hart and George S. Kaufman's comedy entirely in close-up. "That's hard to do when you've got thirteen people onstage," observes Browning. "But Ellis was convinced, and he was absolutely right, that the only way to capture the play's energy was to see one thing at a time and be absolutely specific about each moment."

William Ball's highly physicalized *commedia dell'arte* production of *The Taming of the Shrew* presented another kind of challenge. Browning believed the show would look "grotesque" on the screen, until he thought of treating the camera as an innocent child seated in the first row at a circus and gazing up in wonderment at the action.

CAPTURING THE STAGE VERSION ON TELEVISION

Browning's approach to *Our Town* is a model of what televised drama can be. His objective, evident in every cut and camera angle, was to articulate, not appropriate, stage director Gregory Mosher's original vision. The television version of Mosher's 1989 Lincoln Center Theater production was shot in the empty Lyceum Theatre, the Broadway house that had just played host to the live theatrical run of Thornton Wilder's small-town New England classic. Browning and Mosher frankly acknowledge the Lyceum environment. In addition to the open wing space and bare back wall, the camera takes in action that occurs in the theater's ornate boxes and orchestra seating area.

After George Gibbs (Eric Stoltz) and Emily Webb (Penelope Ann Miller) are married, they charge up the Lyceum's center aisle into the shadowy uncertainty of their future. That image is echoed in the third act, when the theater's ranks of empty seats, shrouded in drop cloths, form a kind of extended graveyard at Emily's funeral.

The impact of Wilder's famously minimal settings—two ladders for the young lovers' facing upper-story windows, a table and chairs to create a kitchen—is subtly underscored by Browning's collaboration with Mosher. "We wanted the theater itself to represent Grover's Corners," Browning says. "You still recognize it as a theater, but the space is also abstracted."

Mosher's production drew some heated reactions, both pro and con, especially for the casting of the monologuist Spalding Gray (*Swimming to Cambodia*) as the Stage Manager. Browning's rhythms seem particularly attuned to Gray's laconic interpretation of the role. As casually as this Stage Manager pops into the frame, the camera cuts away from him while he's talking, to catch Mrs. Webb (Roberta

"Our Town holds a secure place within the handful of lasting masterpieces written for the American theater in this century. This production brilliantly reminds us why."

— John J. O'Connor
NEW YORK TIMES

"Television doesn't get much better than Our Town. . . . It could be said, to borrow an anti-television canard, that this production of Our Town, performed on a stage devoid of scenery or props, is merely talking heads. But what talk! The most vivid images in this 1938 play are the haunting ones conjured in the viewer's imagination by Wilder's incomparable words."

—Greg Dawson
ORLANDO SENTINEL

RIGHT: Spalding Gray in *Our Town*.

Maxwell) preparing breakfast or the church choir at practice in one of the Lyceum boxes.

With characteristic modesty, Browning credits Mosher and the cast for the affecting ensemble work in *Our Town*. "As long as you take care to let the actors know exactly what the camera is doing, how it's moving, and when it's in close-up, they will sense what to do.

"It's very difficult to say how a performance should change from the stage to television," Browning continues. "It's dangerous simply to tone everything down. Sometimes an actor can give the exact same performance he or she gave onstage. Other times, the actor will need to internalize more. It's a matter of taste and judgment."

Sometimes the taste and judgment come in saying no. Browning successfully argued against a GREAT PERFORMANCES taping of the Off-Broadway play *Strider*, in which the actors portray horses. "You totally accept it in the theater," he says. "But the moment you put a camera on them they're no longer horses. They're actors dressed up in leotards pretending to be horses."

Browning tapes most scenes three times. "The first is almost like a dress rehearsal. In the second the actors are tired and the equipment is working beautifully. Then you take a break and do it a third time."

Again and again, Browning has made that third time the charm.

CAPTURING THEATRICS ON CAMERA
KEVIN KLINE'S *HAMLET*

Kevin Kline had played *Hamlet* twice before the GREAT PERFORMANCES production, once in 1986 and then again in 1990. On television it would be very different. Under the camera's mobile scrutiny, Kline does things no star of William Shakespeare's tragedy, himself included, could ever manage in a theater. He whispers. He confides in Rosencrantz and Guildenstern while lying flat on his back. He lets a single tear carry a torrent of emotion in the "To be or not to be" speech.

But the most astonishing moment in the performance is also the most theatrical. Approaching a praying King Claudius (Brian Murray) from the deep background, Kline's Hamlet closes in on his uncle, raises a dagger as if to strike, then roars out his own argument with himself about whether to murder the man who killed his father.

In a scene most actors play as if the king won't hear, this Hamlet shouts and rages inches away from Claudius, who remains lost in futile prayer. It's a hypnotically mad moment, at once bizarre and emotionally true, that goes to the heart of what Kline, as both leading actor and codirector of this *Hamlet*, has achieved.

"I never meant to adapt the play for television and lose the theatrical essence," says Kline. "There's something at its core that goes beyond naturalism and realism. The poetry transcends all that."

His minimally furnished, modern-dress production was conceived—first for the New York Shakespeare Festival and then for GREAT PERFORMANCES—with the focus firmly on Shakespeare's lan-

"It is the genius of the Lincoln Center Theater production directed by Gregory Mosher . . . that Wilder's conception has been meticulously respected while the play's darker aspects are confronted unflinchingly."

—John J. O'Connor
NEW YORK TIMES

"When Kevin Kline is at center stage in a Shakespeare production, New York audiences can for once relax, secure in the knowledge that they will be seeing a classical actor of exceptional gifts and the highest integrity."

—Frank Rich
NEW YORK TIMES

LEFT: Kevin Kline as Hamlet coldly watches Diane Venora's Ophelia.

guage. But while the camera allows intimate subtleties, this can also become a trap. "The language tends to become conversational, almost banal, and lose the grandeur," explains Kline. "Sometimes I found myself pulling the camera back and saying, 'No, you've got to let it rip.'"

Kline heeds his own advice with thunderous eruptions and soliloquies honed to a murmurous intensity. He also taps his abundant comic resources, teasing the sober Polonius (Josef Sommer) with an array of rubbery mocking faces.

DASHING BETWEEN DUAL ROLES

Acting and directing created some heady demands, especially on a ten-day shooting schedule that made even a modestly budgeted film seem leisurely by comparison. "We had to shoot twenty minutes of tape a day," says Kline. "On a film you might shoot two." He remembers dashing back and forth from the control room to the stage during the frenzied scene Hamlet plays with his mother Gertrude (Dana Ivey) in her bedroom. "I'd jump into the scene, run out to look at the playback, and run back. Sometimes what I saw was pretty alarming. But we had about an hour, and we had to make it work." Kline credits codirector Kirk Browning, his designers, the cast, and crew for extreme resourcefulness under pressure.

For all the logistical madness, Kline is temperamentally suited to the dual roles he took on with this *Hamlet*. "As an actor, much to the chagrin of some directors, I've always felt that you really direct yourself. So much of directing is reminding the actor of something he did right in rehearsal or five takes before." Kline learned that, he says, when John Cleese asked him to direct a scene in *A Fish Called Wanda*.

The character of Hamlet, as Kline sees him, may justify working on both sides of the camera. "He's at the mercy of certain events, but he also observes and orchestrates them." Hamlet, as Kline points out, directs the play-within-the-play that catches the conscience of the king. "He writes lines. He gives notes to the players."

Kline pauses and admits, with a laugh, that he may be rationalizing. "I suppose since I was going to do *my* Hamlet," he says, "the one sure way to do it was to direct it. It was probably really cheeky, perhaps foolish, but it just seemed like the right thing to do."

DRIFTING TOWARD WAR

SHAW'S HEARTBREAK HOUSE

George Bernard Shaw's vision of England's leisure class morally adrift in World War I was, by his own reckoning, his masterpiece. Thirty years after the publication of *Heartbreak House*, he called this scalding, furiously funny, and deeply humane 1919 work his *King Lear*.

If time has dulled the edge of Shaw's political sword somewhat, it has only enhanced the warmth and satiric wit of his Chekhovian "fantasia in the Russian manner on English themes." The play, a dizzying round of romantic betrayals and crisp philosophical argument set in an aged sea captain's quirky Sussex home, is one of the English theater's choice and most challenging

"Nothing gets between the audience and the play. . . . Even the most familiar passages—the set pieces—sound fresh, and there is no skimping on eloquence, especially from Mr. Kline."

—Edith Oliver
NEW YORKER

RIGHT: Rex Harrison's Captain Shotover captivates Amy Irving as Ellie Dunn.

ensemble pieces.

Rex Harrison heads the cast of the 1986 telecast, based on director Anthony Page's 1983 production at New York's Circle in the Square. As eighty-eight-year-old Captain Shotover, Harrison presides over a chaotic crew that includes a bohemian Rosemary Harris and upper-crust Dana Ivey as his daughters, Remak Ramsay as his nefarious son-in-law in sheik's clothing, and a glowing Amy Irving as the trusting young visitor who grows into astute self-possession before the viewer's eyes.

Harrison brings a distinguished Shavian provenance to the project. He met Shaw on the set of the 1941 *Major Barbara* film, earning the playwright's praise for the easy naturalism of his acting. In the musical *My Fair Lady*, based on Shaw's *Pygmalion,* Harrison made Henry Higgins his indelible signature role. And he had played Shotover in London before Circle in the Square's *Heartbreak House*.

Harrison was also loyal, insisting that the American company, rather than a proposed all-English cast, be used in the televised *House*. Page was retained to direct the production for the small screen.

Even with the excision of one character and some healthy cuts in Shaw's script, *Heartbreak House* packs a demanding range of ideas and exposition into three acts. Page makes a clear and conscious decision to animate the play by focusing tightly on the faces and expressive nuances of the cast. The director's heavy reliance on close-ups of the superb cast yields a kind of living portrait gallery.

Harrison, at seventy-seven, is a remarkable Captain Shotover. With his grizzled gray beard and eyes narrowed to horizon-seeking slits, he wears his years at sea as plainly as the navy blue cap on his head. As Shotover, Harrison is at times brusque, cutting others off midsyllable and showing not the slightest flicker of recognition of his own daughter when she returns home.

The camera catches his impish mode as well, as he darts offstage to fortify his tea with shots of rum. Musing on the leaky ship of state, Harrison widens his eyes and slows his cadence to a rueful dirge. It is no mystery why Irving, as young Ellie Dunn, wants to marry the old man after her engagement to the coarse industrialist Boss Mangan sours. Harrison is the vital, sad soul of *Heartbreak House*.

As his romantic but clear-eyed daughter Hesione, Rosemary Harris gives a funny and sympathetic performance. "Have I broken your heart?" she coos to one frustrated lover. "I didn't know you had one." Ivey, her head comically elevated over a high ruffled collar, plays her stuffy sister Ariadne with a tremor that can turn either haughty or humble.

Tears well easily in Irving's eyes, when Ellie's first love turns out to be her best friend's husband. But then her features and voice gradually take on a steely resolve, as she calmly outmaneuvers another selfish suitor (George Martin as Boss Mangan) and marries the captain. LEFT: From *Heartbreak House.*

The production builds to its climax in carefully registered moments: a cigar planted like a fuse at the center of Martin's florid face; a panicky Jan Miner flailing a servant's warning to turn out the lights in an air raid; the ghastly gray cast on the screen when a bomb explodes near the house. But even something as decisive as a bomb strike can't quiet the churning, ambiguous longings in *Heartbreak House.* "What a glorious experience!" Harris marvels of the lethal planes. "I hope they'll come again tomorrow night."

LUIS VALDEZ

TRUE GRASS ROOTS THEATER: *LA PASTORELA*

FOR SOME THEATER COMPANIES, "GRASS ROOTS" IS MORE OF A POPULIST MARKETING TOOL than a reality. Not so for El Teatro Campesino, the farmworkers' theater company formed during the 1965 Delano grape strike in San Juan Bautista, California. Founder Luis Valdez discovered his theater's mission in the soil—the fruit and vegetable fields worked by migrant laborers.

Valdez and El Teatro have kept the faith for over thirty years, giving voice to the Latino experience in scores of barbed and splashy stage works. Valdez gained wider notoriety with the 1978 musical *Zoot Suit* and the 1987 film *La Bamba*, both of which he wrote and directed.

In *La Pastorela*, Valdez frames a traditional Christmas shepherds' play with a contemporary *Wizard of Oz*–like story about a farmworker's daughter who dreams the events of the play. Linda Ronstadt appears as the armored archangel San Miguel, soaring through the sky with sword drawn to vanquish Satanas (Paul Rodriguez). In the following interview, writer-director Valdez talks about the origins and production of the piece, which was filmed in and around San Juan Bautista.

Q: *What got you interested in this tradition?*

A: *Pastorelas* are probably the oldest medieval works brought over to Mexico with the conquest, and a cornerstone of the Hispanic theater. They had enormous popular appeal but fell out of use here in the nineteenth century. The battles of the angels and devils make them daunting to do—that and the high-flown, archaic Spanish they're written in.

The mother of one of our company members had a typed manuscript of a *pastorela* from her village in Mexico. The language and characterizations were quite accessible. It was a play, not just a pageant.

Q: *You did this first as a puppet play in the early 1970s.*

A: Yes, to see if we could get a handle on the material. Then we began doing it in the streets of San Juan Bautista. The audience would follow along on the shepherds' journey. It was very boisterous and broad, which may be why the church fathers were a little reluctant to let us use the mission church when it rained one year.

Q: *Did you consider filming it in the San Juan Bautista Mission for* GREAT PERFORMANCES*?*

A: I always felt this should be done as a movie, with exterior locations. I do a lot of walking in these hills, so I know them well. It was once a major sheep and cattle area. So there was a natural connection.

Q: *And what's the* Wizard of Oz *connection?*

A: Everybody rips off something. Actually, I saw it as a way to uphold one tradition by inviting another one in.

Q: *Your devils are very modern, too. They ride Harleys and spy on the shepherds with binoculars.*

A: Devils need to be as devilish as they can be in popular dramas, and the only way to do that is to make them modern, to make them present tense. I don't really believe that bikers are devils, you know. They tap into an image, one that also satirizes itself.

Q: *Some of the special effects are quite ingenious—a devil leaping into one shepherd's body and bloating him up, the battle in the heavens between San Miguel and Satanas.*

A: The tricky part was to make it work within the budget, about $1.2 million. The computer-generated imagery was important, but sometimes making a movie is just hard and old-fashioned. One of the night shoots had to be done at 4:00 A.M., and it was very cold.

Q: *Your version of hell looks an awful lot like a major earthquake.*

A: That may have been subconscious. I was out walking that afternoon in 1989 when the big quake hit here. It was hellish, it was fantastic. We're terrified of the destruction, but that energy is feeding us, too, it's feeding us all the time.

"[San Juan Bautista is] some of the loveliest country in California. Here was a tremendous opportunity to aim the camera at this landscape. A lot of people here don't understand why I insist on going back to this dinky little town. . . . Those people who do make it to San Juan Bautista understand."

—LUIS VALDEZ

LEFT: Cheech Marin and Paul Rodriguez in *La Pastorela.*

[*29*]

Great Adaptations of Literary Works

GREAT PERFORMANCES ASSUMES WHAT MOST TELEVISION PROGRAMMING SEEMS DETERMINED TO disprove: that its viewers actually read. Many of the series' most successful adaptations spring from unlikely works that defy conventional wisdom about capturing and holding a television audience at home.

CURTAIN CALLS FOR
VERNA: USO GIRL

She sings flat and dances like a kid who has just strapped on tap shoes for the first time. These wobbly skills, combined with a dewy-eyed conviction about her talent, make Verna, as Sissy Spacek portrays her, a beguiling leading lady in this 1978 made-for-TV film about a World War II USO troupe. Being bad has never won so many hearts.

Based on a short story by Paul Gallico, *Verna* follows a low-rent show around the besieged American army posts in Europe. The film was actually shot in Hammelberg and Baumholder, Germany, where hundreds of 1970s GIs served as the grateful audience for the title character's endearingly inept charms. Verna plays third fiddle to Sally Kellerman's velvet-voiced chanteuse and Howard da Silva's Catskills comic. Neither of these seasoned show-biz vets can convince Verna that her Broadway dreams will never come true.

"You're not even second rate," Eddie (da Silva) levels with her.

"How do you know?" she shoots back.

"Because *I'm* not even second rate."

A then-unknown William Hurt plays a farmboy army captain who falls in love with Verna as she croons "Someone to Watch Over Me" in her pale reedy soprano. She loves him back but declines his proposal. Marriage, Verna tells him with a wistful smile, will just interfere with all the parties and publicity and opening nights that are sure to be hers. Her "gift" has to come first.

The two create a sweet, innocent chemistry in their brief affair. Hurt's blond locks, cleft chin, and adoring looks make him guileless and vulnerable. Spacek, a telekinetic icon in Brian de Palma's high school horror film *Carrie* two years before, gives Verna a hoofer's determination—even offstage she never stops tapping. But she is as delicate as she is blithely dense about herself. The slightest crackle of distant gunfire sends Verna into a terrorized trance.

Albert Innaurato's teleplay and Ronald F. Maxwell's direction are models of tactful restraint and understated irony. By cutting in period black-and-white stills of Bob Hope and other USO luminaries, the film places Verna in charmed company for her perilous moment in the limelight. In an affecting climax, Verna has to master her fears in order to perform in an underground bunker as mor-

"Hurt is at his best—sexy, tender, sweet. . . . Spacek is unforgettable. . . . She brings to the role a concept-of-self so strong that even the viewer expects a miracle: the heartfelt hope that one morning Verna will wake up to find she has become a 'star.' No glitzy staging or props take away from this tightly crafted little film."

—Penny L. Nickle
SAGINAW NEWS

LEFT: Sissy Spacek delights the troops as the good-hearted if flat-footed Verna.

[*31*]

tar shells explode above. With the worn, war-stressed faces of the soldiers looking on, Spacek shoulders her cane, conquers the most authentic case of stage fright she's ever had, and finally flings her arms high in triumph.

Then, like the punch line to one of Eddie's bad jokes, Verna promptly dies when her jeep rolls over a land mine in a mishap far from the front. Her hero's funeral in Paris offers a deadpan irony about the way war inverts the rational order of things. For the viewer, it also makes a perfect curtain call. Now Verna will never have her dreams destroyed.

Verna: USO Girl was rebroadcast in 1992 and celebrated once again as one of GREAT PERFORMANCES' early triumphs in dramatic adaptation.

A DEADLY GAME
TINKER, TAILOR, SOLDIER, SPY

The title of John le Carré's 1974 espionage novel comes from a child's ditty. But on the page and in the meditative BBC miniseries based on the book, *Tinker, Tailor, Solider, Spy* is a mature and challenging work for adults.

Alec Guinness stars as George Smiley, a silver-haired London secret agent whose unprepossessing looks and self-effacing manner make him the antithesis of that fantasy image of British spy stories, Ian Fleming's James Bond. Where Bond comes accessorized with gadgets and pneumatic women, Smiley has only his beady intelligence and deliberate deductive powers to flush out a Russian double agent, the "mole" who has been planted at the Circus, the summit of British intelligence.

Le Carré's plots are famously complicated, and this one is no exception. Host Robert MacNeil offers some kindly encouragement through the six-part series. "It's no disgrace to be confused," he counsels. Keeping up with the betrayals, double dealing, and blind alleys in adaptor Arthur Hopcraft's astute dramatization of the Cold War narrative is only one small part of the pleasure *Tinker, Tailor* provides. Directed by John Irvin with a somber, film noir-inflected mood, the show's six hours probe le Carré's themes and characters with a cumulative depth and resonance.

The pursuer, his elusive prey, and the supporting players are rendered in economical strokes, keenly realized by a superb cast. In addition to Guinness, who makes a duly celebrated television debut in the series, a calculating Michael Aldridge, pouting Bernard Hepton, grimly retributive Ian Bannen, and faltering but tenacious Alexander Knox create distinct impressions.

Ian Richardson, cast as the double agent, gives off a chilling, amphibious calm in his early scenes, fussily clapping a saucer over his teacup to keep his tea warm or narrowing his eyes with a lizardlike detachment at a fellow agent or a painting he admires. When Smiley finally corners him, Richardson admits to his betrayals—which include sleeping with Smiley's wife—with a bracing clarity. "Do you mind if I finish my drink, George?" he asks. In prison, he lays out his revulsion for a Western democracy riddled by greed, moral and political constipation, and "the economic repression of the masses in America." With that, he turns Smiley into a messenger boy, conveying notes of

"Just when you think you've utterly lost track of the plot and half the characters, everything snaps back into bracing, if fleeting, clarity. Tinker, Tailor proves not so much a merely captivating tale as an induced compulsion. A paranoid's delight. A thinking person's Shogun. Chess with soul. A glass of port on a chilly, rainy night."

—Tom Shales
WASHINGTON POST

RIGHT: Alec Guinness as George Smiley faces off with the enigmatic Karla played by Patrick Stewart.

farewell, one to his girlfriend and another to his male lover. Richardson's bisexual connoisseur acquired a real-world counterpart around the time of the series premiere in England, when news broke of Anthony Blunt, the homosexual art scholar and spy who had worked for the Queen.

A FIGURE IN ECLIPSE

Le Carré thought the "small, podgy, and at best middle-aged figure" of Smiley could never transfer successfully to the screen. Guinness, who captures the author's image of "a man searching for his own lost innocence among the sins of his companions," made a believer of le Carré. Guinness brings a chromatic richness to Smiley without straining for a single note. In portraying a man banished from his beloved Circus, then summoned back to purge it of the betrayer's stain, Guinness allows pride, indignation, suppressed fury, and a guileless trust to play across his bland, seemingly impassive face.

Smiley is a figure in eclipse, in both his career and his marriage, as the story opens. At moments, in some sad, half-empty restaurant, he almost seems to disappear behind his horn-rimmed glasses; even a hand lifted to call for a check goes unnoticed. His strength, however, comes from just this quiet but deeply felt sense of the tenuous nature of all human connections.

In a beautifully pitched reunion with a woman Smiley once worked with (Beryl Reid), Guinness brings a melting tenderness to the screen. His face-off with his Russian rival (a scowling, silent Patrick Stewart) ends with the Russian making off with a cigarette lighter inscribed with a message of love from his wife. Even after Smiley has solved the case and seized control of the Circus, mastery is an illusion.

In the show's only scene with Smiley's wife Ann (Sian Phillips), a pivotal offstage character, it's she who gets the last word. Turning to Smiley on a windswept lawn, she sighs, "Poor George. Life's just a puzzle to you, isn't it?"

Le Carré's instincts about television as a "talk medium" more appropriate for *Tinker, Tailor, Soldier, Spy* than film were confirmed. The cryptic conversations, many of them shot in a shadowy half-light, build the story's claustrophobic momentum. Brief interludes in a Portuguese village and the English countryside, even the random barking of a dog somewhere, deftly imply the larger world outside this overheated mind game.

Smiley knows it's a game, but a deadly serious one that can never be resolved and never won. The only refuge is the truth. To his Russian rival he offers "no claims about the moral superiority of the West." What they share, he says sadly, are "new forms of the old misery."

THE REIGN OF *BRIDESHEAD REVISITED*

"My theme is memory," the narrator of *Brideshead Revisited* says, "that winged host that soared above me one gray morning of wartime. Those memories—for we possess nothing certainly except the past— are always with me."

The lines come deep into the massive eleven-part dramatization of Evelyn Waugh's 1945

"I really don't pay much attention to the differences between motion pictures and television. I believe it is silly to think in those terms. . . . An outstanding role is equally worth playing on stage, for TV, or movies. In some instances, a story can only be told properly on TV—Shogun and Tinker, Tailor, Soldier, Spy, for example."

—ANTHONY HOPKINS

LEFT: Anthony Andrews as Sebastian Flyte, Diana Quick as Julia Flyte, and Jeremy Irons as Charles Ryder in front of Castle Howard, the real setting for *Brideshead Revisited.*

novel. But they might well serve as a burnished frontispiece for a production that captivated viewers on both sides of the Atlantic in the early 1980s. In both sentiment and tone, those words evoke the elegiac rhythm of this remarkable work as it recounts one man's journey into the many-chambered heart of a privileged English family between the two world wars.

Jeremy Irons stars as the camera-eye main character, Charles Ryder, a young artist enthralled by the Marchmain family of Brideshead Castle. Infatuated first by the family's beautiful son Sebastian and then by the elder daughter Julia, each of them a tormented soul, Ryder sees his hopes initially dissolve and then find unexpected redemption through the story's long arc. Laurence Olivier, John Gielgud, Claire Bloom, and such gifted newcomers as Anthony Andrews and Nickolas Grace lend their luster to the cast.

The series became famous for many things, from its sumptuous visual style and all-star cast to its doting fascination with upper-class mores and a cult for teddy bears that one of its characters provoked. In John Mortimer's rigorously faithful adaptation, the action shuttles from the soaring vistas at Brideshead Castle to the twisted streets of Morocco, from Venice to Mexico, from the spires of Oxford to the skyscrapers of New York. Foxhunts, champagne suppers, the British General Strike of 1926, and a love affair on a storm-tossed luxury ship are all disclosed in flattering cinematography. Addictive, sybaritic, sexy, and insidiously funny, this was, as both critics and ratings testified, a major television event.

The most astonishing thing about the *Brideshead* phenomenon—and it was nothing less than that in its reign on British and American TV—may be that it ever came about in the first place. For all its lavish grandeur, the themes turn relentlessly inward, to obsession, the nature of religious faith and doubt, thwarted love, emotional privation, and memory's persistence. Steeped in Catholic theology and nostalgia for a bygone way of life, Waugh's novel, which some critics had found overwrought and sentimental, seemed an unlikely candidate for a sprawling, high-budget translation to the screen. The author's own attempt to adapt *Brideshead* for Hollywood had failed.

In bringing it to television, Mortimer, directors Michael Lindsay-Hogg and Charles Sturridge, and their collaborators give the novel, flaws and all, a full accounting. The voice-over narration preserves Waugh's moody authorial presence, while the accumulated detail renders the narrative and emotional texture with a density few adaptations even attempt.

Mortimer wanted viewers to experience the book "at the length and, as nearly as possible, in the way the author intended." In what the *Times* of London's Michael Ratcliffe called "a triumph of beauty, fidelity and relevant embellishment," *Brideshead Revisited* succeeds in doing just that.

A WORLD IN TRANSITION

The story opens in 1944, in the mind and memory of Ryder as a British army captain. Passing with his troops near Brideshead, he is flung backward in time to his first memories of the family that would shape so much of his life.

The early episodes are devoted to Charles's idyllic friendship with the Marchmain son Sebastian Flyte (Anthony Andrews), first at Oxford and then at Brideshead, in sun-dappled Venice, and

"There are so few basic pleasures in life, really: sex, money, chocolate, and Brideshead Revisited. It's a tribute to the mercurial allure of the program that, finally, its appeal and its magical spell cannot be fully explained."

—Tom Shales
LOS ANGELES TIMES

"Brideshead Revisited is, in every frame, a moveable feast. To celebrate its arrival, you might re-create the grand Parisian dinner. Or stock up on peaches and berries, whip up some potted shrimps, or fix a treacle tart. Then, settle back for eleven weeks of this exquisite Baroque binge."

—Regina Nadelson
CHRISTIAN SCIENCE MONITOR

elsewhere. While the teddy-bear-toting dandy Sebastian is portrayed as plainly homosexual, the nature

of his relationship with Charles, who later marries and subsequently falls in love with

Sebastian's sister Julia (Diana Quick), is one of the story's blurred ambiguities.

In flashbacks within flashbacks, the plot embraces a widening circle of characters

and slowly darkening events. Bloom plays the family's pious and manipulative mother, Lady

Marchmain. Olivier's shadowy offstage presence comes richly to the forefront in the final

chapter, when his roguish Lord Marchmain, with his mistress (Stephane Audran), returns

from Italy to die at home. Gielgud, in a feat of sustained comic malice, plays Charles's piti-

less father. Nickolas Grace amply fills one of many vivid minor roles, playing the brilliant

and caustic Anthony Blanche with a wickedly articulate stammer.

The story's central action turns slowly on Sebastian's descent from a bibulous Oxford

aesthete to a full-blown alcoholic, made harrowing in Andrews's performance. Sebastian's loss

becomes, through Charles's watchful lens, a whole world in transition—toward war and the

meaner, grimmer existence that will succeed it. When Charles loses Julia to the mysteries of a Catholic

faith he scorns and at last dimly apprehends, *Brideshead Revisited* reaches its deeply reflective coda.

"Advisory to fund-hungry public TV execs: think sex. Right after the steamy sex scene (with frontal nudity, if you can imagine!) in episode nine of Brideshead Revisited, Channel Thirteen's phone-in fund-raising effort received the most money ever during a single commercial break—$52,000 from a total of 1,275 callers."

— James Brandy
NEW YORK POST

ABOVE: Sebastian (Anthony Andrews) and Charles (Jeremy Irons) recall happier days in *Brideshead Revisited*.

FROM A ROCKY START TO A "RARE EVENT"

Four years in the making, at a cost of over eight million dollars, the series was stalled by a technicians' strike, a change in directors, and Irons's shooting schedule for *The French Lieutenant's Woman.* And not everyone was taken with it: the *Washington Post's* Jonathan Yardley called the series "soap opera for the gentry," and Charles Champlin, in the *Los Angeles Times,* pronounced it "a sumptuous bore." But for the millions who watched it and for the critics who cheered, *Brideshead* remains a rare and treasured event—"the best series ever seen on American television," as one critic plainly put the case. A decade and a half later, its images, and layered effects, and above all, its pervasive atmosphere live on.

Who remembers what Charles and Sebastian said as they lolled under a tree eating strawberries, or what insult fell from Julia's lips in the velvety shadow of a Brideshead fountain at dusk? But who can forget how it felt to see, hear, and sense everything so completely in the moment? *Brideshead Revisited,* in making memory its central theme, created something unforgettable in the process.

THE MYTHS OF TINSELTOWN
TALES FROM THE HOLLYWOOD HILLS

"Hollywood *is* America," the novelist and screenwriter Budd Schulberg wrote, "only bigger, brighter, louder, speeded up." That's a fitting epigraph for *Tales from the Hollywood Hills,* a series of six short-story adaptations that explored, in brightly contrasting tones and temperaments, the pervasive Tinseltown myth. The writers, including Schulberg, F. Scott Fitzgerald, John O'Hara, and William Faulkner, knew Hollywood's seductive allure firsthand. Most had been bruised by it, too, having sold their talent to star-driven studios that routinely treated writers as a lower life-form.

While a number of the tales take a decidedly dark view of Hollywood's sun-spangled glamour in the 1930s, farce and sharp-eyed satire find a home here as well. In "The Old Reliable," P.G. Wodehouse zooms in on a former silent film star, played by Rosemary Harris, who "slept her way to the middle," then threatened to tell all in her memoirs. The fine British farcemeister Michael Blakemore, director of *Noises Off,* here directs Robert Mundy's teleplay based on the Wodehouse story.

Schulberg, author of the essential Hollywood novel *What Makes Sammy Run,* teamed up with Stan Silverman on the adaptation of "A Table at Ciro's." This is the story of a studio head, modeled on the author's father, Paramount mogul B. P. Schulberg, who throws a party for a throng of parasites. A graceful Darren McGavin plays the lead.

In the ruefully funny "Pat Hobby Teamed with Genius," writer-director Rob Thompson combines three of the seventeen Hollywood stories Fitzgerald wrote in the last two years of his life. Christopher Lloyd, a fixture on the TV series *Taxi,* got a breakthrough role as the hack writer Pat Hobby in a battered Panama hat.

Rita Moreno stars as an aging fifties starlet who hires an arty director to save her career in underrated Gavin Lambert's "The Closed Set." Faulkner's "Golden Land," based on his only Hollywood short story, studies the effect of a young actress's sex scandal on her obtuse father (James Sikking).

The six tales were widely praised for their evocative and well-paced direction. Palm

"Looking back, it was a most unusual era. We would all be in the back room of Stanley Rose's bookstore, which was on Hollywood Boulevard, near Vine. There were maybe a half-dozen of the best writers in America. There was William Faulkner, writing away for Fox; there was Fitzgerald; and there was William Saroyan, Dorothy Parker, Johnnie O'Hara, Nathanael West, and Horace McCoy, who wrote They Shoot Horses, Don't They? *. . . I could go on and on and name maybe twenty . . . all drinking Stanley Rose's cheap orange wine in the back of that bookstore and talking about life and the movies."*

—Budd Schulberg

RIGHT: The fame and beauty of Natica Jackson, played by Michelle Pfeiffer, fail to bring her happiness in *Tales from the Hollywood Hills.*

trees, swimming pools, mansions, swank vintage cars, and dreamy period costumes give the stories a delicious glaze. Nuggets of hard-bitten dialogue and wry cynicism add the appropriate crackle and snap.

John O'Hara's "Natica Jackson," adapted by Andy Wolk and superbly directed by Paul Bogart, is the most memorable episode of the series. In spinning out the story of a lonely, glamorous star who falls in love with a married family man, O'Hara offers a parable about the industry of dreams and the nightmares it can create.

With a radiantly unhappy Michelle Pfeiffer in the title role, the story translates beautifully to the screen. From the first shots of Natica driving herself to work down a canyon's winding roads, Pfeiffer's solitary beauty works like a drug on the viewer. The effect is reinforced when the camera pulls back on the star playing a weepy log-cabin love scene on a crowded soundstage. Passion, for Natica, is always artificial and remote.

Everything changes when she crashes into the car of a chemist (Brian Kerwin) on her way home from work. Natica may act tough after their first night in bed—"Don't start asking about my experiences," she warns him; "by tomorrow morning you'll be one of them"—but as Pfeiffer's deep, swimming eyes reveal, Natica is falling in love and falling hard. "I'm crazy mad about this fella," she purrs.

The affair is doomed, the viewer senses, but not just because Natica's lover gets cold feet and pulls back for a while. As the camera slowly pans his pregnant wife's midsection, the story takes a startlingly tragic turn. The wronged woman gets her revenge by leaving her two small children in the ocean to drown. Across town, meanwhile, her husband cavorts in a swimming pool with Natica.

Bogart's direction mirrors O'Hara's ironies and clean narrative concision right to the end. "Natica Jackson" doesn't linger in any maudlin aftermath. It delivers the heroine right back to where she lives. In the final scene, Pfeiffer tools up to the studio gate. Looming overhead is the billboard for her latest film. Its title, *Dark Voyage,* is pure Hollywood eloquence.

RESILIENCE AND PASSION

THE MAHABHARATA

Length was the inevitable first topic when *The Mahabharata* aired in the spring of 1991. At six hours, Peter Brook's theatrical transformation of the Sanskrit saga clocked one of the longest running times, after *Brideshead Revisited,* in the annals of theater on GREAT PERFORMANCES. Audiences who had attended the original stage production, first mounted in an abandoned stone quarry near Avignon, France, in 1985 and later at the Brooklyn Academy of Music and other venues, could boast an even greater commitment. The live version of the Indian classic took nine hours to perform.

There are other impressive numbers attached to *The Mahabharata* (pronounced ma-ha-BAH-ra-ta). Brook and Jean-Claude Carrière spent ten years developing a script from the two-thousand-year-old poem; this epic of one hundred thousand verses about the history of humankind is fifteen times as long as the Bible. A multiracial cast from more than a dozen countries reflects the dizzying range of characters and plot complications. Only the ratings for

"[The Mahabharata] *presents nothing less ambitious than the Hindu story of mankind; its plot has the degree of difficulty of Shakespeare's history plays, and it shines with a spiritual significance akin to that of the Bible. . . . And like the Bible and the Bard, it weaves some juicy tales of higher deities and heroes, of love, war, murder, madness, greed, rape, and incest."*

—Glenn Collins
NEW YORK TIMES

LEFT: Jeffrey Kissoon as the vengeful Karna sits guard over a hermit, Velu Vishwanadan.

the first night of *The Mahabharata* show numbers that are relatively low, since the first of its three parts went up against the 1991 Academy Awards telecast.

But numbers provide no measure of this singular viewing experience. With its agile narrative, expansive spirituality and philosophy, clamorous spectacle, insinuating music, and sheen of miraculous events, Brook's production opens a universe that operates by its own natural and inevitable laws. Of course a man can become a gazelle, a woman can give birth to an iron ball that in turn becomes one hundred children, and a warrior can catch a flying arrow in his teeth. Witnessing *The Mahabharata* becomes a way of believing. "If you listen carefully," the poet narrator advises, "at the end you'll be someone else."

The story of two warring clans of royal cousins is told by the graybeard Vyasa (Robert Langdon Lloyd) to a wonderstruck young prince who enters a candlelit cave in order to hear it. The elephant-headed god Ganesha serves as scribe. In the exposition-packed first half of the first section, "The Game of Dice," the poet quickly weaves the ancestral fabric of the main characters' lives.

Human flaws and supernatural curses stitched into the early part of the story are destined to reappear in the pattern for centuries. Because a princess closes her eyes at the sight of a scruffy lover, her son is born blind. That son's wife will veil her eyes to join him in a sightless marriage. Similarly, the warrior Arjuna (a compelling Vittorio Mezzogiorno) is doomed to a monastic, effeminate life for rejecting a woman.

Sex is the work's bounteous and potent wellspring. Erotic energy shimmers on the screen. It's in the avid almond eyes of Draupadi (Mallika Sarabhai), a woman who marries five brothers, and in the delirious embrace of the strongman Bhima (an ebullient Mamadou Dioume) that levitates him and his bride off the dusty clearing where they meet and promptly produce a full-grown son.

The fates of the rival families are fixed in a crooked dice game. In Part Two, the avaricious Kauravas take control of the kingdom, while the virtuous Pandavas spend twelve years in exile. In Part Three, the families go to war. Played out in a mythic realm of firelight, snowy mountain peaks, and a sun staring through swirling clouds, love scenes, tense familial dramas, and battles are tumbled together with meditative dialogues.

Brook, the legendary stage and film director who heads the International Center of Theater Research in Paris, where *The Mahabharata* was filmed, says the tale is about the conflict between "order and chaos, between dharma and its opposite." Its wisdom may spring from a Hindu worldview, but the dramatic truth feels at once universal and mysterious.

In one quietly captivating scene, the Pandava leader Yudhishthira, played by the sublime Andrzej Seweryn, has a catechismal exchange with a talking lake. Ignorance is grief, we learn, and desire is poison. "What is inevitable?" the lake asks. Yudhishthira answers without dropping a beat: "Happiness."

Lives end and illusions fall away in *The Mahabharata*. Even paradise, which Yudhishthira reaches by a rope ladder in the final scene, can be a disappointment. What endures is the drama's resilient sense of life.

"Mr. Brook, who should never be underestimated, has transformed the epic Indian poem, a saga encompassing the Hindu story of mankind, into brilliantly theatrical television. . . . This is a wonderfully rich and complicated tapestry. . . . In the end, The Mahabharata *is a treatise on wisdom, on realizing ultimate illusions about suffering and happiness, war and peace."*

—John J. O'Connor
NEW YORK TIMES

"Words are never innocent. They're loaded with a shrewd subconscious imagery. Buddha describes the subconscious as something like our sympathetic nervous system. The word is defined in The Mahabharata *as the 'secret movement of the atman'—very difficult to translate. To try to explain the 'atman' would take me an hour. It's neither soul, nor spirit, but means at once the moral value of an individual and his place within a group. It's a very Indian, very complicated idea."*

—JEAN-CLAUDE CARRIÈRE

RIGHT: A scene from *The Mahabharata.*

[*42*]

EDITH WHARTON'S STORIES

Like all keen observers of the social pecking order, Edith Wharton knew the color and plumage of her chosen species down to the last feather. Style—in clothing, food, wine, flowers, and interior decoration (the subject of her first book in 1897)—revealed where Wharton's characters stood in a world that processed lives, women's lives especially, as commodities.

In this 1981 trilogy that helped fuel the Wharton revival, the gorgeous costumes are abundant and closely observed. From flower-trimmed hats to tightly cinched corsets, fluted muslin gowns to lace-filigreed gloves, the women are splendidly turned out. But there's not a trace of empty costume drama here. Whether in the glittering New York society of *The House of Mirth* or a stifling New England small town in *Summer,* women are measured by what they wear. Wharton herself, played by Kathleen Widdoes in *Looking Back,* revisits her past in a memory-glazed vision of satin, chiffon, and diamond chokers.

THE HOUSE OF MIRTH

"I'm horribly poor and very expensive," says the glamorous but not-so-young heroine of *The House of Mirth,* Wharton's masterful 1905 novel about a woman's quest to marry well. Played by Geraldine Chaplin with a ghostly smile and an eerie premonition of doom, Lily Bart flits through a forest of cynical old-money and grasping parvenus. One prospective suitor after another eludes her.

The man who truly loves her (William Atherton as the candid Lawrence Selden) lacks money. Others who want her don't offer the social connections or romantic allure she's after. Amid the garden parties, dinners, open adulteries, and secret letters, Lily is trapped by her own failings and the ruthless self-interest of others. In the end, she poisons herself.

Director Adrian Hall sees Lily's decline as a function of intently, sometimes grotesquely examined surfaces. The camera drinks in the details with hallucinatory fascination: Lily's features twitching nervously in the shadow of a broad straw hat, cigarette smoke pouring from her nostrils, the guests at an elegant dinner party working noisily at their food.

The costumes, by Karen Roston, offer a sumptuous catalog of Edwardian splendor. They also anchor several striking, subliminally powerful scenes. Lacing up another woman's corset, Lily pulls fiercely and grimaces at this daily task, considered essential for a woman's beauty and marketability. Later on, reduced to working in a milliner's shop, Lily is scorned for failing to sew some sequins on properly. In the end, the beautiful things Lily has craved so much are the very substance of her humiliation and defeat.

"Wharton has been called the American Jane Austen. Yet I feel her range was wider than Austen's. She not only pinned New York society like a butterfly in a case, but she also wrote wonderfully and compassionately about the gaunt, barren world of the New England mountain people scratching out futile lives in the stony soil— the stuff of O'Neill. . . . GREAT PERFORMANCES in this trilogy gave us both sides of the Wharton coin."

—Cecil Smith
LOS ANGELES TIMES

LEFT: Geraldine Chaplin as Lily Bart in Edith Wharton's *The House of Mirth.*

SUMMER

The blooming teenage heroine of *Summer* comes from a distant world. Born among rough New England mountain folk, Charity (Diane Lane) is adopted and raised by a widowed lawyer (John Cullum) in sleepy North Dormer. Charity, like Lily Bart, longs for a richer existence. She glimpses it one day when she sees a hat blow off the head of a stylish architect (Michael Ontkean) visiting from New York.

Freed from the confines of a high ruffled collar, Charity's neck becomes a potent signal of her sexuality. Both the duplicitous architect and ravenous lawyer are drawn to it. Sexual jealousy gets its spontaneous expression when Charity rips the blouse a friend is sewing for Charity's rival. And nothing fixes the distance Charity hopes to put between herself and her past like the rough felt hats and shapeless clothes her mountain relatives wear.

Summer gets a soft-focus ending that's less ambiguous than Wharton's own. But Dezso Magyar's deliberate production catches the emotional sense of the tale, the intense yearning of a girl to style her own life as she pleases.

LOOKING BACK

Wharton herself finally accomplished that, leaving behind a boorish husband and repressive American society to live her last twenty-six years in France. In *Looking Back,* the author pays a last visit to the Mount, the Massachusetts Berkshire estate she occupied for many years. Steve Lawson's script pieces together various details and important figures from Wharton's life—including a jovial Henry James (Richard Woods) and her smoldering lover Morton Fullerton (Stephen Collins)—into a sepia-tinted memory piece.

RIGHT: A garden party scene from Edith Wharton's *The House of Mirth.*

"I won't be buried alive," she tells her doltish husband Teddy (John McMartin), in a flashback to their breakup. As Wharton, Widdoes never brandishes the green parasol she carries, but at any moment, it seems, she might. The furnishings of a woman's wardrobe, in the life and works of Edith Wharton, have a terrible power.

RE-CREATING A CLASSIC
ALICE IN WONDERLAND

Make it look just like the books, Eva Le Gallienne had said. With that disarmingly simple request, the director of *Alice in Wonderland* sent her designers scurrying to re-create, in three dimensions, the world's most famous storybooks. Few tales are as closely linked to their illustrations as Lewis Carroll's classic Victorian fantasies, *Alice's Adventures in Wonderland* and *Through the Looking Glass,* are to John Tenniel's indelible black-and-white drawings of the fanciful characters. Audiences *knew* what this show should look like before they ever took a look at it.

No one had a tougher assignment than Patricia Zipprodt, the costume designer of one Broadway landmark after another. Zipprodt has conjured up everything from the garb of a Russian peasant village for *Fiddler on the Roof* to the Weimar decadence of *Cabaret.* But "this was completely new," the designer recalls. "I'd never tried to translate someone else's drawings into costumes for actors who would be moving and breathing and dancing inside them. It was a monstrous job."

Zipprodt explains that merely scaling the three- to four-inch-high figures up to human size would never have worked. "The dodo birds would have been twelve feet tall. The White Rabbit's ears

would have been impossibly large. They would have weighed too much. And how would they be cleaned? Or stored?"

If Zipprodt was cramped by practical concerns, the viewer remains blissfully unaware. *Alice in Wonderland*, which aired on GREAT PERFORMANCES after its brief 1982 engagement on Broadway, is a parade of witty theatricalizations of Carroll and Tenniel's original conceptions. And part of the fun of the show comes from watching one well-known actor after another turn up in delectable cameos.

Eve Arden does her deadpan stare as a boxy Queen of Hearts. Kaye Ballard is the bellowing, big-mouthed Duchess. Donald O'Connor, surprisingly agile inside his massive Mock Turtle shell and flippers, tosses off a jolly lobster quadrille. A stressed and stammering Nathan Lane worries his long Mouse tail with his paws. Colleen Dewhurst is the Red Queen opposite Maureen Stapleton's White Queen. In the show's tenderest scene, Richard Burton plays an addled but noble White Knight to his daughter Kate Burton's winsome Alice.

Alice in Wonderland keeps dealing out little double-shocks of recognition. First, through Zipprodt's uncannily accurate costumes, comes the image from the book. Then we recognize some familiar face peering out from inside the creature.

"There isn't one word in the play that isn't Carroll. . . . Not one word. And there isn't anything you see that is not a Tenniel drawing. My idea of the production was to make people feel they were seeing the two books come to life."

—EVA LE GALLIENNE

ABOVE: Kate Burton as Alice talks with Austin Pendleton's White Rabbit as the Queen of Hearts (Eve Arden) looks on.

[48]

Zipprodt began by enlarging photocopies of the Tenniel drawings, then decided what to include, what to change, and what to leave out. "Some of the crosshatching is there and some isn't," she says. "That's where the artistry came in. We wanted just the touches that would convey the feel of an illustration." Color was added in spots to harmonize with John Lee Beatty's sets, some of which scroll like a Japanese screen.

Zipprodt says that computers could probably help now in projecting the sculptural dimension of the costumes—the White Rabbit's comically low-slung hips, the Caterpillar's bulbous snaky form. In 1982, it was all done by trial and error and with laborious fittings, some of which took three hours or more.

"The real burden of my work is carried by the costume makers," Zipprodt says. "I don't make them. I stand around and say, 'No!' 'Yes!' 'Stop this!' 'That's terrific!'"

Le Gallienne's *Alice*, which she had staged first in 1932 and then revived in 1947, was not a success on its return to Broadway in 1982. Critics praised the design but found the production static. Streamlined, given a new backstage frame, and bolstered with star power for television, it got a livelier second life.

"It could have been awful," Zipprodt says. "The camera doesn't give you any choice of where to look. In this case it worked. The show looked great onstage, but it didn't move. On television it did."

"The set designer John Lee Beatty and the costume designer Patricia Zipprodt have done an extraordinary job of bringing to life the celebrated storybook illustrations of John Tenniel. Virtually every drawing has been rendered to the stage perfectly intact. . . . Every detail is in place—even the curls of line on the sole of Humpty Dumpty's shoe—and all are lovely."

—Frank Rich
NEW YORK TIMES

BELOW: Alice (Kate Burton) talks with Tweedledee and Tweedledum (Alan Weeks and Andre De Shields).

A Great Tour of the Musicals

From *The Gospel at Colonus* to *Sweeney Todd*, Great Performances surveys the invigorating range of the American musical theater. Visits backstage and behind the curtain add the drama, discipline, and giddy electricity of the artists putting it all together.

BENEDICTION AND CATHARSIS IN
The Gospel at Colonus

Resplendent in an African print preacher's robe, Morgan Freeman steps up to a Plexiglas pulpit and declares, "I take for my text this evening the book of Oedipus." And so he does, in adapter-director Lee Breuer's audacious fusion of Sophocles' benedictory Oedipus at Colonus and an ecstatic Pentecostal church service. As composer Bob Telson's gospel, blues, soul, and rock-and-roll score reverberates around the arena, Oedipus, played by the celebrated blind singer Clarence Fountain in a sharkskin suit, rages and wails and finally accepts his own death.

The Institutional Radio Choir of Brooklyn sings and sways and claps out gospel affirmation. The J. D. Steele Singers and J. J. Farley and the Soul Stirrers add their infectious rhythms and falsetto exclamations. "There's hope for me," Oedipus sings. "There's a prophecy." The choir and musicians excitedly concur.

Breuer called his creation "a synthesis of opposed values" or "classicism with a jive stance." He also cited Greek theater scholars who believe a fifth century B.C. amphitheater performance might have felt something like a modern-day church meeting.

In truth, the Breuer-Telson *Gospel* needs no historical justification. It communicates directly to the heart, with the raw power of the Oedipus myth unleashed in the music. Casting Clarence Fountain and the Five Blind Boys of Alabama as a composite Oedipus creates the inspired link to Sophocles' sightless hero. Fountain sounds possessed by something unearthly, a pain and resignation that set his voice cascading upward with a thrilling quaver. The Blind Boys, seated around a white grand piano, provide the assenting harmonies.

Led by Freeman's authoritative Messenger, who also enacts some of Oedipus's lines, the cast features Kevin Davis as Oedipus's perfidious son Polynices, Robert Earl Jones as the quietly lethal King Creon, and Carl Lumbly as the beneficent Theseus. Isabelle Monk, her eyes streaming Greek-tragedienne tears, is a vivid Antigone in a brilliant yellow dress.

Taped in a steeply banked auditorium at the American Music Theater Festival in Philadelphia, GREAT PERFORMANCES' *Gospel* captures the feverish delirium of a live performance. The audience can be seen fanning themselves and waving and can be heard calling back to the performers. Director Kirk Browning's cameras drink in the bright plumage of the choir's African costumes, dart in on the acrobatic conductor J. D. Steele, and tremble from the stamping feet of the crowd. Freeman's

"The Gospel at Colonus is surely the best musical offering we have had this season, pure excitement and thrill and so compelling that, although you may be exhausted at the end, you've never seen ninety minutes go by so fast."

—Jerry Krupnick
STAR-LEDGER

LEFT: Morgan Freeman prays with power in *The Gospel at Colonus.*

sober, forgiving face and rumbling bass delivery provide the show's emotional center of gravity.

The piece explodes in one musical frenzy after another. The cathartic energy peaks one last time when choir soloist Carolyn Johnson White leads the way into a soaring, tambourine-thumping cry of "Hallelujah." With that, Oedipus accepts his fate. "Let the Weeping Cease" settles like a final amen over the crowd.

The Gospel at Colonus premiered at Brooklyn's New Wave Festival in 1983, aired on GREAT PERFORMANCES in 1985, and has been presented in theaters around the country ever since. By spanning the centuries, *Gospel* has acquired a durable life in the theater of its time.

A DELICIOUS THRILL
SWEENEY TODD

To Stephen Sondheim, it seemed like a fiendishly comic idea for a musical. Primed by a jolly new adaptation of a Victorian thriller he'd just seen in London, the creator of *Company, Follies, Pacific Overtures,* and other elegantly sophisticated musicals suggested *Sweeney Todd: The Demon Barber of Fleet Street* to director Harold Prince.

Prince, the famed director and producer who had already staged four Sondheim shows and numerous other hits, wanted no part of it at first. A musical about a revenge-crazed barber who murders his customers and has them cooked into meat pies was about as far from funny as Prince could imagine. He also didn't care much for the Victorian period. "A man comes out in a stovepipe hat," he once said, "and I fall asleep." Yet two decades later, as Prince looks back on a collaboration that may prove to be his most enduring contribution to the musical theater, he remembers how stimulating the *Sweeney* idea must have been, even as it repelled him.

"The number of times that you challenge yourself to envision something and articulate it in a new way are very rare in this business," says Prince. "This was one of those opportunities." The director was determined to create a musical set in Victorian England with none of the sentimental varnish of *Oliver!* "'Food Glorious Food,'" as he says, "this isn't."

RIGHT: Angela Lansbury as Mrs. Lovett and George Hearn as Sweeney toast their new meat pie business in Stephen Sondheim's darkly brilliant *Sweeney Todd.*

"THE RAVAGES OF THE MACHINE AGE"

Sweeney needed a governing idea, Prince felt, a political outlook on the material that would create a context for the show's horrific events. He found it in the Industrial Revolution. "This is a disturbed society," Prince says, "a terrible, inequitable society brought about, in our estimation, by the ravages of the Machine Age."

The set, an actual abandoned factory that designer Eugene Lee bought in Rhode Island for twenty-five thousand dollars, became the audacious frame for Prince's vision. Sprawling across the stage, the steel girders, along with the cluttered machine parts and movable bridges that Lee added, bring an epic dimension to the show.

Prince's trickiest directing chore was handling a chorus that comments bitterly on the action, while gobbling up the pies. Prince explains, "I needed to be able to say to the chorus, 'You share in this devastating view of the world. You are eating human flesh. You've all ceased to see daylight, sit in the

grass, look at animals, except the carnage of them. You've been shoved into a world where you see the sky through filthy glass. And that pervades everything.'"

Prince told the chorus he welcomed their own individual searches for a character. One young woman suggested wearing a heavy iron brace on her leg. That's one of many small but devastating emotional shocks that registers in the televised production, taped during a run of the show at the Dorothy Chandler Pavilion in Los Angeles.

A MONSTROUS HERO AND HIS PARTNER IN CRIME

In the title role, first played by Len Cariou and then by George Hearn, who appears in the televised version, Sondheim and book writer Hugh Wheeler created a hero at once monstrous and sympathetic —a capital-R Romantic figure, in Prince's view. Sweeney embarks on his murderous spree after a judge imprisons him and seizes his wife and daughter for his own pleasure.

Hearn has a lighter, more sympathetic touch than Cariou. But when he prowls downstage and looks for new victims—"Not a hundred can assuage me"—Hearn makes even the viewer at home feel a nervous flutter in the throat.

The show's other great character is the baker Mrs. Lovett, Sweeney's amorously purring partner in crime. Angela Lansbury created the part, making murder liltingly her own five years before *Murder She Wrote*. Prince says Mrs. Lovett emerged as the necessary comic leavening in the show after a read-through of the first act. "But of course she's not remotely funny. She's a very disturbed lady, and she's disturbed for the same reasons everyone else in the show is disturbed."

"When the old Follies *performers sing of old times in period Broadway styles, chances are they are going to find heartbreak, if not psychological torment buried within the Tin Pan Alley clichés. The result was not a stroll down memory lane through pastiche numberts, but one searing theatrical aria after another"*

—Frank Rich
NEW YORK TIMES

AN ENDURING SUCCESS

Prince likes the televised version, first aired in 1982 and then on GREAT PERFORMANCES in 1985, regretting only that the close-ups came at the expense of doing full justice to the production's physical environment. But the camera's relentless eye also magnifies details to deliriously creepy effect: the glint of light on Sweeney's razor, a trustingly bared neck, the sudden gush of stage blood.

L E F T: Mandy Patinkin in *"Follies in Concert."*

Prince admits that working on *Sweeney Todd* never became easy. "My wife sort of had to kick me out of bed every morning to go to work. But at some level I must have enjoyed it, because I delivered." And so he did. In one amazing burst of inspiration, Prince conceived the show's bone-jarring final image two hours before the first preview. Risen from the dead, Sweeney slams a steel door shut to end the show.

Sweeney Todd won eight Tony Awards and proves as searing today as it was on opening night in 1979. "To this day," says the director of *The Phantom of the Opera, Evita,* and the acclaimed *Show Boat* revival, "this is still the show people mention more than any other."

SOME PARTY!
"FOLLIES IN CONCERT"

The tickets, all 5,500 of them, sold out in three hours. For two nights only, in September of 1985, one of the modern Broadway musical's lost treasures was returned to a privileged throng. For Stephen

Sondheim devotees as well as theater lovers too young or otherwise innocent to have seen it the first time around, a chance to catch the composer-lyricist's enthralling 1971 musical *Follies* in a special concert version was not to be missed.

The two nights at Lincoln Center's Avery Fisher Hall accomplished two things. First, as a kind of black-tie recording session, the concerts yielded a permanent and complete record of Sondheim's haunting ode to the vanished world and time-tarnished memories of glamorous showgirls and stage-door Johnnies. The original cast album, from the Broadway production, had made substantial cuts in the score.

Second, *Follies* this time around was destined to become an event in its own right, a magical coming together of talent that otherwise couldn't have happened. Sondheim veterans Lee Remick, George Hearn, Mandy Patinkin, and Elaine Stritch joined forces with cabaret legend Barbara Cook, film and television stars Carol Burnett and Phyllis Newman, opera singer Licia Albanese, and a pair of latter-day vaudevillians, Betty Comden and Adolph Green, best known as a Broadway book-and-lyric writing team. The New York Philharmonic, a far cry from a pickup pit band, played the rich pastiche score.

The *Follies* album that resulted is just what Sondheim, producer Thomas Z. Shepard, and all the artists hoped for: a definitive account of a show that is probably too costly and impractical to be mounted again on Broadway. The televised "*Follies* in Concert," which aired the following spring, added something else, an atmospheric testament to the making of this milestone.

"*Follies* in Concert" opens with the backstage buildup of rehearsal shots and interviews. Elaine Stritch, in shorts and a battered fishing hat, tries to keep the troops loose with her throaty wisecracks: "I heard the cameraman say, 'Move the bag.' I thought he was referring to me." But the nervous tension builds. Lee Remick stumbles through the verbal land mine of "The Story of Lucy and Jessie." Carol Burnett has a shaky first go at "I'm Still Here" and wins an encouraging ovation from her rehearsal-hall colleagues. George Hearn muses on the art of trying to "compress an emotion" in a Sondheim song, then admits, "I'm scared to death."

But by the time the show's "Beautiful Girls" are caught trading hugs on opening night, the collective adrenaline has kicked in. *New York Times* critic Frank Rich described an audience that "erupted in pandemonium," and it happens again and again as "*Follies* in Concert" runs one highlight into another.

With her uncanny timing and gleeful growl, Stritch conquers the crowd in "Broadway Baby." Remick brings a rueful, acidic edge to "Could I Leave You?" Patinkin, snatching a hat on and off his head as he mimics two chorus girls, tears through "Buddy's Blues" like Robin Williams with a Juilliard-trained voice. And when Cook delicately floats the high notes of "In Buddy's Eyes," this *Follies* becomes heartbreaking in a way even the show's most ardent fans couldn't have fully expected.

"I liked everyone but you," Newman teases Stritch after the performance. The banter is part of the glow. *Follies* was, as Patinkin says, "some party."

GUYS AND DOLLS: OFF THE RECORD

When the camera catches up with Nathan Lane during the Broadway cast-album recording session of *Guys and Dolls,* he just can't resist: "Little children all over America will be listening to me and want to go into show business because of me and ruin their lives," he moans.

This is all just so much off-the-cuff shtick from the actor who played Nathan Detroit in the 1992 revival of Frank Loesser's classic American musical about high-roller sinners and Salvation Army saints. But like most good ad-libs, Lane's has more than a grain of truth.

Cast albums are an essential part of Broadway's vitality, the first tantalizing flavor of a show that many audience members get. Hearing the cast album, now in CD form, is supposed to lure customers to the theater. It also serves as the permanent, immutable record of a transitory art.

Everyone who turns up in *Guys and Dolls: Off the Record,* Gail Levin's crisp documentary about the musical's one-day marathon recording session, senses the importance of what they're doing. Every note counts. If the voice cracks on the stage, cast member Josie de Guzman explains, it might go unnoticed in the heat and light of a performance. "You don't want people to hear that whenever they put on the record."

"I hope we can pull it off," worries Peter Gallagher, the rangy stage and film actor who plays Sky Masterson. As Gallagher points out, there's no stage business to fall back on. "We've got to tell the same story we do eight times a week with just the voice." Gallagher sounds terrific on "My Time of Day" but, fearing he has missed an interval, asks for one more crack at the opening bars.

For Faith Prince, who won a Tony Award for her performance as Nathan Detroit's long-suffering girlfriend Adelaide, the vocal technique—"certain things you have to take out and certain things you have to put in"—is quite different for a recording session. "It's a transition, because people are hearing it, not seeing it." But Prince still relies on a stage-prop hankie to help her through her adenoidal sniffles in "Adelaide's Lament."

Director Jerry Zaks understands the recording-day pressures. The jokes and banter may flow for the cast, as he says, but "there's a certain amount of terror."

Like most good documentaries, this one does its share of eavesdropping. Zaks and record producer Jay David Saks have a whispered conference about the danger of one of Prince's songs turning either too bland or too hokey. Orchestrator Michael Starobin wants to lose a series of rim shots that sound out of place to him with no stage movement. "I disagree," says music director Edward Strauss.

The fifteen-hour session may have had its share of tense moments, but what comes across in the documentary is joy, the exhilaration of great Broadway singing seen up close. When Prince and Lane lovingly squabble their way through "Sue Me" at their separate microphones, they do just what Zaks wants them to do in pure musical terms: they "pass the ball."

LEFT: Faith Prince, Nathan Lane, Josie de Guzman, and Peter Gallagher in *Guys and Dolls: Off the Record.*

In the documentary's climax, the chorus charges through a pulse-pounding "Sit Down, You're Rockin' the Boat." The street clothes and clutter of microphones don't matter. That's high-voltage Broadway electricity coming off the screen.

Biographies of the Great and Gifted

If every life story is unique, so is the way of telling it. The struggles of playwright Lorraine Hansberry shine with prismatic detail in *To Be Young, Gifted and Black*. And the brash but elusive soldier and diplomat T.E. Lawrence emerges, then slips away again, in the carefully layered narrative of *A Dangerous Man*.

AN IMPULSE FOR SELF-DISCOVERY
TO BE YOUNG, GIFTED AND BLACK

It's altogether fitting that seven different actors—black and white, male and female—portray Lorraine Hansberry at various points in this biography told "in her own words." Best known as the first black woman to have a play produced on Broadway, *A Raisin in the Sun*, Hansberry was a complex and multi-faceted artist just beginning to come into her own when she died of cancer at age thirty-four in 1965.

To Be Young, Gifted and Black was assembled by Hansberry's husband and literary executor, Robert Nemiroff, and opened Off Broadway in 1969. The televised version is framed as a communal reading of the script by a group of actors in an empty theater. Scenes from Hansberry's plays, dramatized episodes of her life, speeches, and documentary clips create a portrait rich in period detail and shot through with the writer's fiery impulse for self-discovery. The cast, headed by an arresting Ruby Dee, includes Barbara Barrie, Blythe Danner, Al Freeman Jr., Lauren Jones, Claudia McNeil, and Roy Scheider.

Born into a middle-class Chicago family, Hansberry moved from childhood innocence of slavery to an impassioned commitment to social change. Asked about Martin Luther King's nonviolent protests in 1962, Hansberry replied, "I have no illusion that it is enough." Her impatience with her own race was elegantly put: "The acceptance of our condition is the only thing that discredits us."

Hansberry wrote the text for *The Movement: Documentary of a Struggle for Equality*, a book of photographs created by the Student Nonviolent Coordinating Committee. But she was, at heart, an artist, not a spokeswoman. "One, I am a writer," Dee, as Hansberry, says straight into the camera's eye. "Two, I am going to write."

And of course she did, stirred by "the comfort and agitation" of Shakespeare, the "shriek of misery" in Sean O'Casey, and most immediately by the civil rights movement dawning in houses and neighborhoods across the country. *A Raisin in the Sun*, quoted here in a long scene from her 1959 hit, focuses on a black family that is offered money not to move into a white neighborhood.

In one of many incisive letters and journal entries, Hansberry tells her mother that the play "tells the truth about Negroes, that we're just as complicated and mixed up" as whites. *Raisin* made Hansberry famous. She hoped it would make her mother proud.

LEFT: Ruby Dee plays Lorraine Hansberry in the biographical drama *To Be Young, Gifted and Black*.

Just as fascinating are the selections from Hansberry works hardly anyone knows. *The*

Drinking Gourd, a teleplay commissioned by NBC but never aired, presents a slave couple tumbling together in a hayloft and contemplating a flight to freedom. Hansberry offers this dryly ironic analysis of why NBC killed the piece: "We haven't made up our minds yet who won the Civil War."

Another choice line comes in an extract from her intriguing 1964 flop about Greenwich Village intellectuals, *The Sign in Sidney Brustein's Window.* Barrie, playing a woman with decidedly limited sympathies, blanches at the news of another woman's fiancé: "He's not a Communist anymore," she's told, "but he's still a Negro."

Clearly Hansberry, at the time of her death, was just getting started as an artist. *Les Blancs,* her ambitious play about colonialism in Africa, remained uncompleted. The lines that conclude *To Be Young, Gifted and Black* have a prophetic, poignant ring: Write of the world "as it is and ought to be," she tells an audience of young black writers. "Think of the world that awaits you."

A DANGEROUS MAN:
LAWRENCE AFTER ARABIA

In his forty-six years, T. E. Lawrence knew enough triumph and intrigue, celebrity and carefully cloaked secrets to fill several lifetimes to overflowing. The enigmatic World War I hero's popular reputation endures largely through David Lean's sweeping 1962 film epic, *Lawrence of Arabia.*

"A Dangerous Man: Lawrence After Arabia" studies Lawrence in repose, after his exploits in the Arabian desert were through. Played out against a finely drawn canvas of the 1919 Paris Peace Conference, David Puttnam's production fuses personal and political detail in a rich, multifaceted portrait of a complex man and his times.

Ralph Fiennes's Lawrence is brilliant, self-critical, loyal, vain, treacherous, neurotically vexed by his homosexuality, and deeply ashamed of his illegitimate birth. The performance confirmed the twenty-eight-year-old Fiennes as a major star-in-the-making and took on its full, resonant clarity in the ideal frame created by director Christopher Menaul and director of photography Witold Stock.

"[Peter O' Toole] didn't really worry me—not because I thought I could do better. . . . The film is so firmly placed as a great huge piece of cinema.

A Dangerous Man is on a much smaller note. It's much more interior both physically and metaphorically, so I was more daunted by trying to do T.E. Lawrence—his courage and intelligence and imagination."

—RALPH FIENNES

comparing his own T.E. Lawrence to Peter O'Toole's performance in *Lawrence of Arabia*

An early scene neatly establishes Lawrence's double-edged nature and reputation. As a scruffy and unnoticed Lawrence watches with a mix of revulsion and pride from the rear of a London lecture hall, the American journalist Lowell Thomas (Adam Henderson) trumpets the exploits of this "sort of supernatural being." Black-and-white footage of Lawrence in the desert flickers on a movie screen.

The heroism of a "breathless youth" who helped drive the Turks from the Holy Land assumes a more muted and ambiguous tone at the Paris conference. When Lawrence attempts to secure the Arabs' independence promised by his own British government, high-stakes diplomacy kicks into gear to thwart him. A dour Clemenceau (Arnold Diamond) has arrived to claim Syria for France. The steely British prime minister Lloyd George (Bernard Lloyd) wants to protect his country's oil interests in the Persian Gulf. Woodrow Wilson (Robert Arden) and Winston Churchill (Michael Cochrane) further solemnize the proceedings.

ABOVE: Siddig El Fadil plays the Emir Feisal and Ralph Fiennes plays Colonel T. E. Lawrence in "A Dangerous Man: Lawrence After Arabia."

Fiennes, his agate eyes flashing, looks trapped across the negotiating table from all these sober, jowly faces. When it comes to Hashemite prince Emir Faisal, who had fought beside him in the desert, Lawrence's vital, conflicted feelings emerge. Lawrence regards Faisal, played by the intense Sudanese-born actor Siddig el Fadil, as a comrade, rival, political inferior, and perhaps even potential lover. Their scenes together—striding through the countryside, riding horses, entering a champagne reception in matching Arab robes—have a robust sense of urgency. Even a shot of the two riding together in a taxi has a kinetic tension. Both men want, without declaring themselves, to be recognized as "the uncrowned king of Arabia."

As the layers of diplomatic intrigue build, so does the portrait of Lawrence. He can peer at pictures of himself with a kind of innocent admiration, then greet the seductive advances of a woman with an incredulous, half-mad giggle. "I cannot respond to you as I feel you'd wish," Lawrence tells the woman waiting for him in his bed. "It is simply not within my power to do so." It may be the most smoothly diplomatic line he utters.

Menaul's pacing is deliberate, but Stock's resourceful camera work helps propel "A Dangerous Man." In one scene of languid resignation just before he's branded a traitor, Lawrence is seen from behind in a bath, the vapors rising around him like the cloud of obscurity that will soon engulf him.

"It's very, very hard to disappear," Lawrence remarks. Then, as if in confirmation, he's watching himself on the silent movie screen again. It's the Lawrence of Arabia image that neither he nor his public can quite get out of their minds.

[*63*]

Preserving Performances
That Won't Come Again

⸎

THIRTEEN YEARS AFTER HIS BROADWAY PERFORMANCE PIECE RAN ON GREAT PERFORMANCES in 1984, Bill Irwin scouted up a tape of *The Regard of Flight*. "For the first twenty minutes, all I saw were the mistakes," Irwin says. "Then something wonderful happened: I became fond of the piece all over again. The show preserved something that won't come again, and I'm very glad we did it."

For twenty-five years, GREAT PERFORMANCES has been making audiences very glad, too. In recording a quarter century of plays and players, the series has created an incomparable chronicle of live theater and dramatized literature. Even the most tireless traveler couldn't have caught up with a fraction of the productions from Broadway, regional theaters, England, and beyond that have aired on GREAT PERFORMANCES.

Theater, as Irwin acknowledges, is a transitory enterprise. Shows close. The connections among artists change. Inspiration moves them in new directions. Television can't stop that process, of course, any more than it can or even should attempt to duplicate the experience an audience has in a theater.

The *Hamlet* or *Heartbreak House* that plays on GREAT PERFORMANCES is not the same one that happens live on a given night. The camera selects, composes, juxtaposes, and reshapes. It also opens new expressive possibilities, from the zealous intimacy of *The House of Mirth* to the filmic splendor of *Brideshead Revisited*.

There are heroes, too, of tact and sensitivity. GREAT PERFORMANCES would not have deserved its title were it not for the work of master television directors like Kirk Browning. Without his singular contributions, Browning's stage colleagues acknowledge, their art would have faltered and faded on the screen.

Irwin remembers the madness of shooting *The Regard of Flight* for the telecast. "We had two nights to do it, with some cameramen, borrowed from *MacNeil-Lehrer* at the last minute, who weren't used to swiveling and moving around." Irwin says executive producer Jac Venza, who was on the set, "looked positively ashen." But *The Regard of Flight* flew, like the astonishing preponderance of shows in the GREAT PERFORMANCES library, and as a result it reached an audience it could never have achieved on its own.

LEFT: Clown, mime, and dancer Bill Irwin (right) and Michael O'Connor are the hilariously hapless pawns of large forces in *The Regard Of Flight*; FOLLOWING PAGE: Robin Williams *in Seize the Day*.

"The theater is a wonderful community," says Irwin, "but it's also a small and insular one. GREAT PERFORMANCES has given us all, artists and audiences, a larger world."

GREAT PERFORMANCES
Drama Programs

The following format has been used to describe the drama programs:

LFLC = LIVE FROM LINCOLN CENTER

TITLE
(Author)
Cast
Theater/Acting Group
Season
Awards

ABIDE WITH ME
(J. Mitchell)
1977–1978

AH, WILDERNESS!
(Eugene O'Neill)
Richard Backus, Geraldine Fitzgerald
Long Wharf Theater, 1976–1977

ALICE IN WONDERLAND
(adapted from Lewis Carroll)
*Kate Burton, Colleen Dewhurst, Donald O'Connor,
Eve Arden, Fritz Weaver, Geoffrey Holder,
James Coco, Maureen Stapleton, Nathan Lane,
Richard Burton*
1983–1984

ALL OVER
(Edward Albee)
William Prince, Myra Carter
Hartford Stage Co., 1975–1976

ANTIGONE
(Jean Anouilh)
Genevieve Bujold, Stacy Keach
1973–1974

THE ARCATA PROMISE
(David Mercer)
1977–1978

ASINAMALI!
(Mbongemi Ngema)
1987–1988

BACALL ON BOGART
Documentary
1987–1988
Chicago International Film Festival

BERNSTEIN CONDUCTS *WEST SIDE STORY*
rehearsals and recording sessions
Kiri Te Kanawa, Jose Carreras, Tatiana Troyanos
1984–1985

BEST OF BROADWAY
Star-filled Gala, 1984–1985

BEYOND THE HORIZON
(Eugene O'Neill)
*Richard Backus, James Broderick, Geraldine
Fitzgerald, John Houseman, Maria Tucci*
McCarter Theater Co., 1975–1976

BIG BLONDE
(adapted from Dorothy Parker)
Sally Kellerman, John Lithgow
1980–1981

BLACK AND BLUE
Ruth Brown, Linda Hopkins
1992–1993

A BOWL OF BEINGS
(Culture Clash)
Culture Clash
1991–1992

BRIDESHEAD REVISITED
11-part series, (adapted from Evelyn Waugh)
Jeremy Irons, Anthony Andrews
1981–1982

BROADWAY SINGS: THE MUSIC OF JULE STYNE
. 1986–1987
Emmy

BROTHER TO DRAGONS
(adapted from Robert Penn Warren)
Richard Kneeland, Pamela Payton-Wright
Trinity Square Repertory Co., 1974–1975

BUDDENBROOKS
(adapted from Thomas Mann)
1983–1984

THE CEREMONY OF INNOCENCE
(Ronald Ribman)
James Broderick, Richard Kiley, Jessie Royce Landis
American Place Theatre, 1973–1974

THE CHARTERHOUSE OF PARMA
(adapted from Stendhal)
Marthe Keller
1982–1983

CHILDHOOD
5-part series
BAA BAA BLACKSHEEP
(adapted from Rudyard Kipling);
A GREAT DAY FOR BONZO
(adapted from H.E. Bates);
EASTER TELLS SUCH DREADFUL LIES
(adapted from Barbara Waring);
POSSESSIONS
(adapted from George Ewart Evans);

AN ONLY CHILD
(adapted from Frank O'Connor);
1976–1977

THE CHRISTMAS CHESTER MYSTERY PLAYS
Tom Courtenay
1976–1977

THE COLLECTION
Harold Pinter
*Alan Bates, Malcolm McDowell, Helen Mirren,
Laurence Olivier*
1978–1979

THE COLLEGE OF COMEDY WITH ALAN KING
Panel discussion
*Tim Conway, Buddy Hackett,
Paul Rodriguez, Judy Gold*
1997–1998

THE COLORED MUSEUM
(George C. Wolfe)
*Danitra Vance, Loretta Devine, Reggie
Montgomery, Tommy Hollis, Vicklyn Reynolds*
Crossroads Theatre Co., 1990–1991

COMEDY OF ERRORS, LFLC
(William Shakespeare)
Flying Karamazov Bros.
1986–1987

THE COMMON PURSUIT
(Simon Gray)
Andrew McCarthy, Tim Roth, Stephen Fry
1992–1993

THE CONTRACTOR
(David Storey)
Reid Shelton
Chelsea Theater Center, 1973–1974

COUNT DRACULA
(adapted from Bram Stoker)
Louis Jourdan
1977–1978

CREATING RAGTIME
Documentary
1997–1998

CYRANO DE BERGERAC
(Edmond Rostand)
Peter Donat, Marsha Mason, Marc Singer
American Conservatory Theater, 1973–1974

A DANGEROUS MAN:
LAWRENCE AFTER ARABIA
(Tim Rose Price)
Ralph Fiennes
1991–1992
INTERNATIONAL EMMY

THE DINING ROOM
(A.R. Gurney)
Frances Sternhagen, John Shea
Astor Place Theatre, 1984–1985

DR. FISCHER OF GENEVA
(adapted from Graham Greene)
Alan Bates, Greta Scacchi, James Mason
1985–1986

EARLY DAYS
(David Storey)
Ralph Richardson
1985–1986

THE EASTER CHESTER MYSTERY PLAYS
1976–1977

ECCENTRICITIES OF A NIGHTINGALE
(Tennessee Williams)
Blythe Danner, Frank Langella
Old Globe Theater, 1975–1976

EDITH WHARTON
3-part series:
THE HOUSE OF MIRTH
William Atherton, Geraldine Chaplin;
SUMMER
John Cullum, Diane Lane, Michael Ontkean;
LOOKING BACK
Stephen Collins, John Cullum, John McMartin,
Kathleen Widdoes, Richard Woods;
(adapted from Edith Wharton)
1981–1982

END OF SUMMER
(S.N. Behrman)
Helen Hayes, Lois Nettleton
Asolo State Theatre, 1976–1977

ENEMIES
(Maxim Gorky)
Kate Reid, Frances Sternhagen
Repertory Theater of Lincoln Center, 1973–1974

AN ENGLISHMAN ABROAD
(A. Bennett)
Alan Bates, Coral Browne
1984–1985

AN EVENING WITH ALAN JAY LERNER
1989–1990

FEASTING WITH PANTHERS
(Richard Cumming and Adrian Hall)
Richard Kneeland, Jobeth Williams
Trinity Square Repertory, 1973–1974

THE FIRST BREEZE OF SUMMER
(Leslie Lee)
Moses Gunn
Negro Ensemble Co., 1975–1976

FOLLIES IN CONCERT
(Stephen Sondheim)
1985–1986

FORGET-ME-NOT LANE
(Peter Nichols)
Geraldine Fitzgerald, John McMartin
Long Wharf Theatre, 1974–1975

THE GERSHWINS' PORGY AND BESS
(George and Ira Gershwin)
Willard White, Cynthia Haymon
Glyndebourne Festival, 1993–1994

GIRLS IN THEIR SUMMER DRESSES
AND OTHER STORIES: GIRLS IN THEIR SUMMER
DRESSES; THE MONUMENT
Jeff Bridges, Carol Kane, Charles Durning;
THE MAN WHO MARRIED A FRENCH WIFE
Claudine Auger, Pierre Santini;
(adapted from Irwin Shaw)
1980–1981

THE GOLDEN YEARS
3-part series:
THE EBONY TOWER
(adapted from John Fowles)
Laurence Olivier, Greta Scacchi, Roger Rees;
MONSIGNOR QUIXOTE
(adapted from Graham Greene)
Alec Guinness
CHRISTOPHER AWARD;
DECEMBER FLOWER
(adapted from Judy Allen)
Jean Simmons, Mona Washbourne
CHRISTOPHER AWARD;
1986–1987

THE GOOD DOCTOR
(Neil Simon)
Edward Asner, Richard Chamberlain, Lee Grant,
Marsha Mason, Bob Dishy
1978–1979
(Richard Chamberlain as The Good Doctor)

THE GOSPEL AT COLONUS
(Bob Telson)
Morgan Freeman
Brooklyn Academy of Music, 1985–1986
INTERNATIONAL FILM & TV FESTIVAL OF
NEW YORK

GROWN UPS
(Jules Feiffer)
Charles Grodin, Jean Stapleton, Marilu Henner,
Martin Balsam
1985–1986

GUESTS OF THE NATION
(adapted from Frank O'Connor)
Frank Converse, Estelle Parsons
Colonnades Theater Lab, 1980–1981

GUYS AND DOLLS OFF THE RECORD
Documentary on original cast recording session
1992–1993

HAMLET
(William Shakespeare)
Kevin Kline, Dana Ivey, Diane Venora
New York Shakespeare Festival, 1990–1991

HAPPY DAYS
(Samuel Beckett)
Irene Worth, George Voskovec
New York Shakespeare Festival, 1979–1980

HARD TIMES
4-part series, (adapted from Charles Dickens)
Edward Fox, Jacqueline Tong, Timothy West
1976–1977

HEARTBREAK HOUSE
(George Bernard Shaw)
Rex Harrison, Rosemary Harris, Amy Irving,
Dana Ivey, Remak Ramsay
1985–1986

HENRY V AT SHAKESPEARE'S GLOBE
Documentary plus excerpts
(William Shakespeare)
Mark Rylance
1997–1998

HOGAN'S GOAT
(William Alfred)
Faye Dunaway, Kevin Conway, Robert Foxworth,
Rue McClanahan
1972–1973

THE HOUSE OF BERNARDA ALBA
(Frederico Garcia Lorca)
Glenda Jackson, Joan Plowright
1991–1992

THE IMPORTANCE OF BEING EARNEST
(Oscar Wilde)
Wendy Hiller, Alan Hay, Ann Thornton
1985–1986

IN FASHION
(adapted from Georges Feydeau)
Charlotte Rae
Actors Theatre of Louisville, 1973–1974

IN FROM THE COLD
Documentary, in 2 parts
Richard Burton film clips, interviews
1989–1990

**IN THE WINGS: ANGELS IN AMERICA
ON BROADWAY**
Documentary
*George C. Wolfe, Tony Kushner,
and original Broadway cast*
1992–1993

THE INNOCENTS ABROAD
(adapted from Mark Twain)
1982–1983

JAMES STEWART: A WONDERFUL LIFE
film clips, interviews
1986–1987
INTERNATIONAL FILM & TV FESTIVAL OF NEW
YORK, CINE'S GOLDEN EAGLE CERTIFICATE

JAMMIN': JELLY ROLL MORTON ON BROADWAY
Documentary
*Gregory Hines, George C. Wolfe,
and original Broadway cast*
1992–1993

JENNIE: LADY RANDOLPH CHURCHILL
7-part series, (Julian Mitchell)
*Lee Remick, Barbara Parkins, Ronald Pickup,
Christopher Cazenove*
1975–1976
EMMY

JERRY HERMAN'S BROADWAY AT THE BOWL
1993–1994

JOHN GIELGUD: AN ACTOR'S LIFE
Documentary
1988–1989

JUNE MOON
(George S. Kaufman and Ring Lardner)
*Jack Cassidy, Kevin O'Connor, Estelle Parsons,
Susan Sarandon, Stephen Sondheim*
1973–1974

KING LEAR
(William Shakespeare)
James Earl Jones, Raul Julia, Paul Sorvino
New York Shakespeare Festival, 1973–1974

LA PASTORELA
based on the traditional holiday Shepherds Play
*Linda Ronstadt, Cheech Marin, Paul Rodriguez,
Freddy Fender*
El Teatro Campesino, 1991–1992

LARGO DESOLATO
(Vaclav Havel)
F. Murray Abraham, Phoebe Cates, Sally Kirkland
Wilma Theater, 1989–1990

LAURENCE OLIVIER: A LIFE
Documentary
1985–1986
EMMY, ACAPULCO WORLD FESTIVAL

LES MISÉRABLES IN CONCERT
(Alain Boublil and Claude-Michel Schönberg)
1995–1996

LETTERS FROM THE PARK
(adapted from Gabriel Garcia Marquez)
1989–1990

A LIFE IN THE THEATRE
(David Mamet)
Peter Evans, Ellis Rabb
1979–1980

LIFE ON THE MISSISSIPPI
(adapted from Mark Twain)
David Knell, Robert Lansing
1980–1981

THE LOST LANGUAGE OF CRANES
(adapted from David Leavitt)
*Brian Cox, Eileen Atkins, Angus MacFadyen,
Corey Parker, Rene Auberjonois, John Schlesinger*
1991–1992

THE MAHABHARATA
3-part series:
GAME OF DICE; EXILE IN THE FOREST; THE WAR
(adapted from Peter Brook's theater production
of the Indian epic poem)
1990–1991
INTERNATIONAL EMMY

MAN FROM MOSCOW
3-part series, (Greville Wynne)
Andrew Carr, Christopher Rozycki
1984–1985

MASTER HAROLD . . . AND THE BOYS
(Athol Fugard)
Matthew Broderick, Zakes Mokae
1985–1986

A MEMORY OF TWO MONDAYS
(Arthur Miller)
*Tony LoBianco, George Grizzard, Barnard Hughes,
Harvey Keitel, Estelle Parsons, Dick Van Patten,
Jerry Stiller, Kristofer Tabor, Jack Warden*
1973–1974

MIRACLE IN ROME
(adapted from Gabriel Garcia Marquez)
1990–1991

THE MISER
(Molière)
1987–1988

MOLIÈRE
5-part series, (Ariane Mnouchkine)
Philippe Caubère
1979–1980

MONKEY, MONKEY, BOTTLE OF BEER
(Martha Sheiness)
Cincinnati Playhouse in the Park, 1973–1974

THE MOST HAPPY FELLA
(Frank Loesser)
Sharon Daniels, Richard Muenz, Giorgio Tozzi
1979–1980

THE MOTHER
(Paddy Chayefsky)
*Anne Bancroft, Joan Cusack, Stephen Lang,
Adrian Pasdar, Anne Meara, Mary Alice*
1994–1995

THE MOUND BUILDERS
(Lanford Wilson)
Brad Dourif
Circle Repertory Theater, 1975–1976

MOURNING BECOMES ELECTRA
5-part series, (Eugene O'Neill)
Bruce Davison, Joan Hackett, Roberta Maxwell
1978–1979

MRS. REINHARDT
(Edna O'Brien)
Helen Mirren, Brad Davis
1981–1982
(Helen Mirren as Mrs. Reinhardt)

MUSIC BY RICHARD RODGERS
1989–1990

**MUSICALS GREAT MUSICALS:
THE ARTHUR FREED UNIT AT MGM**
1996–1997

THE MYSTERIOUS STRANGER
(adapted from Mark Twain)
Julian Mitchell
1982–1983

THE NORMAN CONQUESTS
3-part series, (Alan Ayckbourn)
Tom Conti, Penelope Keith, Penelope Wilton
1977–1978

ON GIANT'S SHOULDERS
(Michael Robson and Marjorie Wallace)
Judi Dench, Terry Wiles
1979–1980

ON THE RAZZLE
(adapted from Johann Nestroy)
Ciaran Madden, Alfred Lynch
1985–1986

ONCE IN A LIFETIME
(George Kaufman and Moss Hart)
Edward Petherbridge, Kristofer Tabori,
Niall Buggy, Zoe Wannamaker
Royal Shakespeare Festival, 1987–1988

OUR TOWN
(Thornton Wilder)
Spalding Gray, Eric Stoltz, Penelope Ann Miller
Repertory Theater of Lincoln Center
1989–1990

OUT OF OUR FATHER'S HOUSE
(adapted from Eve Merriam)
Carol Kane, Jan Miner, Dianne Wiest
1977–1978

PARADISE LOST
(Clifford Odets)
Jo Van Fleet, Fred Gwynne, Bernadette Peters,
Eli Wallach
1973–1974

THE PATRIOTS
(Sidney Kingsley)
Ralph Clanton, Philip Le Strange
Asolo State Theater, 1975–1976

PORGY AND BESS: AN AMERICAN VOICE
Documentary
1997–1998

THE PRINCE OF HOMBURG
(Heinrich Von Kleist)
Frank Langella
Chelsea Theater Center, 1976–1977
(Frank Langella as the Prince)

PRINCESS GRACE REMEMBERED
Nancy Reagan, narrator
1983–1984

THE PRIVATE HISTORY
OF A CAMPAIGN THAT FAILED
(adapted from Mark Twain)
Edward Herrmann, Pat Hingle
1980–1981

PROFESSIONAL FOUL
(Tom Stoppard)
Peter Barkworth, John Shrapnel
1977–1978

PURLIE
(Gary Geld, Ossie Davis, Philip Rose)
Robert Guillaume, Melba Moore,
Sherman Hemsley
1983–1984

QUARTERMAINE'S TERMS
(Simon Gray)
Edward Fox, John Gielgud
1986–1987

THE REGARD OF FLIGHT
Bill Irwin
American Place Theatre, 1982–1983

RELATIVELY SPEAKING
(Alan Ayckbourn)
Nigel Hawthorne, Michael Maloney, Imogen Stubbs
1989–1990

THE RIMERS OF ELDRITCH
(Lanford Wilson)
Rue McClanahan, Susan Sarandon,
Frances Sternhagen
Circle Repertory Company, 1972–1973

ROSENCRANTZ AND GUILDENSTERN ARE DEAD
(Tom Stoppard)
Gary Oldman, Richard Dreyfuss, Tim Roth
1991–1992

THE ROYAL FAMILY
(Edna Ferber and George S. Kaufman)
Rosemary Harris, Eva Le Gallienne, Ellis Rabb
APA-Phoenix Theater, 1977–1978
EMMY

RULES OF THE GAME
(Luigi Pirandello)
David Dukes, John McMartin, Joan Van Ark
APA-Phoenix Theatre, 1974–1975

SARAH
Profile of Sarah Bernhardt, (Suzanne Grossman)
Zoe Caldwell
1977–1978

THE SCHOOL FOR SCANDAL
(Richard Sheridan)
Blair Brown, Larry Gates
The Guthrie Theater, 1974–1975

SEA MARKS
(Gardner McKay)
Manhattan Theatre Club, 1975–1976

THE SEAGULL
(Anton Chekhov)
Blythe Danner, Lee Grant, Frank Langella,
Kevin McCarthy
Williamstown Theatre Festival, 1974–1975

SECRET SERVICE
(William Gillette)
Mary Beth Hurt, John Lithgow, Meryl Streep
APA-Phoenix Theatre, 1976–1977

SEIZE THE DAY
(adapted from Saul Bellow)
Robin Williams, Jerry Stiller, Eileen Heckart,
Glenne Headly, Jo Van Fleet
1986–1987

SHE LOVES ME
(Jerry Bock)
Gemma Kraven, Robin Ellis
1979–1980

SHOOTING THE CHANDELIER
(David Mercer)
Denholm Elliott, Edward Fox
1977–1978

SHOW BOAT
(Jerome Kern, Oscar Hammerstein II)
Eddie Bracken, Rebecca Baxter, Richard White,
Shelly Burch, Lee Roy Reams, Lenora Nemetz
Paper Mill Playhouse, 1989–1990

THE SILENTS (1): THE THIEF OF BAGDAD
restored film
Douglas Fairbanks
1986–1987

THE SILENTS (2): OUR HOSPITALITY
reconstructed film
Buster Keaton
1987–1988

THE SILENTS (3): THE EAGLE
restored film
Rudolph Valentino
1988–1989

THE SILENTS (4): THE BROKEN BLOSSOMS
refurbished film
Lillian Gish
1989–1990

SIR NORBERT SMITH: A LIFE
spoof on Olivier biography
1990–1991

SOME ENCHANTED EVENING:
CELEBRATING OSCAR HAMMERSTEIN II
1994–1995

SONDHEIM: A CELEBRATION AT CARNEGIE HALL
American Theatre Orchestra, 1992–1993

STAYING ON
Trevor Howard, Celia Johnson
1980–1981

SUDDENLY LAST SUMMER
(Tennessee Williams)
Natasha Richardson, Maggie Smith, Rob Lowe
1992–1993;

SWEENEY TODD:
THE DEMON BARBER OF FLEET STREET
(Stephen Sondheim)
Angela Landsbury, George Hearn
1984–1985
EMMYS

**SYLVIA FINE KAYE'S
MUSICAL COMEDY TONIGHT**
Jerome Kern
1985–1986
EMMYS

THE TAILOR OF GLOUCESTER
adapted from Beatrix Potter
1990–1991

TAKING MY TURN
(Will Holt)
1984–1985

TALES FROM THE HOLLYWOOD HILLS
(3 teleplays from American short stories):
NATICA JACKSON
(adapted from John O'Hara)
Michelle Pfeiffer, Brian Kerwin;
A TABLE AT CIRO'S
(adapted from Budd Schulberg)
Darren McGavin, Ann Magnuson;
PAT HOBBY TEAMED WITH GENIUS
(adapted from F. Scott Fitzgerald)
Christopher Lloyd, Colin Firth;
1987–1988

TALES FROM THE HOLLYWOOD HILLS
(3 more teleplays from American short stories):
THE OLD RELIABLE
(adapted from P.G. Wodehouse)
Lou Jacobi, Lynn Redgrave, Rosemary Harris;
GOLDEN LAND
(adapted from William Faulkner)
Audra Lindley;
THE CLOSED SET
(adapted from Gavin Lambert)
Rita Moreno, D.W. Moffett, Penelope Ann Miller;
1988–1989

TALKING WITH
(Jane Martin)
*Kathy Bates, Beverly D'Angelo, Marcia Gay
Harden, Celeste Holm, Frances McDormand,
Mary Kay Place*
1994–1995

THE TAMING OF THE SHREW
(William Shakespeare)
Marc Singer, Fredi Olster
American Conservatory Theater, 1976–1977

TARTUFFE
(Molière)
*Patricia Elliott, Victor Garber, Tammy Grimes,
Donald Moffat*
Circle in the Square, 1977–1978

THANK YOU, COMRADES
(James Hawkins)
Connie Booth, Ben Kingsley
1978–1979

THREE JOHN CHEEVER STORIES:
THE SORROWS OF GIN
*Edward Herrmann, Rachel Roberts,
Sigourney Weaver;*
O YOUTH AND BEAUTY!
Michael Murphy, Kathryn Walker;
THE FIVE FORTY-EIGHT
Mary Beth Hurt, Lawrence Luckinbill;
(adapted from John Cheever)
1979–1980

THE TIME OF YOUR LIFE
(William Saroyan)
Kevin Kline, Patti LuPone
The Acting Company, 1975–1976

TINKER, TAILOR, SOLDIER, SPY
7-part series, (adapted from John le Carré)
*Alec Guinness, Ian Richardson, Beryl Reid,
Hywell Bennett, Alexander Knox*
1980–1981

TO BE YOUNG, GIFTED AND BLACK
(adapted from Lorraine Hansberry)
*Ruby Dee, Barbara Barrie, Blythe Danner,
Roy Scheider*
1972–1973

TO THE LIGHTHOUSE
(adapted from Virginia Woolf)
Rosemary Harris, Kenneth Branagh
1984–1985

A TOUCH OF THE POET
(Eugene O'Neill)
*Geraldine Fitzgerald, Nancy Marchand,
Roberta Maxwell, Fritz Weaver*
1973–1974

THE TRIAL OF THE MOKE
(Daniel Stein)
Howard Rollins, Franklyn Seales
Milwaukee Repertory Theater, 1977–1978

A TRIBUTE TO BILLY WILDER, LFLC
Film Society of Lincoln Center, 1981–1982

A TRIBUTE TO JOHN HUSTON, LFLC
Film Society of Lincoln Center, 1979–1980

UNCLE VANYA
(adapted from Anton Chekhov)
*David Warner, Ian Holm,
Mary Elizabeth Mastrantonio*
1990–1991

UNCOMMON WOMEN AND OTHERS
(Wendy Wasserstein)
Jill Eikenberry, Swoosie Kurtz, Meryl Streep
APA-Phoenix Theater, 1977–1978

VERNA: USO GIRL
(adapted from Paul Gallico)
*Sissy Spacek, William Hurt, Sally Kellerman,
Howard da Silva*
1977–1978
EMMY

WAITING FOR GODOT
(Samuel Beckett)
Dana Elcar, Donald Moffat, Ralph Waite
Los Angeles Actors Theatre, 1976–1977

WHEN HELL FREEZES OVER I'LL SKATE
(Vinnette Carroll)
Lynne Thigpen, Cleavant Derricks
1978–1979

WHO'S HAPPY NOW?
(Oliver Hailey)
Betty Garrett, Rue McClanahan, Albert Salmi
Mark Taper Forum, 1974–1975

THE WIDOWING OF MRS. HOLROYD
(adapted from D.H. Lawrence)
Frank Converse, Geraldine Fitzgerald
Long Wharf Theater, 1973–1974

THE WINSLOW BOY
(Terence Rattigan)
Michael Darlow, Emma Thompson, Gordon Jackson
1989–1990
(Emma Thompson in The Winslow Boy)

THE WORLD OF JEWISH HUMOR
Documentary
*Neil Simon, Joan Rivers, Milton Berle, Billy
Crystal, Jackie Mason, Sid Caesar, Carl Reiner*
1990–1991

THE WORLD OF JIM HENSON
Documentary featuring clips from
The Muppets and Henson's films
1994–1995
PARENTS' CHOICE HONOR

THE YEAR OF THE DRAGON
(Frank Chin)
Pat Suzuki, George Takei
American Place Theatre, 1974–1975

YOU CAN'T TAKE IT WITH YOU
(George Kaufman and Moss Hart)
Jason Robards, Colleen Dewhurst
1984–1985

ZALMEN OR THE MADNESS OF GOD
(Elie Wiesel)
Joseph Wiseman
Arena Stage, 1974–1975

DANCE

BY JENNIFER DUNNING

THE CREATION OF
DANCE IN AMERICA
An Extraordinarily Exciting Time

⌘

GREAT PERFORMANCES' *DANCE IN AMERICA* SERIES, WHICH BEGAN IN 1976 ON PBS, was the first long-running television program in the United States devoted entirely to dance. Over its long, rich history, the series has been many things to many people. To American choreographers, it has offered the chance to work with top-level directors, producers, camera operators, and editors in an atmosphere that has made them feel unusually cherished and important. As the producers emphasized from the start, each program was to be a collaborative effort.

The series has also provided an evening of ballet or modern dance, broadcast in prime time, to millions of Americans who would not or could not have ventured into a theater. And dance companies, worried initially that the program might draw audiences away from their live performances, have discovered that just the opposite has occurred.

Finally, *Dance in America* has embodied the heady promise of an art form newly popular in the 1970s, and it has marked a golden era for public television. "It was an extraordinarily exciting time," reflects Merrill Brockway, the series' first producer (with Emile Ardolino). "The wonderful thing was that we knew that we were having a wonderful time. We didn't have to wait twenty years to find that out. We didn't know where we were going, but we knew that we were making history."

FOSTERING NEW TALENT

A relatively small event that went unnoticed by history may actually reflect the greatest impact of *Dance in America*. When an eleven-year-old boy in Queens, New York, sat down in front of his family's television and tuned in to a public television program, he discovered his future. On the screen, then and in months to come, he saw male athletes spinning and soaring in moves that were very different from hip-hop, the only kind of dance he knew. He recognized that this is what he would do with his life: he wanted, he told his mother, to become a professional dancer.

LEFT: Jerome Robbins coaching Natalia Makarova in *Other Dances*, seen on "Two Duets"; PREVIOUS PAGES: New York City Ballet performing *Serenade* in "Balanchine in America."

That teenager was Desmond Richardson, who would become a principal dancer with the Alvin Ailey American Dance Theater and one of the great dance artists of his generation. In time he would appear with the Frankfurt Ballet in Germany, with the American Ballet Theatre, and with Alvin Ailey's company—on *Dance in America*. The "athletes of God" (as Martha Graham described dancers) to whom *Dance in America* originally introduced him included Rudolf Nureyev and Mikhail Baryshnikov. Richardson would never have seen them otherwise.

"I would not have been able to go to the theater at all," he says. "There was no money for that. Thank God for things like GREAT PERFORMANCES."

Richardson's story is not unique. "There are hundreds of Desmond Richardsons," says Judy Kinberg, who succeeded Brockway and Ardolino as the program's producer. "There are many, many people who were first exposed to dance because of *Dance in America.*"

THE UNION OF TWO VISUAL MEDIA

The first *Dance in America* team was determined to unite dance and television—two highly visual media that were very much alike but that had seldom been connected in the public mind—in order to bring beautifully produced, serious dance to Americans throughout the country.

By the 1970s, television had established itself as the preeminent form of mass communication in America. But dance had played only a small and usually frivolous part in commercial television programming. Variety shows generally included a bit of chorus-line dancing, and Ed Sullivan would sandwich classical dance "acts" like "The Dying Swan" into his lineup with some regularity. Programs such as *Camera Three,* where Brockway was producer for eight years, did present concert dance straightforwardly and with imagination, but its Sunday morning time slot guaranteed that it preached only to the converted.

"Dancers were doing something suitable for television, with a few exceptions," Jac Venza, then director of performance programs for Thirteen/WNET, says. "No one had a showcase for concert dancers doing what they do. And many of the finest dancers were not even considered television material. They were not all-American boys and girls." If dancers were dark-skinned, Venza adds, the opportunities were even scarcer.

THE GROWING POPULARITY OF DANCE

But change was in the air. In 1963, nearly a decade before the birth of GREAT PERFORMANCES, the Ford Foundation announced a $7.7 million program "to strengthen professional ballet in the United States." The largest grant ever made to American dance, the program made front-page news throughout the country. More awards, which went to modern dance as well as ballet companies, followed. Two years later President Lyndon Johnson founded the National Endowment for the Arts as a kind of public validation of the arts in America, and still more private support emerged. Agnes de Mille headed the NEA's dance panel, and a dance-loving visionary named Nancy Hanks became the chairperson of the endowment in 1969.

By the mid 1970s, there was considerable evidence that dance was beginning to enjoy a new popularity in the United States: tours by the Royal Ballet of England and the mighty Soviet Bolshoi Ballet had convinced Americans that ballet could be glamorous and exciting after all; the highly publicized defections of Rudolf Nureyev, Natalia Makarova, and Mikhail Baryshnikov added to that glamour; and if all else failed, the burgeoning ticket sales were an infallible

"My feeling about television is that it is the most potent media of our time. Its impact is undeniable on the culture of this country, but very little has been done to enrich what that impact could be in an educational sense. We don't always need to be instructional, but I believe that GREAT PERFORMANCES— with the theater, dance, and music programming we present—has brought a new experience to people who may never have thought they would enjoy any of these things. And I think that this is going to nourish what happens in the attendance at the community level across the country. I think that a good ballet program on television would certainly encourage someone to go see their own hometown company."

—JAC VENZA

"Television dance is able to reach millions of viewers in a single broadcast, introducing an art form once perceived as elitist. While audiences across America are now able to attend live performances of dance companies, my guess is that the very first exposure for the majority was on TV, specifically to some broadcasts of the GREAT PERFORMANCES series."

**—Richard Philp
DANCE MAGAZINE**

barometer of popularity. Some one million tickets to dance had been sold in 1964, but sales had jumped to 11.6 million a decade later. In 1975, the *New York Times* described dance as "the most vital American art form of the 1970s."

BRINGING DANCE TO THE AMERICAN HOME

Dance in America grew out of Nancy Hanks's determination that dance should be accessible to all Americans—not just to those living in the big cities where ballet and some modern dance companies occasionally appeared on tour. "She felt that if dance were presented properly on television, the endowment could get what it supported out everywhere, and for free," Venza recalls. The NEA and the Corporation for Public Broadcasting discussed the need for such a program at a conference held in Washington, D.C., in October 1974. As a result, public television stations were asked to submit proposals.

Thirteen/WNET in New York City was chosen, and the new series, to be called *Dance in America,* was announced the following June. The endowment joined with Exxon and the Corporation for Public Broadcasting in awarding three million dollars for eight programs over two years. ("The endowment wanted quality, the corporation wanted quantity, and Exxon wanted tutus," Brockway comments wryly. In the end, everyone was satisfied.) Although the problems of raising money for the expensive work of televising dance would change over the next decade—and by the 1990s, they would grow worse in a national climate generally unfavorable to the arts—the atmosphere surrounding the creation of *Dance in America* was full of excitement and hope.

The first companies to appear in the series would be the City Center Joffrey Ballet (as it was then known), the Twyla Tharp Company, and the Martha Graham Dance Company. The carefully chosen creators of *Dance in America,* eventually a four-person team that included Venza, Brockway, Ardolino, and Kinberg, all had backgrounds in television and video production, cultural programming, and, specifically, dance. Venza had produced a number of cultural programs for Thirteen/WNET, among them shows on José Limón, the Jacob's Pillow Dance Festival, Alvin Ailey, and 1973's "American Ballet Theatre: A Close-Up in Time." Brockway, a musician with a master's degree in musicology, had been working in television since 1953 and had been named executive producer of *Camera Three* in 1967. Ardolino, the series coordinating producer, was a film editor who had made many dance movies for the Jerome Robbins Film Archive at the world-famous Dance Collection of the New York Public Library for the Performing Arts at Lincoln Center. And Kinberg, associate producer, had been trained as a production assistant on *Camera Three,* working closely with Brockway, who taught her such concepts as suiting the format to the subject of the show. This unusual concept would form the foundation for *Dance in America.*

THE PROCESS TAKES SHAPE

The *Dance in America* team began with a nearly open mandate: to reach the broadest possible audience with a wide range of programs that would at least loosely follow the format of Venza's

"Dance in America *is a tribute to the depth, richness, and diversity of American dance so evident to all of us. It's clear that dance in this country has come to its visible flowering. We all believe it's time to share this flowering with spectators throughout the country and the world.*"

—JAY ISELIN
Former President of WNET
announcing the new *Dance in America*
series in June 1975

"Dance in America *is the most ambitious, potentially far-reaching television series on dance ever undertaken. . . . The potential audience for dance of one hundred million through television could make the present increase of the live dance audience to eleven million seem like a drop in the bucket.*"

—NANCY HANKS
Former Chairperson of the
National Endowment for the Arts,
at the unveiling of the *Dance in America* series, 1975

[77]

program on the American Ballet Theatre; this show had been a mix of documentary and performance. Merrill Brockway describes the proposal written by Emile Ardolino and Joan Mack, a development executive at Thirteen/WNET, as "so vast we could do anything." So, now they had the money—what exactly would they do?

The choreography, everyone felt, was to be the most important ingredient. And the dances must be performed by the best casts. Most of all, each choreographer was to be a full collaborator in the process of "translating" the dances for television, as the team preferred to put it. According to George Balanchine, no one had ever asked for his opinion in the early misadventures he'd had with the medium. This was to change with *Dance in America.*

"We bent over backwards to be respectful of the work," Brockway says, "even to the point of being boring. But the choreographers began to try to find ways of making it not boring. The creator had to do it. There were so many decisions to be made that you could take it all off track very easily. We [directors and producers] had to be, in many ways, faceless. As a musician, I had accompanied singers and other musicians; in a sense, we were accompanists."

A process began to evolve: Brockway, Ardolino, and Kinberg would study work tapes made and selected for a particular program by the dance company. These were generally primitive videotapes that served simply as records of rehearsals and performances. At the same time, the production team held intense conversations with the choreographer about the point of each dance and how best to communicate its unique personality. The studio was used for taping most shows during the early years, but later programs were also shot from live theater performances or were documentaries.

Video technology had become simpler, cheaper, and more accessible by the early 1970s, when GREAT PERFORMANCES began. For programs shot in the studio, small home-video cameras could be taken into rehearsals to create a director's tape that would suggest the look and shape of the final television version.

The actual studio work, involving three cameras, was the most expensive phase of the process. By the third program the series had begun to use the large, well-appointed new studios at the Grand Ole Opry in Nashville. "They didn't realize they were building the ideal studios for dance," Venza comments.

During the final studio process, most dances were shot in three- to five-minute segments, in and out of sequence. The camera operators, who by now knew each dance thoroughly, met with the director each morning to discuss the piece and the work to be done that day. These camerapeople quickly learned to anticipate rather than follow movement and to be extra-sensitive to the framing of each shot. In Nashville, they became a crucial part of the collaboration. Brockway recalls how he snapped early on at Ed Fussell, who would become a longtime *Dance in America* camera operator, because Fussell kept adjusting his frames. "I thought he was just screwing around," Brockway said. "Merrill, this rehearsal is for me, too," Fussell replied.

"Putting dance on television has always been a slightly awkward undertaking. Like trying to squeeze a left foot into a right shoe, the two just didn't seem to fit: A ballet on TV has a way of becoming a series of blurred figures leaping on and off screen—sometimes losing the tops of their heads, the bottoms of their legs, and their continuity of movement in the process.

"Finding a solution to this uneasy alliance could never be a simple matter, but the public television series Dance in America *. . . has proved that it can be done, and done very successfully. The main reason is the show's format: This is no mere attempt to present a dance in front of television cameras; instead, it is a cooperative effort by dance companies and television crews to create a program that serves the needs of both media."*

—Alex Ward
CULTURAL POST
National Endowment for the Arts

LEFT: Yuriko Kimura as Martha Graham's Clytemnestra.

To an unusual degree, the dancers were also taken into consideration. Television studio floors tend to be made of concrete, a stable surface for the camera but dangerous for dancers; for the *Dance in America* shoots, the floor was specially built from layers of resilient wood and foam padding. The normally chilly temperature in television studios was raised, and room for stretching was made available. Taping was timed as much as possible to keep the performers warmed up, and appropriate food was provided. "You can't send them out in their tutus to McDonald's," Venza says.

Finally, *Dance in America* clearly needed to be edited by someone with a special sensitivity to the rhythms of dance, both live and on the screen. And the team found just the right person in Girish Bhargava, who has edited most of the programs.

Still, not everyone was convinced by such empathy and wholehearted involvement. Television was a "vulgar medium," Lincoln Kirstein, who had founded the New York City Ballet with Balanchine, told Brockway. The City Ballet would never become involved with *Dance in America,* he predicted. Paul Taylor shied away from becoming artistically involved with what seemed like a complex process. His life, he said, was on the stage, not on "that box." Even among the choreographers and dancers who were involved in the earliest programs, there was a general reluctance to take charge of the process with the television unit.

But eventually they all came around. The diversity of programs in the first year alone was impressive, ranging from the Joffrey Ballet, a major urban company, to the Pennsylvania Ballet, a leading regional troupe, and from Martha Graham, the formidable matriarch of American modern dance, to Twyla Tharp, a brainy young upstart whose work represented the cutting edge of modernism.

A HARBINGER OF RICHES TO COME

Dance in America's first program was dedicated to the history and repertory of the Joffrey Ballet. In many ways, it encapsulates the range of contributions the series has made ever since. In its youthful, bouncy spirit, the Joffrey was considered about as American as classical ballet could get. Robert Joffrey approached ballet not only as a gifted choreographer and historian but also as a connoisseur with the irresistibly exuberant passion of a fan. There was a little of almost everything in that first program, from Kurt Jooss's *The Green Table* and Léonide Massine's *Parade*—two historical ballets by major choreographers that Joffrey rescued from near oblivion—to *Trinity,* a rock ballet by the resident Joffrey choreographer Gerald Arpino and the only work seen in its entirety on the program.

The show not only captures three master artists—Massine, Jooss, and Joffrey—who are now dead but also serves as a performance record of Joffrey stars who have since died or retired from the stage. In addition, the Joffrey Ballet, two decades after that first program, has expanded its modern repertory, leaving Americans fewer chances to savor the landmarks of twentieth-century ballet. This kind of archival preservation has always been one of *Dance in America*'s aims. Another has been its early introduction of up-and-coming companies and choreographers, including

"There are two schools of thought, and one is that dance never works outside the theater, and that it should not be translated at all. We just don't accept that theory. The fact that dance exists in the theater doesn't mean that it can't exist in television, too. There are people who will never be able to get to a theater to see dance, for one thing. We have reached more people in one night with the Joffrey program than that company has reached in all the years of its existence!"

—EMILE ARDOLINO

"Jac Venza, who directed the Joffrey telecast, obviously knows and appreciates the laws of dance. Unlike too many of his colleagues, he never amputates a torso in quest of an unnecessary closeup; he never obscures essential patterns by focusing upon irrelevant detail. He conveys the basic relationships, the basic rhythms, even the basic styles, faithfully."

—Martin Bernheimer
LOS ANGELES TIMES

RIGHT: Cathy McCann and Elie Chaib in Paul Taylor's *Speaking in Tongues.*

the visionary Dance Theater of Harlem, an unclassifiable little troupe called Pilobolus, and an immensely gifted youngster named Mark Morris. Still, in the beginning, doubters remained about the collaboration of television and dance. Reassurance came from a surprising source: the critics themselves.

THE CRITICS' RESPONSE

At first some people were wary—even alarmed—by television's encroachment on the sacrosanct province of the dance. "There was a terrible noise from the dance community," Brockway remembers. "We were venturing into a secret society." An article by Anna Kisselgoff, dance critic of the *New York Times*, "broke the spell," he adds, by stressing that the two media were not in competition. Kisselgoff's was one of many reviews and features about the new series, published throughout the nation, that helped to sway most doubters.

Some worried that fewer audiences would buy tickets to live performances if they could see dance in the comfort of their homes. A survey by the National Research Center of the Arts conducted during the Joffrey Ballet's spring 1976 season put that concern to rest, finding that just under half of the audience in the theater had seen the Joffrey program on *Dance in America* late the year before. Of first-time audiences, 59 percent cited the show as a significant influence on their decision to attend.

Others wondered how the expansive, space-eating art of live dance could ever be captured— or even suggested—on a tiny screen. But cultural reporters and critics around the nation soon recognized what the series could do for American dance. "The day when television audiences can choose between an old Paul Newman movie and an evening with the Joffrey Ballet may not be far off," Janice L. Ross trumpeted in *Performing Arts*, a San Francisco arts monthly. Early in 1976 Dorothy Thom, writing in the Englewood, New Jersey, *Press Journal*, addressed her comments to new dance audiences: "These programs will offer a not-to-be-missed opportunity to have a whole New World opened to you. Try it, you'll like it. Then you will go to see the dancers in the theater and find that a live performance is even better."

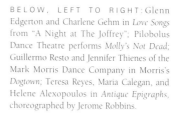

BELOW, LEFT TO RIGHT: Glenn Edgerton and Charlene Gehm in *Love Songs* from "A Night at The Joffrey"; Pilobolus Dance Theatre performs *Molly's Not Dead*; Guillermo Resto and Jennifer Thienes of the Mark Morris Dance Company in Morris's *Dogtown*; Teresa Reyes, Maria Calegan, and Helene Alexopoulos in *Antique Epigraphs*, choreographed by Jerome Robbins.

In the *Milwaukee Journal*, Louise Kenngott urged viewers to watch *Dance in America* if they had ever been interested in dance. "For that matter," Kenngott continued, "even if you've never been interested, watch *Dance in America* anyway." And Clive Barnes, then dance and drama critic of the

New York Times, called *Dance in America* "the most ambitious dance program ever conceived anywhere."

Sali Ann Kriegsman, the former head of the NEA's dance program who went on to direct the Jacob's Pillow Dance Festival, agrees. "*Dance in America* brought dance that didn't tour or wasn't readily accessible to many parts of the country, to people who wouldn't see it otherwise. People who were house-bound, or couldn't afford the price of a ticket, could see a lot of dance for free.

"I don't think there is any question that the program increased the visibility of dance. It added to the buzz and developed an appetite to go to dance. Many, many people have told me they were inspired to go to a performance because of *Dance in America*. Every single performance was created at such a cost to the people who made it—the artists and the producers. . . . I don't know where we'd be without it."

BUILDING A FUTURE ON THE PAST

In its first twenty-two years, *Dance in America* has presented programs on some twenty ballet, modern dance, and ethnic companies. Modern dance history, postmodernist dance, Broadway, tap, juggling, and hip-hop have all been covered in special documentaries. The New York City Ballet might not tour the United States, but Americans have been able to learn a great deal about the company, its repertory, and its performers through the seventeen different programs presented by *Dance in America*. Now Judy Kinberg dreams of commissioning dances for the camera, and others talk enthusiastically of creating for the camera.

"It would be wonderful to do something for television," says Peter Martins, a *Dance in America* veteran who is now the director of New York City Ballet. "You could use all these dissolves, multiple images. It would be fantastic. Look at the old Fred Astaire films.

"It was always a dream of mine to show *Symphony in C* on television when they get this new wide screen that is the equivalent of Cinemascope in movie theaters. I think you must be very careful of special effects. You still want one image on the screen. But there are moments when you could go very close, in the second movement. Just to get tighter."

There is no mistaking the tone of a convert in Martins's voice, but such conversions, after all, have also been part of the mission of *Dance in America*.

Researchers polled audiences at Joffrey Ballet's Spring 1976 season at the City Center Theater in New York to determine how many had previously seen WNET's *Dance in America* program featuring the Joffrey company, and what their reactions were to the program. The survey found that almost half (45%) of the Joffrey audiences had seen the *Dance in America* program; and the program was perceived by a significant portion of first-time attendees (59%) as a significant influence on their decision to attend the live performances.

AGNES, THE INDOMITABLE DE MILLE
PORTRAIT OF A LEGEND

❧

IN HER TWENTIES AGNES DE MILLE CARVED A SMALL BUT VIBRANT CAREER FOR HERSELF AS a solo dancer, and she never looked back. She began to choreograph for major ballet troupes—the first being Ballet Theatre—in 1937 at age twenty-eight, and five years later she became the toast of

Broadway for her dramatic dances in *Oklahoma!* Not long after, she added writing to her accomplishments, and by then she had already become a sought-after consultant on American dance.

But de Mille would always be the teenager who suddenly realized she was ugly and never got over it, always the young dancer who could never forget that she had far too little training to perform. The niece of film director Cecil B. de Mille, she was armed with a strong sense of self that enabled her to persist, complaining all the way about real and perceived injustices but with such style and biting wit that her complaints were celebrated. They undoubtedly fueled her life with renewed vigor.

This is the de Mille captured in *Agnes, the Indomitable de Mille*, produced by Judy Kinberg and directed by Merrill Brockway. The hour-long Emmy Award–winning documentary, shot in 1986, treats three high points of her career—*Oklahoma!* and her signature ballets *Rodeo* and *Fall River Legend*—at surprising length. It also establishes de Mille as a skillful early television commentator and deepens our insight into her private life.

The family photographs are evocative, and her talk of the father she idolized is poignant and revealing. De Mille was allowed to cut school for big shoots on her uncle's Hollywood sets. As her mother put it to a school administrator, how could she deny Agnes permission to watch Gloria Swanson being thrown to the lions?

Hilarious footage shows de Mille and Ballet Theatre director Lucia Chase hamming it up in de Mille's comic *Three Virgins and a Devil*. Nora Kaye and Christine Sarry dance defining roles in *Fall River Legend* and *Rodeo*. The glamour and solemnity of de Mille's Broadway career are suggested in quick shots of theater posters and sheet-music covers as well as in snatches of dancing. De Mille, with a little help from Simone Signoret, even outtalks a Red-baiting Hedda Hopper in an invaluable clip from an early television talk show.

But in the end it is de Mille herself who is the star, perhaps in ways the wily overachiever might not have intended. She was a pretty child, the documentary shows us, and a vivid dancer. Lizzie's moment of madness in *Fall River Legend* still breaks the heart, and the clear, invigorating open air of earlier times in New England and the American West still bursts through the screen in footage from *Carousel* and *Oklahoma!*

Her career wound down somewhat ingloriously, but we are left with a truly unbreakable woman in *Agnes, the Indomitable de Mille,* filmed just seven years before her death. Off camera, de Mille reads excerpts from her grandly eloquent memoirs. It was the writing that convinced Kinberg that the show should be done."I realized what a unique voice she had," Kinberg says. "I think this is one of our most important programs. Agnes is at her best, her most winning, and we gave her her due."

Talking on-screen, seated in her garden, de Mille looks like a fierce rabbit. Girish Bhargava, the show's editor, cuts away at sensitive moments to greenery and a gnarled tree covered with mushrooms on the grounds of her beloved family country home. "Friends die one by one," she says of old age, "but so, thank God, do enemies." And she has come to forgive herself, she admits, "for not being the success I meant to be."

Bob Fosse

STEAM HEAT

Bob Fosse: Steam Heat manages to "kill off the hero at the top and continue for another fifty minutes," quips Girish Bhargava, who edited the show, employing a bit of Fosse's own panache and wit.

Produced and directed by Judy Kinberg three years after Fosse's sudden death in 1987, the Emmy Award–winning program cuts adroitly back and forth among the life and work of the influential director and choreographer, his theatrical productions and films, his own reminiscences, and those of famous friends in the theater and literature who spoke at his memorial. Fosse's speeches accepting the many honors that came his way, including a number of Oscars and Tonys, form a litany of glory intercut with the sudden devastating failures that, as Fosse quipped, "kept his cynicism intact."

The shy thirteen-year-old vaudevillian, the exuberantly flashy film, television, and stage dancer, and the driven choreographer and director are all evoked through archival photographs and clips from his film biography, *All That Jazz.* Fred Astaire was a major influence. Black tap and eccentric dancing styles were clearly an inspiration for his own taut, coiled movement. His shortcomings—his hunched posture, turned-in legs, and a receding hairline that made him more comfortable dancing in hats—were another.

Fosse traveled from the union workers and ballplayers of his first Broadway hits, *Pajama Game* and *Damn Yankees,* to society's glittering, tawdry castoffs in *Sweet Charity* and *Cabaret,* which brimmed with his trademark chilly eroticism. He returned to everyday people in his last musical, *Big Deal,* tantalizingly represented here by a new loose, lyrical choreography performed during the 1986 Tony Award show. Fosse also became fascinated with the techniques of filmmaking, so different from those of the stage. "Fosse was a risk taker," Kinberg says. "He brought that to his filmmaking. He broke new ground."

Gwen Verdon, Fosse's third wife and star dancer, serves as a guide and interpreter throughout the documentary. But the story is in the visuals. Dance on camera has sometimes been criticized as seeming less spontaneous than live dance seen on the stage. But *Bob Fosse: Steam Heat* suggests the unique potential of film documentaries to reanimate a subject. Jac Venza observes, "Judy was able to take advantage of Bob's candor in discussing himself and his career and to intercut interviews with footage from his work in a way that gave the audience a more intimate and 'inside' experience than they would have had simply watching his dance in a theater."

The Joffrey Ballet

A YOUTHFUL EXUBERANCE

THE FERVOR OF THE NATIONWIDE ACCOLADES THAT GREETED *DANCE IN AMERICA'S* OPENING program in 1976 had a great deal to do with the pioneering concept of the series itself. But "City Center Joffrey Ballet," the first of six shows that the series would produce on the Joffrey, was also the perfect mix of ebullience, passion, and history with which to begin.

AN UNMATCHABLE PHYSICALITY AND EXCITEMENT

Directed by Jerome Schnur and produced by Emile Ardolino, this first program proclaims from its opening moments the importance of American dance, using a drumroll and the powerful turns, runs, and jumps of an athletic male torchbearer to convey the message. The camera catches the dancer, a lead character in Gerald Arpino's signature *Olympics,* slicing across parallel lines on the stage floor— lines that run toward the eye rather than across the stage as they usually do in dance programs. This opening image makes a striking statement: dance offers superb physicality and visual excitement in a way that no other art form can match. The program also shows Robert Joffrey, the company's founder, teaching class to his dancers on the stage, a class that resumes at the end of the show. To dance is to be a student one's entire life, these sequences tell us, and in Joffrey these dancers had a teacher of uncommon meticulousness and skill. Joffrey was also an unabashed balletomane, a man who often began interviews by asking what good dance the reporter had seen lately. He was a fundamentally shy man, yet his eagerness was unfeigned. Like Alvin Ailey, Joffrey took pleasure in putting together dance programs that he himself would like to see.

AN INNATE APPRECIATION FOR A RANGE OF STYLES

Joffrey's innate appreciation and knowledge of dance style is evident in his ballets, from the sensual multimedia *Astarte* to the bittersweet, nostalgic *Remembrances,* both of which are seen on the first program. And he was always on the lookout for interesting choreography, helping Americans to get to know the lyrical, sweet-tempered, and wise ballets of Frederick Ashton. For this reason, it was a special mission, producer Judy Kinberg recalls, to include Ashton's *Monotones II* in the 1989 "A Night at the Joffrey." This program, essentially a tribute to Joffrey, was broadcast by *Dance in America* a year after his death. Also on this program are Arpino's luminous *Round of Angels* and William Forsythe's *Love Songs,* a violent, stylish ballet by a young choreographic upstart whose dramatic gifts Joffrey had noted and cherished when Forsythe danced in the company's corps. "I knew Billy would become a choreographer," Joffrey said years later.

If it had not been for Joffrey, American audiences might not have seen two masterpieces of

"The best thing about putting dance on television is the great numbers of people who can see it. My mother's an invalid, and she had never seen Trinity *before this program. Television reaches places where dance companies simply cannot perform. Most companies can only play in large cities, and this gives them much more exposure."*

—ROBERT JOFFREY

LEFT: Denise Jackson, Rudolf Nureyev, and Gary Chryst in *Petrouchka,* from "Nureyev and The Joffrey Ballet: In Tribute to Nijinsky."

twentieth-century ballet: Léonide Massine's *Parade* and Kurt Jooss's *The Green Table*. Excerpts from these two dances are included in the first *Dance in America* program. On camera in conversation with Joffrey, Jooss is wryly unassuming about the creation of his harrowing antiwar classic, which was performed in its entirety in 1983 on *Dance in America*, along with excerpts from other vivid, rarely performed Jooss works. There is less of Massine in "City Center Joffrey Ballet"; still, the show captures the Joffrey star Gary Chryst at the height of his career as the bizarre Chinese Conjurer in *Parade,* a role with which he would become identified. Chryst is seen again on this program in Arpino's *Trinity,* another signature Joffrey ballet, alongside many of the company's leading dancers of the time.

ARTISTS OF ALL SHAPES AND SIZES

In an age of increasing homogeneity, Joffrey's company stood out for its use of dancers who may not have had "perfect" ballet bodies but who were all individuals; they came in all sizes, shapes, and colors. Their faces are alive—and still memorable two decades later—in *Trinity.* The screen pulses with their fast-moving bodies. Dancers, unlike the rest of us, can fly, this first *Dance in America* program seems to be saying.

The Joffrey programs also introduce television audiences to two of the greatest ballet dancers of the century. In the 1981 "Tribute to Nijinsky," Rudolf Nureyev dances three roles made famous by the Russian dancer Vaslav Nijinsky during the exotic era of Serge Diaghilev's

"This was an actual record, something that would last. It wasn't as if we could shrug it off and say, 'Well, next year we'll try to do this dance better.' It had to be better this time. There was also the matter of matching our shots—if bits of a dance had been shot at different times of the day, one dancer might be sweating in one sequence and not in the next. They had to match up, and they had to maintain the impact and the flow of a whole performance. That's why the editing was such a painstaking process. Our film editor was most patient with us."

—ROBERT JOFFREY

BELOW: *The Rite of Spring* with original cast, Diaghilev's Ballets Russes.

Ballets Russes seventy years before. First, the program brings to potent effect all the whirling color and strangeness of *Petrouchka*, with Nureyev playing the title role. In a taped interview, the dancer talks amusedly of trying for androgyny in *La Spectre de la Rose*, in which he dances the rose that a young girl brings home from a ball. This proved to be a happily failed attempt, for Nureyev's masculine vigor and avuncular tenderness are intriguing in the role. And Nureyev brings a tantalizing irony to the hedonistic faun in *L'Après-midi d'un Faune*, which unfolds against the background of the sumptuous Léon Bakst set, lovingly recreated from the original production. In the 1990s, *Dance in America* would chronicle efforts by the Joffrey and by dance historian Millicent Hodson to retrieve Nijinsky's lost *Rite of Spring*.

ABOVE: The Joffrey Ballet's reconstruction of *The Rite of Spring* in *The Search for Nijinsky's Rite of Spring*.

THE PIONEER OF "CROSSOVER BALLET"

With the 1994 broadcast of "Billboards with the Joffrey Ballet," the controversial rock extravaganza set to music by the composer formerly known as Prince, *Dance in America* captures the Joffrey's pioneering concept of "crossover ballet," in which modern-dance choreographers have been invited to create ballets for the company's classically trained dancers. Robert Joffrey cherished the variety and breadth of dance, and almost no form was foreign to him. This philosophy has been shared by *Dance in America*, and so it was particularly appropriate that a collaboration with the Joffrey Ballet helped launch a series dedicated to celebrating every aspect of American dance.

[*91*]

MARTHA GRAHAM
AND HER DANCE COMPANY
THE JOY AND THE PASSION

MARTHA GRAHAM WAS "MOTHER'S MILK" TO *DANCE IN AMERICA*'S PRODUCER-DIRECTOR
Merrill Brockway, who looked forward with almost unqualified delight to working with the matriarch
of American modern dance during the series' inaugural season. Brockway knew that "with Martha you

always had to make a deal," as he affectionately puts it. Indeed, Graham walked away from her first *Dance in America* show with a brand-new set for her company; even now, this coup remains an otherwise unheard-of event in the program's history. Still, both sides always profited from their collaboration: as they put together the first program, for instance, Graham wanted more close-ups than Brockway thought wise in *Diversion of Angels,* a joyous group work whose effect partly depends on the broad trajectories of bodies surging across the stage. Finally, Brockway told her, "Then build me a close-up, Martha." And she did.

Graham knew exactly which pieces she wanted in the 1976 "Martha Graham Dance Company," the first of four Graham programs in the series. And she entered into the collaboration as an equal and very practical participant with the *Dance in America* team, Brockway recalls. "Do you want to kill them off in the first year?" she asked in mock horror when Ron Protas suggested *Clytemnestra* for the first Graham program. (Protas, then Graham's assistant, would become the company's director following her death in 1991.)

Yet *Clytemnestra,* taped in 1978, is one of Brockway's two favorite programs in the *Dance in America* series. (The other is "Choreography by Balanchine—Part I.") "It's simple, I think," Brockway reflects. "I think I really got out of the way of the material. It's about showing you the piece."

A SERENE INTRODUCTION TO A FIERY ARTIST

The first program with Graham is perhaps as much a portrait of a grande dame who had a sense of humor and a poetic way with words as it is an introduction to Graham's dance. A central solo from *Cave of the Heart* represents the white-heat emotional intensity for which Graham is probably best known. The balance of the first program is relatively serene, a reminder to the cognoscenti that even in her narrative dances there is much joy and a spareness worthy of the postmodernists who would follow her into New York's dance world of the 1960s. *Appalachian Spring,* in particular, unfolds in an atmosphere of spacious air that the camera was well suited to suggest.

REIMAGINING THE STAGE EXPERIENCE

There is airy empty space around the ancient heroes and villains in *Clytemnestra,* too, but here it is charged air. The close-ups in this reconception of the Graham masterpiece suggest a narrative that is being remembered, one that is reoccurring in a tortured heart. The visuals are exotic in a way that complements but does not exactly replicate Graham's stage pictures. This *Clytemnestra* is, as dance critic Deborah Jowitt wrote, "a beautiful and slightly baffling new thing" that confidently reimagines the experience of the dance onstage.

Eight years after the first Graham program, in "An Evening of Dance and Conversation with Martha Graham," *Dance in America* offered the full *Cave of the Heart,* along with *Errand into the Maze* and *Acts of Light.* By then, thanks in part to the series itself, there was less need to reassure dance neophytes, and Graham's full passion is allowed to blaze across the screen.

"Television is a very powerful medium, and I said I'd never do it. Then I realized I was just being stupid. When I worked in it I found it fascinating. The energy it takes is terrific, because everything has to be done and geared from a visual point of view."

—MARTHA GRAHAM

"I'm not just interested in doing designs for the stage. Pretty bodies do pretty things. I am absorbed in man's tragedy and comedy. You have to find the inner movement, that you practically never show."

—MARTHA GRAHAM

LEFT: Peggy Lyman and Takaka Asakawa of The Martha Graham Dance Company in *Diversion of Angels.*

The New York City Ballet

THE COLLABORATION WITH MR. B.

✑

FROM THE BEGINNING, *DANCE IN AMERICA* SET A TOP PRIORITY ON COLLABORATING with George Balanchine, whose dances had forged a fast and unfussy new style of classical ballet. Looking back, Kinberg realizes that Balanchine had been auditioning the *Dance in America* team for some time, waiting to see how the program would tape his ballets when they were danced by other companies. Eventually the television series would create more programs with Balanchine's New York City Ballet than with any other company or choreographer. Seventeen programs were recorded by the twenty-fifth anniversary of GREAT PERFORMANCES, with Paul Taylor and American Ballet Theatre coming in a distant second at seven programs each. The shows featuring the New York City Ballet (also known simply as City Ballet) began in 1977 with the first of four "Choreography by Balanchine" hours; for the anniversary period, they included the two-part "Balanchine Celebration" televised in 1993. Throughout his involvement, Balanchine (or "Mr. B.," as he was called by his colleagues and protégés) played an active role in "reconceiving" the ballets for television, as the credits would put it.

Over the course of the collaboration, *Dance in America* has captured the range of City Ballet's repertory, which includes works by Jerome Robbins, who directed the company with Balanchine for many years; Peter Martins, Balanchine's successor as company director; and Auguste Bournonville, a nineteenth-century choreographer whose dances have some of the speed and lightness of the Balanchine style. In addition, the programs offer a history of City Ballet performers, from the early Balanchine dancers seen in the atmospheric archival footage of the 1984 documentary *Balanchine* to the international guest stars who appear with the company in "Balanchine Celebration." These programs not only offer a chronicle of Balanchine's career, documenting a huge variety of his ballet productions, but they also reveal the development of new skills and an emerging sensitivity to televised dance on the part of both the choreographer and the *Dance in America* team.

AN EMERGING TECHNIQUE FOR TELEVISING DANCE

We can witness this development in the "Choreography by Balanchine" series alone. The ballets in the first two programs are shot pretty much straight on, from a vantage point approximating that of a person sitting in a good theater seat with a pair of binoculars within reach. The frame occasionally crops off the dancers on the sides, and the camera increases the visual interest by moving in and out and by positioning small groups of dancers slightly off center in the frame.

In *The Four Temperaments*, which closes the first show, choreographed entrances and exits

"Lessons could be learned from watching the television version of Balanchine's work. . . . Instead of moving in and out, they follow the dancer, just as we would, if we were sitting out front. Occasionally there's a close-up, but no oftener than as if we were using binoculars. And it's nice because we do enjoy seeing what the dancers look like."

—Judy Flander
WASHINGTON STAR

LEFT: Peter Martins coaching Stephanie Saland and Robert LaFosse in George Balanchine's *Western Symphony,* seen on "Balanchine in America."

[95]

become dissolves; the dancers fade from view rather than disappearing into the offstage wings, which of course do not exist on the television screen. But the overall quality is clearly one of respect for the dance, allowing it to speak for itself without much help from snazzy camera angles, panning with (that is, following) the dancer, and zooming in and out. We are left with the sensation of motion contained in a vessel of air.

In contrast, in the fourth "Choreography by Balanchine" program—which won an Emmy Award in 1979 as the outstanding classical program in the performing arts—two culminating superimpositions enhance the charming fantasy of Balanchine's *The Steadfast Tin Soldier.* Other camera techniques help to pull the viewer into the kinetic energy of the Tschaikovsky medley. For example, in *Elégie,* the hyper-romantic opening section of Balanchine's *Tschaikovsky Suite No. 3,* the camera provides a sensation of soaring and surging with a windswept Sean Lavery, who is pursuing his unattainable muse (danced by Karin von Aroldingen) across a vast deserted ballroom at dusk. In part, this effect is achieved through the time-honored device of dancers moving toward the eye of the camera, but there is also less empty space at the sides. The picture looks less composed and more active.

By the 1990 "Balanchine in America," the shifting patterns of a screenful of women in long classical tulle skirts in *Serenade* have a formal beauty and excitement that come partly from the tension between the stage and the camera action and partly from the richness of the ballet's patterns, magnified to almost Busby Berkeleyesque complexity on the screen.

Balanchine had died in 1983, long before this program was put together, but he would surely have been pleased by such filmic overtones. He had been fascinated by movies while working in Hollywood on four film musicals. He told Merrill Brockway, who directed the first three "Choreography by Balanchine" programs, that he had learned a lot from the work of Gregg Toland, the director of photography on *Citizen Kane* and other landmark films. Dance on film should be created for film, he believed, citing the freshness and inventiveness of Fred Astaire's movie musical numbers.

Balanchine had strong ideas about what he liked and didn't like on film, though some of those ideas changed as he worked with *Dance in America.* Television did peculiar things to space. Dancers did not advance and retreat, Mr. B. said, they just got bigger and smaller. He wanted the camera to back far enough away to record a moving dancer's trajectory without reducing the performer to the size of an ant. He liked to see where a body started on the stage and where it ended. But if the camera followed the dancer, only the scenery seemed to be moving—and if there were no sets, as was true of many Balanchine ballets, the dancer might as well have been standing still.

PROFITING FROM PAST EXPERIENCE

Balanchine's dances had been presented with relative frequency on television in the 1950s and 1960s; he'd had ten specials and a total of twenty excerpts and whole pieces presented on the *Kate Smith* and *Ed Sullivan* Shows and on the *Bell Telephone Hour.* He had learned from these

"I have great faith in the future of Americans in ballet. We're well suited to dance. At least Mr. B likes us. When he came to America he saw that American dancers were taller than the Europeans and they had a facility for speed. Being very wise, he took those bodies and elaborated on them. To this day, people in Europe that do Balanchine ballets say, 'Oh, it's so fast, it's impossible.'

"But, it's not impossible. Not for Americans."

—SUZANNE FARRELL

"Choreography by Balanchine is neither a record film, nor a video piece. It is a collaboration between Mr. Balanchine and Dance in America. . . . His choreographic ideas were translated to television. . . . If you know the piece very well and you see it on television, you may notice changes. He cooperated intimately with us in order that his ideas were not changed."

—JUDY KINBERG

RIGHT: Mikhail Baryshnikov and the New York City Ballet in George Balanchine's *Prodigal Son.*

experiences. "If you want to present these ballets on television, then I think you should tamper with them as little as possible," Balanchine told Bernard Taper in a 1962 interview in *The Eighth Art: Twenty-three Views of Television Today*. He was not in favor of "fancy camera work," he said in this interview, reprinted in the catalog for *A Celebration of George Balanchine: The Television Work*, a 1984 exhibition at the Museum of Broadcasting in New York City. The camera "should be like a spectator who goes into the theater and gets himself a good seat and stays in it—doesn't keep jumping up and down and distracting everybody."

He suspected, too, that directors who treated existing ballets cavalierly really didn't like dance at all. This doubt was reinforced by the difficult experience he'd had while working with German television just before he was approached by *Dance in America*.

WOOING THE MASTER

Balanchine was won over to *Dance in America* in part because Brockway had gray hair and was a musician, as his assistant Barbara Horgan told series producer Emile Ardolino. Brockway's wooing of the reluctant choreographer began with a brief note: the program could not be called "Dance in America" without Balanchine and the City Ballet, Brockway wrote. Could the two men meet, any time, any place?

"We had a three-hour lunch at a French restaurant he liked. He was interested in my musical background. And he wanted to discuss his experience with film. We didn't discuss television until dessert." Balanchine insisted he wasn't the choreographer Brockway was looking for, because television told stories and Balanchine's ballets did not. Instead, Mr. B. suggested that Brockway go to the English ballet choreographer Antony Tudor, who did tell stories.

"We had a convoluted discussion about music. I tried to say that chordal progressions tell a story. He'd never heard that cockamamy theory." Then came Balanchine's two important questions. The choreographer asked Brockway if he knew anything about ballet. Not really, Brockway answered bravely. Surprisingly, Balanchine was reassured. "Good," he told the producer. "I teach you." But one more point needed to be settled. Would Brockway and Ardolino "trust the dancing"? Again, Balanchine seemed satisfied with the answer. He agreed to do two programs.

THE TEAMWORK BEGINS

First they had to discuss which ballets should be selected. And then the studio work on these dances could begin only after Brockway, Ardolino, and Balanchine had worked out a detailed shooting plan, based on extensive study of City Ballet rehearsal tapes. The two director-producers broke down the choreography themselves, writing it out in a private notation system that, while relatively informal, was clear enough that either man, they joked, could have filled in for any of the dancers. Finally came the actual shooting of the ballets, with Balanchine seeming to be everywhere at once. In the cowboy shirts he always favored, he looked right at home in Nashville, where the program was taped.

Brockway recalls that each part of the process was accompanied by fascinating talks with

"Merrill Brockway, series producer for Dance in America, *and his two colleagues, Emile Ardolino and Judy Kinberg, have been proving conclusively that while the experience of dance on television is different from dance in the theater, it is not necessarily inferior. In fact, as evidenced by one of this evening's pieces, it can be better in several respects. Mr. Balanchine, who not long ago was . . . adamant . . . in his disdain for television, apparently is beginning to perceive some potential for the medium."*

—John O'Connor
NEW YORK TIMES

LEFT: Mikhail Baryshnikov in *Prodigal Son*.

Balanchine, which he wishes he had recorded, as they involved "looking and seeing what the pieces were about." "We had marvelous conversations as we waited for the lighting, the costume changes. He'd start with what I call his little essays. A step is not a note, he'd say."

Balanchine wanted to start the first program with *Tzigane,* a piece that began with a long dance for Suzanne Farrell, one of the most exalted of his ballerinas. "You want to start the first program with a nine-minute solo?" Brockway asked incredulously. There was worse to come. Balanchine talked of ending the program with *The Four Temperaments,* which closes with the sort of group dance that is difficult to capture on a television screen. "But there are all these people," Brockway said plaintively. "Yes," Balanchine reassured him, "but they don't stay too long." The phrase became a favorite of the *Dance in America* team.

Brockway dreaded the first shoot. Balanchine told him not to worry. "I fix," he said in his Russian accent. "He went over to the monitor and positioned all these dancers with his finger within the frame," Brockway continues. "Somehow, despite the great distance between them, the dancers seemed to know instinctively whom his finger was pointing at."

The director was touched by Balanchine's simplicity and practicality. He talked to Brockway about his favorite television shows—*Wonder Woman* and the cowboy dramas. He worried about going into overtime, even though he would not be paying the bill. And it was clear that he cared about entertaining the television audiences. "Public will like, public will like," Balanchine told Brockway and Ardolino when they questioned a change or worried that he had gone too far in making a ballet program viewer-friendly.

In fact, he had no qualms about eliminating whole dances from a ballet or changing steps to make the piece work better on the screen. Television was the future, Balanchine told Peter Martins, who danced in many of the Balanchine programs. "Everyone will not want to go out of home," he said, "so we will have to deal with this."

But what about historical accuracy? Martins was disturbed at times by the apparent casualness with which Balanchine reworked his ballets. "What difference does it make?" Balanchine asked. Indeed, he was notorious for living in the present artistically. "When we go home, we do it the way it's supposed to be." But the television version was forever, Martins countered. "No," Balanchine responded. "Let them think that's the way it is."

Brockway and Ardolino also worried about his rechoreographing. "We found a way to control it, to some degree," Brockway recalls. "Do you like this?" Balanchine would ask the collaborative team after one of his bouts of tinkering. "Well, it's not so pretty," Brockway or Ardolino would respond if they thought the new choreography was a mistake. They had discovered that this was usually enough to get him to change things back again.

Balanchine tended to choose ballets for the programs on the basis of who would dance them. One ballet would be "for Kay [Mazzo]," he would say, and that one "for Peter [Martins]." He decided to do *Prodigal Son* on the third "Choreography by Balanchine" program in part because of Mikhail Baryshnikov, who had just joined City Ballet and was eager to work with Mr. B. It

"Mr. Balanchine has been treated splendidly by Dance in America. . . . *More to the point, the work of a great choreographer is being preserved in a form of some permanence, a function that is also important to the dancers, who have relatively short careers. It is essential that [Suzanne] Farrell, Patricia McBride, Kay Mazzo, Colleen Neary, Bart Cook, Robert Weiss, and all the others be recorded in their prime. Some evidence should certainly exist to prove that Peter Martins is a magnificent dancer, among the very best on the contemporary scene."*

—John O'Connor
NEW YORK TIMES

LEFT: Peter Martins and Suzanne Farrell in George Balanchine's *Chaconne.*

was the first time the two had worked together, and footage of the process was later used in the documentary *Balanchine*. Baryshnikov looks nervous and eventually lapses into Russian. Balanchine seems very happy, demostrating what he wants so energetically that some onlookers worried he might hurt himself.

"We never have to do again," he told Brockway contentedly at the end of three days of very hard work. "Thank God," Brockway exclaimed. "It was never right," Balanchine confided. "Now I made it right for Misha."

USING NEW TECHNOLOGY TO FIX OLD PROBLEMS

A similar sense for Balanchine that he might be able, with the help of new electronic technology, to get one of his works "right" at last was the driving force behind the creation of *The Spellbound Child* in 1981. This Ravel piece was based on a story by Colette about a willful child who learns to be kind when the animals and objects he has attacked all turn against him. But there had been four *Dance in America* programs on Balanchine in a little over a year, so Jac Venza put his foot down when Brockway approached him about doing a completely reworked version of the piece.

Venza agreed reluctantly to talk with the two men. Balanchine, who loved theatrical gimmickry, talked eagerly of all the special effects that were now possible in film. Butterflies, furniture, and alphabet letters could all be made to dance on camera, he said. So much could not be done on the stage, though the choreographer had tried to fix the remaining problems several times in previous versions— for Serge Diaghilev's company, for the Monte Carlo Opera (both in 1925), and for City Ballet fifty years later.

"I kept looking at the bill, which Balanchine himself had brought to the meeting," Venza groans at the memory. "The largest orchestra, the hugest cast, the most expensive soundtrack. Then I realized in our discussion of what he had tried to do at City Ballet that we had suddenly switched back to Diaghilev! Balanchine hadn't been able to solve the problems either then or later, when he'd tried once or twice with his own company. Now he wanted to try one more time."

The result was a fantasy that was filled with visual imagination; in one section, wallpaper shepherds suddenly begin to dance. But the piece still didn't work entirely. "Not great," Balanchine said philosophically, "but not lousy."

SUZANNE FARRELL

BALANCHINE'S ELUSIVE MUSE

Suzanne Farrell was as much a product of George Balanchine's practical yet exalted dance aesthetic as any of his ballets. What would Farrell have become without Balanchine and the New York City Ballet? It is hard to imagine that she would not have been a dancer—but just as hard to picture what kind of dancer she would have been without Balanchine's influence.

A shy but knowing teenager, hair scraped back to reveal a sweetly rounded face and avid eyes, glances out from the photographs of Farrell taken at the City Ballet–affiliated School of American Ballet and included in the 1984 *Dance in America* documentary entitled simply *Balanchine,* as well as in *Suzanne Farrell: Elusive Muse,* an Oscar-nominated film directed by Anne Belle and Deborah Dickson and shown on *Dance in America* in 1997.

From that film, made in 1996, we now know the devastating extent of the young Farrell's emotional involvement with her mentor Mr. B. She was not Galatea to Balanchine's Pygmalion, but her fearless technical skills and tantalizing mix of aloofness and immediacy, both on the stage and off, were irresistible raw materials for the master artist. The history of their collaboration as recorded in *Dance in America* programs suggests the ways in which Balanchine made use of his muse.

Farrell appears in the very first Balanchine program, the 1977 "Choreography by Balanchine—Part 1." Here she dances in *Tzigane,* a come-hitherish gypsy concoction that Balanchine created for her on her return to City Ballet after a painful rupture between the two. There is also an excerpt in the second program, broadcast the same year, from *Diamonds,* showing Farrell in a role that she originated in 1967 and that epitomizes both the fire and the cool formal splendor of her dancing. Later, a reckless anomie—the madness, perhaps, of the true artist—pushes up through the ballet's mannerly surface in *Variations,* a 1982 reworking of a solo for Farrell that was the last work choreographed by Balanchine before his death in 1983.

Farrell was all these things during her long career onstage at City Ballet. She was also the little girl from Cincinnati who stayed up until the early morning hours watching, with tears of pleasure, yet another rerun of *The Red Shoes.* That little girl would grow up to witness firsthand an extraordinary moment in cultural history, seeing and absorbing the work of a master from the privileged position of the ballet studio.

Asked by a reporter, in an interview before a broadcast of "Choreography by Balanchine—Part 3," whether she believed classical ballet was becoming unduly modern, she gave a typically sensible yet penetrating answer. "That depends on what you mean by modern," Farrell told Kyle H. Lawson of the Scottsdale, Arizona, *Daily Progress.* "Mr. B. has been doing Mr. B. for a long time. The public just hasn't been with him. We're just now assessing ballets that he did thirty years ago and which still look new."

"I like working with young people. I like reaching them at the beginning. You have to start young in this business because it's a short life—it's going to end while you're still a young human being.

"I feel I have something to say to my students. I'm not trying to impose myself on them but dancers must learn a whole world of knowledge in a short amount of time. I want them to take advantage of what I have learned. That way they won't waste time. They can start from where I am and go further— do things I never will have time to do."

—SUZANNE FARRELL

INSIDE THE DANCES OF

JEROME ROBBINS AND PETER MARTINS

Dance in America was George Balanchine's laboratory, a place where he could indulge the quiet curiosity he had about everything around him. Jerome Robbins and Peter Martins were just as involved in bringing their ballets to television. The series introduced new audiences to their dances, providing insight into the mind, work, and inspiration of each choreographer and even into the art of running a ballet company.

The dances in the six *Dance in America* programs featuring the works of Robbins and Martins

did not require much reconceiving for television, since most of the ballets were either screen-manage-able *pas de deux* or were shot during actual theater performances at Lincoln Center, the Brooklyn Academy of Music, or the Minskoff Theater on Broadway. But the range of pieces on four of the shows suggests a great deal about the choreographers and the art of making dances.

COMBINING THE OLD AND THE NEW

"Two Duets: Choreography by Jerome Robbins and Peter Martins," a 1980 program directed by Emile Ardolino and Kirk Browning, combines dances by Robbins and Martins that reflect the old and the new worlds of classical ballet, matching romantic lyricism with astringent oddity. On the surface, *Other Dances,* created by Robbins for Natalia Makarova and Mikhail Baryshnikov, looks as offhanded as its title suggests, but it is actually a carefully wrought exposition of its two great Russian interpreters and the Chopin piano music to which they dance. Martins's *Calcium Light Night* is a quirky first ballet danced by young Heather Watts and Ib Andersen to a score by the curmudgeonly American musical icono-clast Charles Ives.

"Two Duets" offers rare insights into the sometimes inscrutable Martins and Robbins. In one segment, Martins, a fledgling choreographer at the time the program was filmed, talks with dance writer Tobi Tobias about the difficulties of creating dance while one is still performing it. "I didn't feel like a dancer today at all," he says. "When I feel like a dancer, I can't think about choreographing. It is a big mental split." He also talks about the inspiration for *Calcium Light Night,* which occurs in a bleak, dimly lit space that looks like an empty stage. This was, in fact, the image that inspired the ballet, as Martins recalled the sight of dancers suddenly dashing across the stage to retrieve forgotten possessions after a performance was over, the sets had been struck, and everyone else had gone home. Listening to Martins tell this story, we are allowed into a theater experience from which nonperformers would ordinarily be excluded; we also catch a glimpse of a pragmatic man who for a moment has become a dreamer.

Similarly, the Robbins segment in "Two Duets" includes rehearsal footage that offers an unusually realistic look at the dancers' offstage experience. Often there is a "staged" feeling to rehearsals captured on film, but here Robbins, Baryshnikov, and Makarova interact as if no camera were present, with Robbins fine-tuning their dancing in a piece they have not performed together in a long time. "Ya da da da *dum,*" Robbins hums at one point, teasing a laughing Makarova as he guides her through a difficult sequence of steps.

The choreographer talks of the variables that must be refined in such a coaching session, among them musical phrasing and timing, the distance the dancers travel onstage, and the speed of their journey. He shrugs off the controversial practice of changing steps to suit differ-ent dancers, calling the adjustments "little things that I think clarify the performance for the audience's eye." But this does not imply a cavalier attitude toward his own choreography. He wants Makarova and

"It is probably more difficult to dance on television than on the stage. There is no cohesiveness. You keep doing little tidbits—never the whole thing—and having to warm up over and over. But you learn how to pace yourself and adjust to the different medium."

—PETER MARTINS

"The latest in an impressive series of triumphs for public TV's Dance in America series is the snaring of choreographer Jerome Robbins, who has long played the reluctant dragon with respect to the video medium. In . . .'Two Duets,'. . . Robbins . . . per-mits one of his fine recent ballets to be encapsulated within the small screen—a thing he so long shied away from."

—Alan M. Kriegsman
WASHINGTON POST

LEFT: Natalia Makarova in Jerome Robbins's *Other Dances,* from "Two Duets."

Baryshnikov to "remember the original image," down to counting the exact number of walking steps that will look simply improvised when they perform them onstage.

MARTINS'S TRIBUTE TO BALANCHINE'S BALLERINAS

In 1991, *Dance in America*'s "Ballerinas: Dances by Peter Martins with the New York City Ballet" took another look at Martins, now a full-time choreographer as well as City Ballet's company director. In this program, Martins offers five small pieces that showcase the gifts of the last lead ballerinas who worked with Balanchine. In particular, he commemorates Suzanne Farrell with an unabashedly sentimental waltz choreographed for the two of them to perform on the eve of her retirement from the stage.

PERFECTIONIST AND POET OF THE DANCE

In the 1986 "Choreography by Jerome Robbins with the New York City Ballet" and 1987 "*In Memory Of . . .* A Ballet by Jerome Robbins," both directed by Ardolino, Robbins, the notorious perfectionist of

"When Balanchine did Tschaikovsky Pas de Deux *on television for Misha and Patty [McBride], he choreographed a solo for Misha on the spur of the moment, for the camera. 'Now what can you do here, dear?' he'd say. He made it up as he went along.*

"When I think about television and working with Balanchine, the thing that comes to mind most is his unbelievable flexibility, his casual approach to it all. Not that he didn't know it was important. But he was willing to try whatever worked. If I am ever lucky enough to do anything more on television, that will be my big lesson. A guy who had done so much saying, 'Well, listen, if it doesn't work, the hell with it.'

"You can't be too reverent. If it doesn't work, you make it work. It's not going to come across if you stick to your guns. Why are you doing it in the first place? So you can translate it to a different medium so that people who are watching can enjoy it."

—PETER MARTINS

RIGHT: Kipling Houston in *Fancy Free*, from "Choreography by Jerome Robbins."

American dance, reveals himself as its poetic explicator, as well, in an interview with Rosamond Bernier. Bernier is a writer and lecturer on the arts and clearly a friend with whom the choreographer feels at ease. The two ballets in "Choreography by Jerome Robbins" represent both the new—in the 1984 *Antique Epigraphs*, a dance of murmuring lyricism for eight Grecian maidens set to music by Debussy—and the old, in Robbins's 1944 *Fancy Free*, whose story of three sailors on shore leave became the Broadway musical *On the Town*.

Robbins talks hauntingly of the bronze, enamel-eyed women in a Naples museum whose air of ritual stillness subconsciously inspired *Antique Epigraphs*. He is funny about the "Russianized" Ballet Theatre of the early 1940s, where, as a dancer intent on choreographing, he submitted endless proposals for "little things like five-act ballets" before being guided toward that short and sweet burst of ebullience called *Fancy Free*.

He choreographed *In Memory Of . . .* two years after the death of Balanchine, of whom he speaks affectionately in this *Dance in America* program. The ballet reflects the loss and pain that inspired the score by Alban Berg and that Robbins had experienced in his own life. Robbins nearly abandoned the work, so difficult was the process of creating it. Finding the first phrase of a new ballet may be "murder," as Martins enthusiastically puts it in "Two Duets," but what follows can be even more frustrating, even for a veteran like Robbins. Robbins is candid and explicit about the misery of simply continuing to create during a dry time. But when it works, the rewards are great.

Choreography is like building a bridge, he tells Bernier. It's an arc that reaches out, for a time, over nothing. Making a dance, he continues, is like "knowing an island is out there that you've read and heard about." To finish the ballet is to have explored that island. Later in the interview, however, he pulls back with characteristic caution, for even such a magical metaphor can explain very little. "There are no definitions," Robbins says. "There is no way of explaining dance."

The Paul Taylor Dance Company

FROM *RUNES* TO "THE WRECKER'S BALL"

PAUL TAYLOR HAD BEEN MAKING DANCES FOR TWO DECADES WHEN *DANCE IN AMERICA* director-producers Emile Ardolino and Merrill Brockway approached him about doing his first program for the GREAT PERFORMANCES series. By then, Taylor had a solid place in American cultural history. But he was an infant, and an irritable one at that, in terms of dance on camera.

"I resisted like crazy," Taylor admits. "I did everything I could to get out of it for a long time. It wasn't Merrill or Emile—just the idea of a different medium. I wasn't sure what they'd do to my dances. I sensed that I would not be forceful enough in my part of the job to get what I wanted, and I would have to capitulate to what they wanted. And I did, though more out of respect." Series program director Jac Venza recalls having to walk Taylor around the block while producer Ardolino worked. "He felt we were doing terrible things to his child," Venza says ruefully.

The first program, created in 1978, featured Taylor's *Esplanade* and *Runes*. Both are large dances that spread out across the stage, though *Runes* unfolds very slowly. *Esplanade* presented special problems with its speed and often hurtling, space-gobbling choreography. "I had wanted to do it, but it was an incredible challenge," admits Brockway, a member of *Dance in America*'s creative team. "I put it on my desk and walked around it for a year."

Many of Taylor's dances lend themselves to cinematic treatment because of the linear nature of their actual or implied stories. But the dramatic color in these two pieces comes from Taylor's evocation of atmosphere or mood: explosive joy and a pensive sadness in *Esplanade* and mysterious ritual in *Runes*. In *Esplanade* and to a lesser degree in *Runes*, the camera creates the sensation of small stages, rather like lily pads on a pond, where different parts of the dancing unfold. Still, the eye is guided, as it would be by the action in a live performance.

Despite his doubts, Taylor was drawn into the process, completing four more programs before he and *Dance in America* ventured into the new territory of *Speaking in Tongues* in 1991 and "The Wrecker's Ball, Three Dances by Paul Taylor" in 1996. "Paul didn't want to like us in the beginning," Judy Kinberg says. "But Emile was so lovable and so deeply appreciated Paul's work—he was so sensitive to Paul and how to present his work—that Paul could not help giving himself over. And Paul is smart. I think he realized that this was something he needed to do for his company. It would have been foolish for him to have been left out when we clearly wanted to acknowledge his commanding presence in American dance."

LEFT: The Paul Taylor Dance Company in *Company B*, performed on "The Wrecker's Ball: Three Dances by Paul Taylor."

TAKING THE VIEWER INSIDE THE DANCE

Taylor's journey from the airy formalism of the first program to the cinematic re-envisioning of "The

Wrecker's Ball" in 1996 mirrors a similar development in *Dance in America*. As in the earliest shows on George Balanchine, the viewpoint in the first five Taylor repertory programs remains close to that of the theater audience, though an audience able to shift its perspective and distance from the stage. "We referred to the process as 'translation,'" Merrill Brockway recalls; what mattered most was "to create

as complete as possible a picture of a piece onstage." In *Speaking in Tongues* and "The Wrecker's Ball," however, dance is shown in a way that would never be possible from a seat in a theater. For Ed Fussell, a long-time and highly committed camera operator for the series, *Speaking in Tongues* was "the first time *Dance in America* broke the plane of the audience and went inside the dance." With "The Wrecker's Ball," Taylor and *Dance in America* moved even further from the world of *Esplanade*.

On the other hand, the earlier *Dance in America* programs capture the near-infinite variety of Taylor's work, with twelve dances that span more than three decades and include some of his greatest and most vivid masterpieces. One early show features the loping lumps of the 1960 *Three Epitaphs*—creatures covered in black and accented with small mirrors. They are ambiguous but endearing and very Tayloresque. Watching them, a viewer might find it hard to decide whether their dance is "the saddest or the funniest thing you ever saw," as Robert Rauschenberg, who designed the costumes, said.

SADNESS AND A WICKED SENSE OF HUMOR

Taylor is a choreographer who wears his large and complicated heart hidden in the folds of a rippling sleeve, but much of his sad, funny, and savage glory has been represented on *Dance in America*. The lyrical, tender sweetness and joy of Taylor's 1962 *Aureole* may be seen blooming on a much larger scale in the later *Arden Court, Mercuric Tidings*, and *Roses*, all captured on video by *Dance in America*, along with performances by such important middle-period Taylor dancers as Carolyn Adams, Elie Chaib, Christopher Gillis, David Parsons, and Lila York.

The choreographer is unabashedly melancholic in *Sunset*, a portrait of young men at war and the women they have left behind. And he is eerily, wickedly funny in dances like *Big Bertha, Le Sacre du Printemps*, and *Snow White*, which tell their stories in a corrosive cartoon style. But each dance was allowed to tell its tale in a familiar way—until the fifth Taylor program on *Dance in America*, in 1988, which included *Last Look* and *Roses*.

A TELEVISION BREAKTHROUGH FOR TAYLOR

Last Look was the dance that convinced Kinberg, who coproduced the show with its director, Thomas Grimm, that it was time to "take things a little further and use the camera more aggressively to express what Paul did on the stage." An apocalyptic last encounter for searching and collapsing lost souls, *Last Look* would translate well to the screen, Kinberg believed. "I just felt the power of the piece would not be sacrificed on camera." On the screen, the dance's despairing ritual is both trapped within and extended by the mirrors that surround it.

Kinberg convinced Taylor to come to Denmark, where the program was being shot, in order to work closely with her and Grimm, who had already directed many other *Dance in America* programs. "It's not really as effective to talk to choreographers about your ideas," Kinberg says, "as it is to show them." With *Last Look*, something clicked. "Paul started seeing the camera for what it could do and stopped thinking of it as the enemy," Kinberg goes on. "His attitude about what was possible really changed."

A NEW TRANSLATION OF *SPEAKING IN TONGUES*

Speaking in Tongues, a chilling claustrophobic tale of a fundamentalist preacher and his rural congregation that Taylor choreographed in 1988, came along just in time to benefit from this change in attitude. The setting and relationships would lend themselves to film, the *Dance in America* team felt. Would Taylor consider treating the dance differently by shooting it on location? Taylor agreed. And Kinberg found a new young director who she thought would be perfect for the job.

Matthew Diamond had been a modern dancer and choreographer before getting involved with television, where he had directed episodes of the soap opera *Guiding Light* and sitcoms such as *The Golden Girls, Family Ties,* and *Designing Women.* Diamond and Taylor hit it off almost immediately. When it became obvious that it would be too expensive to shoot *Speaking in Tongues* on location, Diamond began to work with the Broadway and film designer Santo Loquasto on an austere studio set that suggested not just the slatted-wood enclosure of the original design but many shifting interiors and exteriors. Among them were a barn, a bar, a bedroom, a church, and a confined space that seems to represent the preacher's tortured soul. In several shots one can see more than one person dancing in more than one space; the superimpositions create a sense of ghostly spatial echoing.

"Santo and I developed a treatment for the ballet, based on set ideas and shots, section by section," Diamond says. "The dance lent itself so wonderfully to that. I don't think I would say that [Balanchine's] *Agon* lends itself to another step. There, dance exists on a stage. Nothing about it suggests anything other than the sheer brilliant design of the choreography." But *Speaking in Tongues* was different, as its *Dance in America* production shows.

DANCING TO THE MUSIC OF THREE DECADES IN "THE WRECKER'S BALL"

Almost immediately after the shooting of *Speaking in Tongues* was completed, talk began of another Taylor-Diamond collaboration. Taylor's *Company B,* an evocation of the music and world of the Andrews Sisters that was choreographed in 1991 seemed a likely subject for the next program, but the dance was not long enough to fill the hour slot of most shows in the series. "Why one hour?" Taylor asked. Why not just a half hour, leaving time for "whatevers," like interview material and credits? "They didn't go for that," he admits.

Several years passed, during which Taylor choreographed *Funny Papers,* drawing on material created by his dancers, and *A Field of Grass,* a haunting evocation of hippie life during the Vietnam War era. *Funny Papers* is danced to goofy rock music that comes for the most part from the

"A dance is not like a realistic play or movie. Dance is supposed to be a poetic form. You don't worry about changing the locale. You can be in a rose garden one minute and the next minute in hell. You take your imagined scenery along with you. But the camera lends itself to much more realistic views. That's one reason why 'Wrecker's Ball' worked. Those dances are set in specific times and places."

—PAUL TAYLOR

1950s. *A Field of Grass* is performed to the 1960s songs of Harry Nilsson. Putting these two together with *Company B* would provide an evening of dances to music from three distinct decades.

Loquasto conceived an imaginary setting for all three pieces, placing them in an abandoned building, about to be torn down, that had once been a USO-type dance hall, then a movie theater, and finally a seedy home for young squatters—hence the title of the program, "The Wrecker's Ball." Diamond saw the show beginning outside the building, with the theater door being pushed open to reveal the past by a bum, played by Taylor.

Shot in the auditorium of a girls' school on the Lower East Side of New York City, the three dances are quite different in tone and look from the original staged versions. The camera and editor seem to be just as much the choreographer as Taylor, plunging the viewer into the midst of tumultuous action. With "The Wrecker's Ball," *Dance in America* proved that it could not only capture dance in a relatively straightforward, sometimes documentary way but also show it to be a stylized, intimate form of popular entertainment.

FROM THE STAGE TO THE SMALL SCREEN: THE TRANSFORMATION OF A CHOREOGRAPHER

In reconceiving both *Speaking in Tongues* and "The Wrecker's Ball" for television, Paul Taylor worked as an equal partner with director Matthew Diamond and designer Santo Loquasto, from the shooting of the programs through the editing. By this time, he had become fascinated with the whole process, both in its mechanical details and in the larger philosophy required to recreate dance on film.

Taylor had discovered that, rather than the rectangular space of the stage, space for the camera is a triangle, with the camera positioned at the apex. "But when it came to respacing the dance, I couldn't understand why they couldn't just move the camera or why it was important to let the viewer know at all times where in the space the dancer was.

"A dance is not like a realistic play or movie. Dance is supposed to be a poetic form. You don't worry about changing the locale. You can be in a rose garden one minute and the next minute in hell. You take your imagined scenery along with you. But the camera lends itself to much more realistic views. That's one reason why "Wrecker's Ball" worked. Those dances are set in specific times and places."

Taylor also became increasingly concerned about how to counteract the flattening effect of film and make his dances look three-dimensional on the screen. The screen "does away with perspective," he points out. "There is no sense of kinetic energy. No goo. No dynamics. Fast things look faster, slow things slower."

ADDING AND TIGHTENING: NECESSARY INVENTIONS

Taylor had done almost no tightening of the dances in the programs before "The Wrecker's Ball." In fact, he had actually added a dance to *Speaking in Tongues* to help make the piece fit its fifty-six-minute time slot and to give Christopher Gillis, a senior dancer in the Taylor company, something special to perform. As is often the case in dance, this last-minute practical necessity resulted in imaginative invention. Taylor choreographed a small and very interesting duet in which a "hayseed," danced by

ABOVE: Linda Kent and the Paul Taylor Dance Company in Taylor's *Last Look*.

Christopher Gillis, courts a sexily rumpled wench, danced by Denise Roberts. The lighting and sense of air and open space give the dance the innocent look of a movie musical number, but the choreography, barnyard noises, and the crudity of Gillis's sensual passes reflect the underlying darkness of many of Taylor's dances. Denise Roberts remembers that Taylor wanted to include gestures from the club-dance style called vogueing, so the choreographer took the two dancers to see *Paris Is Burning*, a documentary on drag queens in New York in which the men vogue.

For "The Wrecker's Ball," several sections had to be cut from each dance in order to create the program's smooth, continuous flow. Taylor also had to come up with steps to get the dancers from one part to another—steps that would make as full use as possible of the space and the equipment. Taylor was intrigued but undone by having three monitors to watch during the shoot. "I was supposed to be deciding which shot I liked best, but I found it totally confusing to watch three monitors," he admits. "I guess young people can." At times he just gave up and wandered off to play cards with the crew, but this nearly caused a fiasco at one point when he stubbed out his 1990s filter-tip cigarette in an ashtray positioned for a shot in a 1940s scene.

Taylor had asked for a headset after a few days on the "*Speaking in Tongues*" set in Nashville so that he could listen to crucial conversations among Matthew Diamond and the camera operators. When he too was miked, he was amazed: "I could talk to Matt or to Judy [Kinberg, the pro-

"The kinds of people I like to work with are not mannequins. They are assertive. They have minds of their own and perhaps even idiosyncratic bodies. When I choose a dancer I look for intelligence, a certain technical capability—it can be from a ballet background or a variety of modern dance persuasions, but mostly I look for somebody who draws your eye."
—**PAUL TAYLOR**

ducer], who was real far away somewhere in a truck. And I could eavesdrop on the cameramen. Their comments about what was going on were very funny."

As the choreographer became increasingly involved, Diamond says, Taylor became more confident about using the terminology, and their work became more efficient—which was a good thing, given the complexities of "The Wrecker's Ball." This program was shot from all around the dancing, including below and above. For one dizzying sequence in *A Field of Grass,* dancer Patrick Corbin was asked to turn with his head tilted up toward an overhead camera, thus relinquishing all of a dancer's steadying spatial references. Corbin also had to negotiate a sea of camera wires as well as the body of camera operator Ed Fussell, who had been choreographed into the dance by Taylor so that he could crawl on the floor beneath the dancer's feet and shoot upward with his handheld camera.

At one point, Ronnie Smith, another veteran *Dance in America* camera operator, had to be covered with garbage so that he couldn't be seen shooting from the floor. And in another sequence, Fussell had to catch one exact and unrehearsable moment. "Two dancers were rolling around on the tops of rickety little round bar tables," he recalls serenely. "At the end, the male dancer ends up posed next to the girl, reaches out his hand, and flicks out a joint. My task was to see him raise his head up from the table, then walk 360 degrees around the table, and at the end zoom in to the flick of this ash. Matthew wanted some things from me that just really pushed me to the limits of my endurance."

One dance in *A Field of Grass* was shot in pouring rain. "It was cold, and the guy who brought the rain in didn't heat it," Taylor recalls. "And it was dangerous. One girl cut her chin but went right on. The dancers were just wonderful."

There were other effects that Taylor could not have created on a theater stage. He had imagined a dancer suddenly bursting into view in one part of *Company B.* In "The Wrecker's Ball," Tom Patrick, as if by magic, leaps off the auditorium's stage and flies into his "Boogie Woogie Bugle Boy" solo. "What was new about the old film tricks," Kinberg says, "was how we used them to further what Paul had conceived of originally for the stage."

By the completion of "The Wrecker's Ball," Taylor could settle comfortably into the "bull sessions" that took place during the final editing, and as Diamond laughingly recalls, these conferences were "plenty vociferous." Fortunately, Taylor says, he did not have to be present until a rough cut had been made. "Matt, Judy, and Girish [Bhargava, the show's editor]—a marvelous, dear man who loves dance—did the work. I find the whole editing process terribly tedious, though they have machines now. You push a button and get dozens of versions, then you pick one and splice it by computer. It's a much faster process." "That box" that Taylor had initially dreaded had become almost as fascinating as his beloved stage. And Taylor's conversion has become one of the great success stories of *Dance in America.*

Mikhail Baryshnikov and American Ballet Theatre

A Breeze Through Cloistered Hallways

Profound changes occurred in American ballet and modern dance during the second half of the twentieth century, and many of them have been chronicled, either intentionally or serendipitously, by *Dance in America* programs. One of these shifts occurred in 1979 when Mikhail Baryshnikov was appointed artistic director of the American Ballet Theatre (also known simply as Ballet Theatre or ABT); it was a position he would hold for a decade.

Baryshnikov's appointment was in many ways a fresh breeze through cloistered hallways. The dancers he chose to feature and the repertory he shaped reflected his unflagging curiosity about unfamiliar forms of dance, which he had been unable to explore as a young dancer in training in the Soviet Union. On the other hand, that training had given him an abiding respect for the discipline and essential immutability of ballet classicism.

Under Baryshnikov's direction, Ballet Theatre acquired modern-dance repertory by such established choreographers as Twyla Tharp and Merce Cunningham and by such avant-garde artists as David Gordon and Karole Armitage. Of course, ABT was not the first classical company to engage in "crossover ballet"; Robert Joffrey and his troupe had initiated this trend, which by now has become almost universal. But Baryshnikov's star status lent an extra prestige to the endeavor, especially as he moved in this direction just at the time when fewer promising ballet choreographers seemed to be coming to the fore. Baryshnikov's choices were often particularly daring ones considering the history of Ballet Theatre and its entrenched classicism—a history so different from that of the Joffrey, with its reputation for high-spirited youthfulness.

FROM THE CLASSICAL TO THE UNEXPLORED

The eight programs that *Dance in America* devoted to Ballet Theatre from 1977 through 1990 richly display the company's range from the old to the new. And all but the first of these programs were created during Baryshnikov's directorship. The shows provide a look at some of ABT's most important and affecting masterworks as well as a record of distinctive dancers now lost to the stage through retirement or death. Here, too, is a record of how the look and goals of the troupe have changed.

LEFT: Mikhail Baryshnikov and Elaine Kudo in *Sinatra Suite*, performed on "Baryshnikov by Tharp."

The company was founded in 1940 by Americans Lucia Chase and Richard Pleasant, who were intent on creating a repertory that included the best that international ballet had to offer. Their sense of the international was unusual for the time, since this was an era when there were few home-grown ballet troupes. Yet their emerging repertory included not only the glittering fare of the foreign touring companies but also American choreography based on American themes, among them the quintessentially American West. One of the first such acquisitions, procured a year before Agnes de Mille's *Rodeo,* was Eugene Loring's *Billy the Kid.* This became the opening work on *Dance in America*'s first ABT program, which bore the straightforward title of "American Ballet Theatre."

The darkness of Loring's portrait of an outlaw hero is balanced on this program by the skimming, amiable *Les Patineurs,* a ballet about skaters in winter choreographed by Frederick Ashton. Ashton had played an important role in the creation of a truly English style of ballet dancing. These two ballets were restaged for television by artists who were close to the heart of the choreography and both of whom have since died. Loring himself did the "translation" for *Billy the Kid,* while Brian Shaw, a lead dancer and teacher with the Royal Ballet of England and a noted interpreter of Ashton's ballets, took on *Les Patineurs.*

Though Frederick Ashton is one of the greatest and most engaging choreographers of twentieth-century ballet, his works are performed less often today than they once were. "American Ballet Theatre" preserves this bit of history, at the same time that it brings new life on video to the gentle Marianna Tcherkassky and the famed virtuoso Fernando Bujones, both now retired from the company, as well as to Clark Tippet and Charles Ward, two interesting lead dancers who died in the 1980s.

Other Ballet Theatre programs that feature the company's more traditional repertory have included the hoary Russian *Paquita* and *Don Quixote,* in stagings by Natalia Makarova and Baryshnikov, as well as *Les Sylphides,* an early twentieth-century piece in which Michel Fokine set out to revolutionize ballet. These ballets star dancers like Baryshnikov, Bujones, and the beloved all-American prima ballerina Cynthia Gregory. In addition, the 1990 *A Tudor Evening with American Ballet Theatre* offers a lovingly scrupulous record of two penetrating classics from the mid 1930s, with reminiscences of the early life and work of their eccentric creator, Antony Tudor, by Agnes de Mille and the English ballerina Maude Lloyd. Both had known Tudor well and worked with him during his London years.

Tudor threw in his lot with Ballet Theatre in its first year of existence and continued to work with the company for the next three decades. At ABT he found a secure home in which to create works that have an essentially European flavor, often odd subject matter, and a highly specific vocabulary. This vocabulary is now sometimes difficult to reproduce with dancers trained in the sleek high-energy style of today's classical ballet.

One of the "Tudor Evening" ballets is *Jardin aux Lilas;* the story of a woman forced to marry a man she does not love, it is a feverish portrait of stifling societal convention, danced to trembling music by Chausson. It is paired with the ballet *Dark Elegies,* which depicts the grief of a community and its resolution, using dark, drab tonalities that communicate all too well the loss of hope and the struggle to regain it. Both dances feature Martine van Hamel, a ballerina of rare musicality and depth who has since retired from the stage.

At the other end of the spectrum are the shows that capture Baryshnikov's willingness to explode the boundaries of what was expected from ABT. In one five-year period (from 1985 to 1989), Baryshnikov and the *Dance in America* team worked together on "Baryshnikov by Tharp with American Ballet Theater," "Balanchine and Cunningham: An Evening at American Ballet Theatre," "David Gordon's Made in U.S.A.," and "Baryshnikov Dances Balanchine." The commissioning of Gordon's cartoonlike comedy *Murder*, one of the dances included on the "Made in U.S.A." program, was one of the most controversial choices of Baryshnikov's directorship. As Baryshnikov recalls in "Balanchine and Cunningham," Balanchine told him, when he sought the choreographer's advice about accepting ABT's invitation to lead the company, "If you think you can make dancers dance *your* way and boards of directors respect *your* mistakes, then do it."

ABOVE: Leslie Browne and Ricardo Bustamante in Antony Tudor's *Jardin aux Lilas* from "A Tudor Evening with American Ballet Theatre."

THE PLEASURE OF UNLIKELY PAIRINGS

It is clear from Baryshnikov's comments on this Balanchine-Cunningham show that part of the pleasure he found in programming dance for television was to pair works that he admired, however unlikely that pairing might seem at first. "The idea was meaningful and exciting from my point of view," Baryshnikov says of pairing Balanchine with Cunningham, for example. "Both choreographers are structuralists. Both dances are neoclassical with an edge of the avant-garde. There are a thousand interesting parallels."

In the Tharp program, Baryshnikov gets to be shamelessly romantic, first in *The Little Ballet,* a breezy evocation of lush ballet music by Glazunov, then in the hip and sensuous *Sinatra Suite,* and finally in *Push Comes to Shove,* with which he had already enjoyed great success. Along the way, Baryshnikov conducts an alphabetic tour through ballet terminology and history. The contrast is delightful: from the black-and-white footage of an ardent teenage Baryshnikov in class in Leningrad with his favorite teacher, Alexander Pushkin, to the confident dancer, choreographer, and company director, smiling easily into an American television camera and saying, "F is for *fondu, frappé,* . . . forget it."

Equally delightful is the story of Baryshnikov being summoned to breakfast in Balanchine's apartment in order to discuss his joining New York City Ballet. As Baryshnikov describes it in "Baryshnikov Dances Balanchine," the choreographer continued to iron his shirts while the dancer ate! Also on this program, we learn that Balanchine was sparing in his praise, but when the praise came, it was transforming. "Excellent," Balanchine told Baryshnikov occasionally, peering into the dancer's dressing room to say good night after a performance. "And," says Baryshnikov, "it was your evening. When you heard those words, the stars were shining for you."

In this program, the luminous Balanchine-Stravinsky masterwork *Apollo* is paired with *Who Cares?,* Balanchine's jazzy evocation of Gershwin music amid a glittering nighttime city—a combination based on the ballets' musical contrast and mutual spareness. On the other hand, the dances Baryshnikov chose for the "Baryshnikov by Tharp" program had each been "a present for my life" from the choreographer. "It's probably the most original work I've done, with respect to Twyla," Baryshnikov says of that program. Tharp had already impressed the *Dance in America* team with her innovative ideas and sophistication about film when they worked together on the 1976 *Sue's Leg/Remembering the Thirties.*

LIBERATED TO PLAY WITH DANCE

There is a special pleasure in the way Baryshnikov talks about "David Gordon's Made in U.S.A.." This suite of three dances begins with *Valda and Misha,* commissioned for the series by *Dance in America.* In this unassuming little romp, Baryshnikov and Valda Setterfield, Gordon's elegant English wife and an avant-garde star in her own right, travel through painted interiors, landscapes, and seascapes. They reminisce touchingly and with gentle wit about their childhoods and other matters, all the while dancing together with an offhanded grace.

Elsewhere in the program, Baryshnikov plays the omnipresent butler, Smith, in *Murder.* And in *TV Nine Lives,* Baryshnikov gets to be a rubber-limbed cowboy cutup dancing with men from Gordon's company. Watching this piece, one imagines that it must have been tremendously liberating for Baryshnikov to arrive in a land where dance and play are not mutually exclusive.

Baryshnikov was especially taken with the daring of Gordon's concept for their *Dance in America* program. "Everything was him," he recalls. "We were trying to make people listen and think and imagine. I was very proud."

RIGHT: Mikhail Baryshnikov and Twyla Tharp preparing for *Zoetrope,* directed by photographer Annie Liebovitz for "GREAT PERFORMANCES 20th Anniversary Special."

Dance Theatre of Harlem

———————————————— ✧ ————————————————

"DANCE THEATRE OF HARLEM," THE FIRST *DANCE IN AMERICA* PROGRAM ON THIS AFRICAN-American ballet company, is a portrait of "aspirations," as the series' program director Jac Venza puts it. In this 1977 show, audiences also find a portrait of company director Arthur Mitchell. Mitchell was determined to provide black children with the advantages that he had enjoyed as a dancer for the New York City Ballet, and so, shortly after the assassination of Dr. Martin Luther King, Mitchell joined with his white ballet teacher and mentor Karel Shook to found the company.

Mitchell had been one of City Ballet's most popular dancers in the 1960s, but he never lost sight of his status as an outsider in the primarily white world of ballet. All of Mitchell's "children"—from the professional dancers in his company to the students at the company's school—are in training not just as dancers but as role models from the time they first point a foot in the light-filled studios of the troupe's headquarters on West 152nd Street in Harlem. It is clear from the dancers' soft voices and idealistic words in this first program's taped interviews that Mitchell drives them as hard as he must have once pushed himself. "I don't say that they must become ballet dancers," Mitchell says in "Dance Theatre of Harlem," "just that they must be able to compete. Do whatever you do better."

The program captures the company's mix of hope, pride, and determined pragmatism. The show opens with a montage of Harlem street scenes shot during one of the company's frequent community street fairs. "To do a regular story just about the ballet and the dancers was not enough," Mitchell says of the program's conception. "What could we do to make it more interesting?" The answer, he goes on, was to start with "a street fair—with what these kids come from."

BREAKING NEW GROUND

When the Dance Theatre of Harlem was first incorporated in 1969, the dancers were an anomaly in the neighborhood, drawing a certain amount of teasing as they went to classes and rehearsals. Onstage, where they found themselves just two years later, they were just as much of an oddity. No one in memory had filled a stage with African-American—along with a few Hispanic and white—classical ballet dancers. But Mitchell went about shaping the company's early repertory with a canniness that softened any resistance to the idea of black classical ballet dancers. They were, after all, as Mitchell says in "Dance Theatre of Harlem," "artists who *happen* to be black."

LEFT: Virginia Johnson as Blanche in *A Streetcar Named Desire.*

The ballets chosen for the program reflect this approach. *Forces of Rhythm,* by the African-American choreographer and classically trained dancer Louis Johnson, juxtaposes ballet and ethnic dance in ways that are funny, touching, and affectingly sentimental. The African "natives," dressed comically at one point in red loincloths and bowler hats, are just as elegant as their ballet counterparts.

Also included is *The Beloved*, a sexually charged dramatic duet created by Lester Horton, a noted white West Coast modern dance choreographer who made a point of working with black dancers. Then there are excerpts from George Balanchine's *Bugaku*, an exotic Asian-flavored love duet; from Geoffrey Holder's throbbing Caribbean ritual *Dougla*; and from Mitchell's own *Holberg Suite*, a handsome, airy abstract ballet tailored to the needs of its young interpreters. Mitchell did little to adapt this ballet for the camera, yet *Holberg Suite* expands comfortably and freshly on the screen.

THE RIGHT PLACE AT THE RIGHT TIME

In 1986, *Dance in America* and the Dance Theatre of Harlem teamed up for one other program, titled "*A Streetcar Named Desire*" for the work it featured. An atmospheric evocation of the Tennessee Williams play created by Valerie Bettis, a white modern-dance choreographer, the ballet more than matches the play's airlessness and emotional tension. Mitchell selected *Streetcar* for television in part to offset his company's growing reputation as "a junior New York City Ballet," as he puts it—a company that only did works by Balanchine. "I think *Streetcar* is a phenomenal ballet," Mitchell says. "It is also a story that everyone is familiar with."

The program demonstrates *Dance in America*'s knack for being in the right place at the right time. First, Bettis herself was able to teach the ballet to the company just before her death. Then, too, Mitchell knew that he had an ideal cast for the piece. As Blanche, Virginia Johnson, a lead ballerina known for her lyricism, establishes herself here as a gifted actress, while Lowell Smith, already acknowledged for his acting skills, presents a Stanley of seething, barely contained emotions. Frederic Franklin contributes a sparkling classical dance, *Sylvia Pas de Deux*, to the program, which also includes Holder's *Bélé*. Franklin, who was the original Stanley in the Bettis work, has long been associated with the Harlem company, restaging historical ballet productions for its repertory.

AN ADVENTURE BECOMES AN EDUCATION

For Mitchell, the two *Dance in America* programs were an adventure. "The interaction and making the camera a part of the choreography were what was wonderful about working with Emile, Merrill, and Judy. They knew what they wanted and how to meld it. The programs themselves are a ballet. Camera work must become an integral part. It is a ballet—choreography—unto itself. But it must blend in. The process must be collaborative. You must take your ego and leave it at the door. And that happened."

"Our eclecticism is a strength, not a weakness, and that is the strength of the American dancer. Twenty years ago you had to be a ballet, modern, or jazz dancer. Now you can just be a dancer."

—ARTHUR MITCHELL

RIGHT: Dance Theatre of Harlem performs *A Streetcar Named Desire.*

Mitchell sees great potential in programs like *Dance in America*: "We have a privileged point of view in New York City. When you are touring, you cannot get enough coverage. We live in a visual society. The last three generations have grown up on television. Kids don't get enough about the arts. How do you get the arts to the people? How do you get the people to come to you? People who have seen the television shows are already interested. You cannot buy that kind of visibility." Today Mitchell requires his new young dancers to watch "Dance Theatre of Harlem," the company's first collaboration with *Dance in America*, as part of their study of dance history. "They know Snoop Doggy Dog, but not Martin Luther King. This way they can see where the company came from and where it is now."

Twenty Years of Dance

ASSESSING THE CONTRIBUTIONS OF DANCE IN AMERICA

As *DANCE IN AMERICA* MOVES INTO THE NEXT MILLENNIUM, WHAT KIND OF PICTURE HAVE its first twenty years given us? We have witnessed the distinctive early history of American dance, suggested by the luscious-looking choreography in the series' 1977 *Trailblazers of Modern Dance*; this era was followed by a drier, pricklier middle period captured in 1980's "Beyond the Mainstream." Throughout, American dance has been peopled by enduring individualists, such as Merce Cunningham, Twyla Tharp, and Mark Morris; by glittering superstars such as Mikhail Baryshnikov, Natalia Makarova, and Rudolf Nureyev; and by hardworking legends of choreography, such as George Balanchine, Martha Graham, and Paul Taylor.

 Dance in America has allowed a vast American audience to see not only ballets fraught with the overpowering but contained emotions of Antony Tudor's works but also the small, carefully wrought dances of Elliot Feld and the experiments of David Gordon that take insouciant liberties with formal dance manners. More than most of the performing arts, dance has opened its door to and been immeasurably enriched by the contributions of African Americans like Alvin Ailey, Katherine Dunham, Arthur Mitchell, Ulysses Dove, Garth Fagan, and Bill T. Jones—all subjects of *Dance in America* programs. Dance has happened on Native American reservations, as shown in 1993's "American Indian Dance Theater: Dances for the New Generations," as well as in clubs such as the one where the unassuming, effervescent virtuosi of all ages gather in 1989's "Gregory Hines: Tap Dance in America."

 New kinds of dance have also sprung up on the streets and in Broadway musicals, allowing choreographers like Agnes de Mille and Bob Fosse to flourish. There has been room in dance for jugglers like Michael Moschen and impudent acrobats like Pilobolus and Momix, for the lush physicality of Lar Lubovitch's modern dance, and the hard, fast dancing of music video choreography. *Dance in America* has allowed us to witness them all.

 What do these divergent strands of the American dance fabric have in common? An unashamed physicality, for one thing, and a commitment to the living moment. And Walter Terry, writing of the series in 1977 in the *Saturday Review,* identified something more, which is represented by an illuminating image that strikes him as symbolic of the series as a whole and of American dance itself. This image, at both the start and the close of Eugene Loring's *Billy the Kid* on the "American Ballet Theatre" program, consists of an "unending processional of American pioneers moving ever forward to new frontiers. Individuals falter," Terry observes, "some return to a remembered security, but the march goes on, the quests continue, the adventure never ends. To me, this is what our American dance, on TV or live, is all about."

LEFT: Gregory Hines and Savion Glover cut loose on "Tap Dance in America."

ALVIN AILEY
AMERICAN DANCE THEATER
THREE BY THREE

ULYSSES DOVE, WHO IS REPRESENTED BY THREE WORKS ON *DANCE IN AMERICA* programs, was one of the many young black men and women whom Alvin Ailey encouraged to create dances. *Episodes*, seen on 1991's "Alvin Ailey American Dance Theater: Steps Ahead," typifies the high energy and intensity of Dove's style. By pairing *Episodes* with *For Bird with Love*—Ailey's bleak but loving portrait of the jazz great Charlie "Bird" Parker—the program suggests the range of repertory that Ailey wanted to celebrate and preserve. This repertory is also captured on *Dance in America's* "Three by Three" (1985), "Two by Dove" (1995), and *Dance Black America*, an invaluable documentary directed by Chris Hegedus and D. A. Pennebaker and broadcast in the 1984–85 season.

ABOVE: The Alvin Ailey American Dance Theater performs Ulysses Dove's *Episodes* on "Alvin Ailey: Steps Ahead."

MUSIC VIDEOS

A BROADER VISION OF DANCE

—◊◊—

MUSIC VIDEOS ARE LIKE DREAMS, SAYS THE WISE LITTLE SPITFIRE TELEVISION CHOREOGRAPHER Rosie Perez in *Everybody Dance Now*, an award-winning documentary produced and directed in 1991 by Margaret Selby and shown on *Dance in America*. Just as dreams, fragmented and sometimes surreal, pass in a flash, so do several decades of popular dance in this program, which covers dance in rock acts, in Hollywood musicals, on urban streets, and in hot smoky clubs. The men and women interviewed here are bursting with do-or-die energy and bravado, and they range from musician James Brown and choreographers Cholley Atkins and Michael Peters to Hollywood directors Michael Kidd and Martin Scorsese, who worked on music videos with Janet and Michael Jackson.

"It seemed to me that, at that time, music videos were the place where young people were hired as dancers and young choreographers got a chance to choreograph," Selby says. "And I wanted to give people a much broader vision of dance." The program succeeded, and it preserved the dance and thoughts of a lively but evanescent urban art form.

"Dance isn't calm. Dance is about passion. Dance is about emotion. You can't put a boundary around it."

—MARGARET SELBY

Producer and Director of *Everybody Dance Now*

ABOVE LEFT: Willie Ninja in the dance video special *Everybody Dance Now*; ABOVE RIGHT: Rap artist M.C. Hammer performs in *Everybody Dance Now*; FOLLOWING PAGE: Diana Gray in Martha Graham's *Clytemnestra*.

GREAT PERFORMANCES
Dance Programs

⁂

The following format has been used to describe the dance programs:

DIA = DANCE IN AMERICA
LFLC = LIVE FROM LINCOLN CENTER

TITLE
Dances, Choreographer
Dance Company, Season
AWARDS

ACCENT ON THE OFFBEAT, DIA
Jazz—Six Syncopated Movements, Martins
New York City Ballet, 1994–1995

AGNES, THE INDOMITABLE DE MILLE, DIA
Documentary
1986–1987
EMMY, CHICAGO INTERNATIONAL
FILM FESTIVAL,
CINE'S GOLDEN EAGLE CERTIFICATE

ALVIN AILEY AMERICAN DANCE THEATER:
STEPS AHEAD, DIA
For Bird with Love, Episodes, Alvin Ailey
American Dance Theater, 1990–1991

ALVIN AILEY AMERICAN DANCE THEATER:
THREE BY THREE, DIA
Blues Suite, Fever Swamp,
Rainbow Round My Shoulder
Alvin Ailey Dance Co., 1985–1986

AMERICAN BALLET THEATRE, DIA
Billy the Kid, Les Patineurs
American Ballet Theatre, 1976–1977

AMERICAN BALLET THEATRE, LFLC
Giselle
American Ballet Theatre, 1976–1977,
EMMY

AMERICAN BALLET THEATRE, LFLC
La Bayadère
American Ballet Theatre, 1979–1980

AMERICAN BALLET THEATRE, LFLC
Les Sylphides, Firebird
American Ballet Theatre, 1977–1978

AMERICAN BALLET THEATRE, LFLC
Romeo and Juliet
American Ballet Theatre, 1987–1988

AMERICAN BALLET THEATRE, LFLC
Sleeping Beauty
American Ballet Theatre, 1978–1979

AMERICAN BALLET THEATRE, LFLC
Swan Lake
American Ballet Theatre, 1975–1976
EMMY

AMERICAN BALLET THEATRE AT THE MET, DIA
Les Sylphides, Triad, Paquita
American Ballet Theatre, 1984–1985

AMERICAN BALLET THEATRE: DON QUIXOTE, DIA
American Ballet Theatre, 1983–1984

AMERICAN BALLET THEATRE IN ARGENTINA, DIA
1997-1998

THE AMERICAN DANCE FESTIVAL: PILOBOLUS, DIA
Walklyndon, Momix, Alraune, Molly's Not Dead
Pilobolus Dance Theatre, 1980–1981

AMERICAN INDIAN DANCE THEATER:
DANCES FOR THE NEW GENERATIONS, DIA
Dances from three regions of Native America: North-
west—Kwakiuti Tribe, The Plains—A Pow-Pow in
North Dakota, Northeast—Iroquois and Penobscot
Tribes/Traditional American Indian Dance
American Indian Dance Theater, 1992–1993

AMERICAN INDIAN DANCE THEATER:
FINDING THE CIRCLE, DIA
Zuni pueblo, 1989–1990

BALANCHINE AND CUNNINGHAM: AN EVENING
AT AMERICAN BALLET THEATRE, DIA
Duets, La Sonnambula
American Ballet Theatre, 1987–1988
INTERNATIONAL FILM & TV FESTIVAL
OF NEW YORK

BALANCHINE CELEBRATES STRAVINSKY, DIA
Agon, Variations, Persephone, Balanchine
New York City Ballet, 1982–1983

BALANCHINE CELEBRATION,
PART I WITH THE NEW YORK CITY BALLET, DIA
Selections from *Theme and Variations*, Selections
from *Apollo, Scherzo a la Russe*, Selections from
Uncle Jack, Selections from *Square Dance*,
Selections from *Walpurgisnacht Ballet, Der*
Rosenkavalier from *Vienna Waltzes*, Balanchine
New York City Ballet, 1993–1994

BALANCHINE CELEBRATION,
PART II WITH THE NEW YORK CITY BALLET, DIA
Western Symphony-Fourth Movement: Rondo,
Selections from *Agon*, Selections from *Who*
Cares?, Selection from *Stars and Stripes*,
Balanchine
New York City Ballet, 1993–1994

BALANCHINE IN AMERICA, DIA
Serenade, Western Symphony, Balanchine
New York City Ballet, 1990–1991,
INTERNATIONAL FILM & TV FESTIVAL
OF NEW YORK

BALANCHINE, PARTS I AND II, DIA
Documentary
1983–1984
CHICAGO INTERNATIONAL FILM FESTIVAL,
27TH ANNUAL INTERNATIONAL FILM AND
TELEVISION AWARDS OF NEW YORK,
MONITOR AWARDS

BALLERINAS: DANCES BY PETER MARTINS
WITH THE NEW YORK CITY BALLET, DIA
Beethoven Romance, Ecstatic Orange-"Purple",
Valse Triste, Barber Violin Concerto, Sophisticated
Lady, Martins
New York City Ballet, 1990–1991

BARYSHNIKOV BY THARP
WITH AMERICAN BALLET THEATRE, DIA
The Little Ballet, Sinatra Suite,
Push Comes to Shove, Tharp
American Ballet Theatre, 1984–1985
EMMYS

BARYSHNIKOV DANCES BALANCHINE, DIA
Apollo, Who Cares?, Balanchine
American Ballet Theatre, 1988–1989
EMMY, CHICAGO INTERNATIONAL
FILM FESTIVAL

BARYSHNIKOV ON BROADWAY
with *A Chorus Line* cast
1986–1987

BEYOND THE MAINSTREAM, DIA
Contact Improvisation, Line-up: excerpts, *Glacial*
Decoy: excerpts, *Trio A, The Matter:* excerpts,
The Chair: excerpts, *Light, Dance, La Bayadère*
1979-1980

BILLBOARDS WITH THE JOFFREY BALLET, DIA
Trust, Purple Rain, Slide, Willing and Able
Joffrey Ballet, 1993–1994

BILL T. JONES/ARNIE ZANE AND COMPANY, DIA
Last Supper at Uncle Tom's Cabin,
The Promised Land, Jones
Arnie Zane and Company, 1991–1992

BOB FOSSE—STEAM HEAT, DIA
Documentary
1989–1990
EMMY, MONTREAUX, CHICAGO INTERNATIONAL
FILM FESTIVAL, OHIO STATE AWARD

BOURNONVILLE DANCES, DIA
Ballabile from *Napoli, Pas de deux* from *Kermesse in Bruges, Pas de trois* from *La Ventana,*
Pas de deux from *William Tell, Pas de deux* from *Flower Festival in Genzano,*
Tarantella from *Napoli,* Bournonville
New York City Ballet, 1981–1982

BOXES
Sydney (Aus.) Dance Co., 1985–1986

THE CATHERINE WHEEL, DIA
Tharp
Twyla Tharp Dance Co., 1982–1983

A CHOREOGRAPHER'S NOTEBOOK: STRAVINSKY PIANO BALLETS BY PETER MARTINS, DIA
Eight Easy Pieces, Tango, Piano Rag Music, Concerto for Two Solo Pianos, Martins
New York City Ballet, 1983–1984

CHOREOGRAPHY BY BALANCHINE—PART 1 WITH THE NEW YORK CITY BALLET, DIA
Tzigane, Divertimento No. 15: excerpts, *The Four Temperaments,* Balanchine
New York City Ballet, 1977–1978

CHOREOGRAPHY BY BALANCHINE—PART 2 WITH THE NEW YORK CITY BALLET, DIA
JEWELS: Emeralds: excerpts, *Rubies:* excerpts, *Diamonds:* excerpts, *Stravinsky Violin Concerto,* Balanchine
New York City Ballet, 1977–1978

CHOREOGRAPHY BY BALANCHINE—PART 3 WITH THE NEW YORK CITY BALLET, DIA
Chaconne, Prodigal Son, Balanchine
New York City Ballet, 1978–1979
CHICAGO INTERNATIONAL FILM FESTIVAL,
DIRECTOR'S GUILD OF AMERICA

CHOREOGRAPHY BY BALANCHINE—PART 4 WITH THE NEW YORK CITY BALLET, DIA
Ballo della Regina, The Steadfast Tin Soldier, Elégie from *Tschaikovsky Suite No. 3, Tschaikovsky Pas de Deux, Allegro Brillante,* Balanchine
New York City Ballet, 1978–1979
EMMY

CHOREOGRAPHY BY JEROME ROBBINS WITH THE NEW YORK CITY BALLET, DIA
Antique Epigraphs, Fancy Free
New York City Ballet, 1985–1986
CHICAGO INTERNATIONAL FILM FESTIVAL,
CINE AWARD, INTERNATIONAL FILM
& TV FESTIVAL OF NEW YORK

CITY CENTER JOFFREY BALLET, DIA
Olympics: excerpts, *Parade:* excerpts, *The Green Table:* excerpts, *Remembrances:* excerpts, *Trinity*
Joffrey Ballet, 1975–1976

COPPELIA, LFLC
Balanchine
New York City Ballet, 1977–1978

DANCE BLACK AMERICA
Alvin Ailey American Dance Theatre
1984–1985

DANCE THEATRE OF HARLEM, DIA
Forces of Rhythm: excerpts, *Bugaku:* excerpts, *The Beloved, Holberg Suite:* excerpts, *Douglas:* excerpts
Dance Theatre of Harlem, 1976–1977
CHICAGO INTERNATIONAL FILM FESTIVAL,
9TH ANNUAL DANCE, FILM AND VIDEO FESTIVAL

DANCE THEATRE OF HARLEM IN A STREETCAR NAMED DESIRE, DIA
A Streetcar Named Desire, Sylvia Pas de Deux, Bélé
Dance Theatre of Harlem, 1985–1986
CHICAGO INTERNATIONAL FILM FESTIVAL,
GOLDEN PRAGUE FESTIVAL

DANCING FOR MR. B:
SIX BALANCHINE BALLERINAS, DIA
Documentary
1989–1990

DAVID GORDON'S MADE IN U.S.A., DIA
Valda and Mischa, TV Nine Lives, Murder, Gordon
American Ballet Theatre
& D. Gordon Pick-Up Co., 1987–1988

DIVINE DRUMBEATS: KATHERINE DUNHAM AND HER PEOPLE, DIA
Rites de Passage, Dunham
1979–1980

THE DREAM
Ashton
Royal Ballet Co., 1979–1980

AN EVENING OF DANCE AND CONVERSATION WITH MARTHA GRAHAM, DIA
Errand into the Maze, Cave of the Heart, Acts of Light, Graham
Martha Graham Dance Co., 1984–1985

AN EVENING WITH AMERICAN BALLET THEATRE, LFLC
Le Corsaire, La Fille mal gardée, Sleeping Beauty: excerpts
American Ballet Theatre, 1980–1981

EVERYBODY DANCE NOW, DIA
Documentary
(Choreography in music videos), 1991–1992
INTERNATIONAL FILM & TV FESTIVAL OF
NEW YORK, PEABODY AWARD, GOLDEN ROSE
INTERNATIONAL COMPETITION-MONTREAUX,
GRAND PRIX INTERNATIONAL VIDEO-DANSE
AWARD, CHICAGO INTERNATIONAL FILM FESTIVAL

THE FELD BALLET, DIA
Excursions: excerpts, *Intermezzo:* excerpts, *Danzon Cubano, La Vida:* excerpts, *The Real McCoy:* excerpts, *Santa Fe Saga:* excerpts, *Half Time,* Feld
Feld Ballet, 1978–1979

GARTH FAGAN'S GRIOT NEW YORK, DIA
City Court Dance, Fagan
Garth Fagan Dance Co., 1994–1995

THE GREEN TABLE WITH THE JOFFREY BALLET, DIA
The Green Table, Jooss
Joffrey Ballet Co., 1982–1983

GREGORY HINES: TAP DANCE IN AMERICA, DIA
1988–1989
EMMY, DIRECTOR'S GUILD OF AMERICA

THE HARD NUT WITH THE MARK MORRIS DANCE GROUP, DIA
The Hard Nut, Morris
Mark Morris Dance Group, 1992–1993
THE NEW YORK FESTIVALS

HYMN: REMEMBERING ALVIN AILEY, DIA
1997–1998

IN MEMORY OF . . .
A BALLET BY JEROME ROBBINS, DIA
In Memory Of . . . , Robbins
New York City Ballet, 1986–1987
CINE'S GOLDEN EAGLE CERTIFICATE,
CHICAGO INTERNATIONAL FILM FESTIVAL

IN MOTION WITH MICHAEL MOSCHEN, DIA
Crystal, S Curves, Torches, Columns Triangle
1990–1991

LA BAYADÈRE
Royal Ballet, 1991–1992

LA SYLPHIDE WITH THE PENNSYLVANIA/MILWAUKEE BALLET, DIA
La Sylphide
Pennsylvania & Milwaukee Ballet Cos.,
1988–1989
CHICAGO INTERNATIONAL FILM FESTIVAL,
MONITOR AWARD

LAR LUBOVITCH DANCE CO. AND MOMIX: PICTURES ON THE EDGE, DIA
Fandango, Pictures at an Exhibition
Lar Lubovitch Dance Co., 1991–1992
INTERNATIONAL EMMY, CHICAGO
INTERNATIONAL FILM FESTIVAL

THE MAGIC FLUTE WITH THE NEW YORK CITY BALLET, DIA
The Magic Flute, Martins
New York City Ballet, 1982–1983
EMMY

THE MARGOT FONTEYN STORY
1989–1990

MARK MORRIS, DIA
Songs that Tell a Story-Robe of White, Prelude, Love, You Have Won, Dogtown, Jealousy, The Tamil Film, Songs in Stereo, Pas de Deux, Gloria, Morris
Mark Morris Dance Co., 1986–1987
CHRISTOPHER AWARD, ACAPULCO WORLD
FESTIVAL, CINE'S GOLDEN EAGLE
CERTIFICATE, INTERNATIONAL FILM & TV
FESTIVAL OF NEW YORK, AMERICAN FILM
AND VIDEO FESTIVAL

MARTHA GRAHAM DANCE COMPANY, DIA
Diversion of Angels, Lamentation, Frontier, Adorations, Cave of the Heart: excerpts, *Appalachian Spring,* Graham
Martha Graham Dance Co., 1975–1976
CHICAGO INTERNATIONAL FILM FESTIVAL

MARTHA GRAHAM DANCE COMPANY:
CLYTEMNESTRA, DIA
Clytemnestra, Graham
Martha Graham Dance Co., 1978–1979
CHICAGO INTERNATIONAL FILM FESTIVAL

MERCE CUNNINGHAM DANCE COMPANY:
AN EVENT FOR TELEVISION, DIA
Minutiae, Solo, Westbeth, Septet, Antic Meet,
Scramble, Rainforest, Sounddance, Video Triangle,
Cunningham
Merce Cunningham Co., 1976–1977

A MIDSUMMER NIGHT'S DREAM, LFLC
Balanchine
New York City Ballet, 1985–1986

A MONTH IN THE COUNTRY
Ashton
Royal Ballet Co., 1978–1979

A NIGHT AT THE JOFFREY, DIA
Monotones II, Love Songs, Round of Angels
Joffrey Ballet, 1988–1989
IMZ GRAND PRIX VIDEO-DANSE,
INTERNATIONAL FILM & TV FESTIVAL
OF NEW YORK, CHICAGO INTERNATIONAL
FILM FESTIVAL, MONITOR AWARD

NUREYEV
Documentary
1992–1993

NUREYEV AND THE JOFFREY BALLET:
IN TRIBUTE TO NIJINSKY, DIA
Petrouchka, La Spectre de la Rose,
L'Après-midi d'un faune
Joffrey Ballet, 1980–1981, EMMY

NUREYEV'S *CINDERELLA*
Cinderella, Nureyev
Paris Opera Ballet, 1988–1989

ON THE MOVE: THE CENTRAL BALLET OF CHINA
Documentary
1987–1988

PAUL TAYLOR DANCE COMPANY, DIA
Esplanade, Runes, Taylor
Paul Taylor Dance Co., 1977–1978

PAUL TAYLOR: *ROSES* AND *LAST LOOK,* DIA
Roses, Last Look, Taylor
Paul Taylor Dance Co., 1987–1988
CHICAGO INTERNATIONAL FILM FESTIVAL

PAUL TAYLOR: THREE MODERN CLASSICS, DIA
Aureole, Three Epitaphs, Big Bertha, Taylor
Paul Taylor Dance Co., 1981–1982

PAUL TAYLOR: TWO LANDMARK DANCES, DIA
Le Sacre du printemps-The Rehearsal, Arden Court,
Taylor
Paul Taylor Dance Co., 1981–1982

PAUL TAYLOR'S *SPEAKING IN TONGUES,* DIA
Speaking in Tongues, Taylor
Paul Taylor Dance Co., 1991–1992
EMMY, INTERNATIONAL EMMY, CHICAGO
INTERNATIONAL FILM FESTIVAL, INTERNA-
TIONAL FILM & TV FESTIVAL OF NEW YORK

PENNSYLVANIA BALLET, DIA
Grosse Fugue: excerpts, *Concerto Barocco:*
excerpts, *Madrigalesco:* excerpts, *Adagio*
Hammerklavier: excerpts, *Concerto Grosso:*
excerpts
Pennsylvania Ballet, 1975–1976

PILOBOLUS DANCE THEATRE, DIA
Monkshood's Farewell, Ocellus, Ciona, Untitled,
Pilobolus
Pilobolus Dance Theatre, 1976–1977

A RENAISSANCE REVISITED, DIA
Documentary
1995–1996
THE NEW YORK FESTIVALS

SAN FRANCISCO BALLET:
A SONG FOR DEAD WARRIORS, DIA
A Song for Dead Warriors, Smuin
San Francisco Ballet, 1983–1984
EMMYS, MONITOR AWARD

SAN FRANCISCO BALLET IN *CINDERELLA,* DIA
Cinderella
San Francisco Ballet, 1985–1986
PARENTS' CHOICE AWARD, CINE AWARD,
INTERNATIONAL FILM & TV FESTIVAL OF
NEW YORK

SAN FRANCISCO BALLET: *ROMEO AND JULIET,* DIA
Romeo and Juliet, Smuin
San Francisco Ballet, 1977–1978
EMMY

THE SEARCH FOR NIJINSKY'S RITE OF SPRING, DIA
Documentary
The Rite of Spring-Le sacre du Printemps, Nijinsky
1989–1990
IMZ GRAND PRIX VIDEO-DANSE, INTERNA-
TIONAL FILM & TV FESTIVAL OF NEW YORK

THE SLEEPING BEAUTY
The Royal Ballet, 1995–1996

THE SPELLBOUND CHILD
WITH THE NEW YORK CITY BALLET, DIA
L'Enfant et Les Sortileges-The Spellbound Child,
Balanchine
New York City Ballet, 1980–1981
DIRECTOR'S GUILD OF AMERICA

STRAVINSKY AND BALANCHINE:
GENIUS HAS A BIRTHDAY, LFLC
Apollo, Orpheus, Balanchine
New York City Ballet, 1982–1983

SUE'S LEG/REMEMBERING THE THIRTIES, DIA
Sue's Leg, Tharp, and Documentary
Twyla Tharp Dance Co., 1975–1976

SUZANNE FARRELL: ELUSIVE MUSE, DIA
Documentary
1996–1997

SWAN LAKE
Bourne
Adventures in Motion Pictures, 1997–1998

THE TAYLOR COMPANY: RECENT DANCES, DIA
Mercuric Tidings, Snow White, Sunset, Taylor
Paul Taylor Dance Co., 1984–1985

THE TEMPEST:
LIVE WITH THE SAN FRANCISCO BALLET, DIA
The Tempest, Smuin
San Francisco Ballet, 1980–1981
EMMY

THREE DANCES BY MARTHA GRAHAM, DIA
Steps in the Street, El Penitente, Maple Leaf Rag,
Graham
Martha Graham Dance, 1992–1993

TRAILBLAZERS OF MODERN DANCE, DIA
Documentary, *Five Brahms Waltzes in the Manner*
of Isadora Duncan, Spear Dance Japonesque:
excerpts, *Soaring, Etude, Mother, Polonaise*
1976–1977
9TH ANNUAL DANCE, FILM AND VIDEO FESTIVAL

A TRIBUTE TO BALANCHINE, LFLC
Vienna Waltzes, Mozartiana, Balanchine
New York City Ballet, 1983–1984

A TUDOR EVENING WITH
AMERICAN BALLET THEATRE, DIA
Jardin aux Lilas, Dark Elegies, Tudor, and
Documentary
American Ballet Theatre, 1989–1990

TWO BY DOVE, DIA
Vespers, Dancing on the Front Porch of Heaven
Alvin Ailey Dance Co.,
Royal Swedish Ballet, 1994–1995
EMMYS

TWO DUETS: CHOREOGRAPHY BY
JEROME ROBBINS AND PETER MARTINS, DIA
Other Dances, Calcium Light Night
New York City Ballet, 1979–1980

TWYLA THARP: OPPOSITIONS, DIA
In the Upper Room, Java Jive, Fever, Tharp
Twyla Tharp Dance Co., 1995–1996

WOLF TRAP PRESENTS THE KIROV BALLET
Swan Lake
Kirov Ballet, 1987–1988

THE WRECKER'S BALL, THREE DANCES
BY PAUL TAYLOR, DIA
Company B, Funny Papers, A Field of Grass,
Taylor
Paul Taylor Dance Co., 1996–1997

MUSIC

BY JOSEPH MCLELLAN

THE TELEVISION
TRANSFORMATION
Making Music That's to Be Seen

IN THE LAST HALF CENTURY, TELEVISION HAS HAD AN INCALCULABLE IMPACT ON EVERY aspect of our society, from merchandising and politics to family relations, education, fashion, and design. And nowhere has television's impact been more clearly perceptible than in music, in genres as diverse as the rap videos shown on MTV and the production of Wagner's *Ring* cycle broadcast by GREAT PERFORMANCES.

Through MTV and other stations like it, television has spawned a new performance genre— the music video—and has led many music lovers to prefer, even to expect, that their favorite songs will be enhanced by a visual dimension. GREAT PERFORMANCES, too, has affected America's perception of music in various ways. Above all, it has brought to the attention of a large public many previously unfamiliar pieces of music. Knowledge of such esoteric masterpieces as Stravinsky's *A Soldier's Tale* and Gian Carlo Menotti's *The Unicorn, the Gorgon, and the Manticore* escalated overnight after they were shown on GREAT PERFORMANCES. Such events have expanded public awareness of what is even possible in music; then, by providing unexpected enjoyment, they have also enlarged public perception of the kinds of music that can give pleasure.

The exposure of classical music on public or commercial television has been a rather haphazard process, but its effects have often been both visible and spectacular. Just a few anecdotes from my quarter century of experience as a music critic for the *Washington Post* demonstrate this point. On commercial television, a few years ago, an instrumental transcription of Puccini's aria "O mio babbino caro" from the one-act opera *Gianni Schicchi* was used in a wine commercial. I was bombarded with letters and phone calls asking what that tune was and where a recording of it could be obtained. The same thing happened after the last episode of *M*A*S*H*, on which Mozart's Clarinet Quintet was played. *M*A*S*H* fans, alerted to the existence and quality of the quintet, put it on the best-seller lists, where it has deserved to be for more than two hundred years.

Of course, newspapers and radio stations are not flooded with such inquiries after a piece of music has been featured on GREAT PERFORMANCES, because the series' producers always make sure that its audiences know what they are hearing. Still, it is sometimes possible to trace a telecast's impact. For example, some twenty years ago, the Baltimore Opera

LEFT: Cartoonist R. O. Blechman's drawing illustrating the Los Angeles Chamber Orchestra's animated production of Igor Stravinsky's *A Soldier's Tale*; PREVIOUS PAGES: A great Mahler champion, Leonard Bernstein leads the Vienna Philharmonic in Mahler's Symphony no. 1 in D major, one of Bernstein's several Mahler concerts broadcast on GREAT PERFORMANCES.

Company was caught in what looked like a catastrophe of unfortunate timing: it was mounting a production of Mozart's *The Magic Flute* just a few days after a televised performance had been shown on PBS. How could a small American company hope to compete with a lavish, star-studded *Magic Flute* from the internationally famous Salzburg Festival? Expecting a disaster report, I called the company's director of marketing—and was told that ticket sales had jumped enormously the day after the telecast. "It was almost as though the telecast was a commercial for our production," the marketing director said. "Many people were buying opera tickets for the first time. Some of them said that seeing it on television made them want to see it in a live, staged performance."

So much of classical music needs only to be known in order to be loved. And America has developed no finer forum than GREAT PERFORMANCES for making good music widely known. When it has lived up to its title's proud claim, the GREAT PERFORMANCES series has established high standards and sparked new dreams for audiences and performers alike. The sight of Yo-Yo Ma playing his cello on your home television screen, for example, can have a range of effects, depending on who you are. If you are a young cellist, it offers you a role model, with a set of goals and ideals to help direct your own development as a musician. If you are a young person who loves music but does not perform, it can nudge you toward taking up an instrument and discovering the joys of making music yourself. And if you are simply a music lover, it gives you a taste of what you can hope to experience when you go to a concert hall to hear a cellist perform.

TAKING THE SNOBBISM OUT OF CLASSICAL MUSIC

Most important, perhaps, is the sense of familiarity that comes when music is brought into your own home. This experience takes away much of the strangeness and—why not say it?—the subliminal terror that have often been associated with classical music. For too long, some classical music commentators and performers have cultivated—usually without realizing that they are doing it—a mystique, a kind of snobbism bred by the use of foreign words and technical terms; this exclusivity has, in effect, told less sophisticated people, "This music is too good for the likes of you." A symptom of this attitude and of people's response to it is the apology I have heard over and over again when people want to talk to me about music: "I don't know anything about classical music, but . . . ," they often begin. The response to this opening gambit is, of course, "If you love it, then you know what you most need to know." By bringing good music into their homes in an easily approachable style, GREAT PERFORMANCES has allowed millions of people to discover their love for it.

SETTING NEW STANDARDS FOR OPERA

Opera on television—opera brought to us over twenty-five years by GREAT PERFORMANCES—has built an American opera audience of unprecedented size and appetite. Many of these people now enjoy opera on records, videotape, and radio, as well as on television. A good per-

centage have gone on to buy tickets for live opera—and a lot more would do so if the prices were more manageable.

One impact of televised opera on live opera is demonstrated by the use of printed supertitles that translate the words of a foreign-language opera—and sometimes even "translate" the words of an opera in English—as it is being sung. Usually, these translations are projected onto a screen above the stage, but the Metropolitan Opera, which was the last major American company to accept this innovation, now has a deluxe system that provides the lyrics electronically on the back of the seat in front of you.

This change—the most important new technical development in opera production since the introduction of electric lighting—has occurred because many opera fans (some long-standing, others won over by seeing opera on television) have become accustomed to the use of subtitles on TV. Now, when they come to the opera house, they want their expensive tickets to purchase the same kind of clear understanding that has been provided free of charge by the subtitles on GREAT PERFORMANCES.

One by-product of the use of titles has been an expansion of the standard repertoire for American opera companies. Many audience members used to avoid operas sung in any language but Italian, French, English, or German. Now, with the introduction of simultaneous translations, there

"What you really want to do is something for each medium that allows each medium to be most itself. You can't demand of television that it should be film. You can't demand of theater that it should be television. So you have to figure out where the possible links are but also figure out where the unbridgeable gulf really lies and not try and violate it."

—PETER SELLARS

ABOVE: Treat Williams performs Duke Ellington's "Satin Doll" on "Ellington: The Music Lives On."

has been a spectacular rise in the number of operas being produced in Russian, Czech, Spanish, Hungarian, and other languages—including Chinese—that were once avoided.

As a result of the opera productions seen on GREAT PERFORMANCES, an increasing emphasis on the visual dimension in American opera productions has developed. Many opera companies used to concentrate almost exclusively on the singers' voices, paying little or no attention to how a production looked. But audiences' exposure, through GREAT PERFORMANCES, to visually first-class opera has set new standards. Stage directors and set and costume designers are now achieving a level of importance and recognition unheard of in opera before the advent of television.

RELISHING THE INTIMACY OF THE CAMERA'S VIEW

Because their visual and narrative elements are so important, opera and musical theater have enjoyed the most obvious benefits from their presentation on GREAT PERFORMANCES. But chamber music is also especially well suited to home viewing because of its intimacy—it fits comfortably into an ordinary-sized room—and because the camera can catch the interaction among the players that lies at the heart of chamber music. Similarly, television offers a you-are-there immediacy to performances of full orchestral music, as well as good visual perspectives on the conductor and players, both individually and in groups; in fact, the only downside is that most television sets do not yet have sound systems that can reproduce the richness of sound generated by a full symphony orchestra.

LASTING EFFECTS OF THE TELEVISION REVOLUTION

The effects of televised music on the future of the art are still in their earliest stages, but in the long run television is likely to have a profound effect on composition, performance, and the way audiences approach music. I believe that a major development of the twenty-first century (seen today only in its most embryonic stages but foreshadowed long ago in Walt Disney's *Fantasia* animations and the GREAT PERFORMANCES telecast of Stravinsky's *A Soldier's Tale* with animated pictures) will be the commissioning of artists to provide a visual component for recordings of classical music. When recording executives realize that video composition will give them a chance to sell four or five different versions of *Scheherazade* or *The Four Seasons,* using the same music but different visuals, this innovation will begin to catch on.

Above all, GREAT PERFORMANCES has influenced classical music in America simply by telling millions of people that it exists in splendid variety, that it has a quality that can communicate with listeners of any culture, age, or social category, and that it is as easy to enjoy as it is life enhancing. The series has made a gift of classical music to many people who might never otherwise have encountered it or known how good it can be. In the ticket lines for classical concerts and browsing the classical bins in record stores all over America are thousands of people who would not be there if they had not tuned in to GREAT PERFORMANCES.

"I have a specially warm spot in my heart for public television. They do so many marvelous things so well, so many things that the commercial networks should be doing, but don't. In a way, I wish public television wasn't necessary, that the networks could give us all those worthwhile programs along with the junk food they feed us every night. But it's all a matter of money, I guess. So thank goodness for PBS!"

—LENA HORNE

Leonard Bernstein

A Media Maestro

———— ✍ ————

LEONARD BERNSTEIN'S CAREER WAS A MEDIA EVENT LONG BEFORE TELEVISION—A MEDIUM for which he seemed to be born—became a fixture in every American home. His conducting debut with the New York Philharmonic on November 14, 1943, took place before a nationwide radio audience under circumstances so dramatic he could hardly have done better if he had scripted it.

Bruno Walter, scheduled to guest-conduct the Philharmonic, was taken ill the day before the concert. Bernstein, twenty-five years old and only recently appointed the orchestra's assistant conductor, was told that he must fill in for Walter before an audience in Carnegie Hall, with live CBS microphones transmitting the program across the continent. He was given no time for a rehearsal.

Bernstein came through brilliantly. The concert was a triumph—in Carnegie Hall, on the airwaves, and on the front page of the next morning's *New York Times*. From that moment on, most of his life was spent in the spotlight. He eventually became the Philharmonic's music director and a key figure in American music for half a century: as a composer whose music still lives on Broadway, in opera houses, and in American and European concert halls; as one of the century's most exciting and imaginative conductors; as a gifted pianist who could have made a career as a soloist or a chamber musician; and not least of all, as one of the century's most effective music teachers through a popular series of televised lectures and young people's concerts. Many American orchestras today are led by conductors who, as children, first got the idea that this was how they wanted to spend their lives from watching Leonard Bernstein on television.

BRINGING MUSIC TO *GREAT PERFORMANCES*

Bernstein's association with GREAT PERFORMANCES dates back to the series' first full season in 1973–74, when his *Mass*, commissioned by Roger Stevens for the opening of the Kennedy Center for the Performing Arts in Washington, D.C., became the first music program that GREAT PERFORMANCES broadcast. In the 1975–76 season, the performance led by Bernstein of Tchaikovsky's Fourth Symphony won GREAT PERFORMANCES an Emmy for outstanding classical music programming; it was the first of over forty Emmys that the series has won over the years.

Bernstein's association with GREAT PERFORMANCES continued throughout his life. *On the Town*, his first big Broadway success, was the subject of his last project for the series and was still in the planning stages when he died in 1990. It was brought to completion by Michael Tilson Thomas and broadcast under the title "*On the Town* in Concert" during the

"If ever there was a man for the medium and a medium for the man it was Leonard Bernstein and television. . . . Television was Bernstein's vehicle for transmitting what may be his most important legacy: that classical music was a joyous experience, one filled with all the passion and emotion of life itself."

—Ed Siegel
BOSTON GLOBE

LEFT: Leonard Bernstein receives applause from Seiji Ozawa, Larry Kurt, and Jerry Hadley on "Bernstein at 70."

1993–94 season. It featured the London Symphony Orchestra and an all-star cast of Broadway and opera singers that included Frederica von Stade, Tyne Daly, Marie McLaughlin, Thomas Hampson, Samuel Ramey, Evelyn Lear, and Cleo Laine.

TELEVISION'S MUSIC MAN

The cast of "*On the Town* in Concert" exemplifies the crossover dimension of Bernstein's art and persona; he was able to engage and challenge the most serious classical artists with his music while he and his work remained accessible to the man and woman on the street. In the early years of his career, youth and good looks as well as a smooth, articulate on-screen personality probably helped to make him television's "music man" par excellence. But it was his ability to communicate in words and music, with simplicity and profundity and to anyone who would listen, that kept him in that position.

"I think [Bernstein is] the only genius I've ever known. It's an extraordinary mind, the most fascinating brain I've ever come across. As a singer, I've seen outpourings of energy from him that are unbelievable. He forces you to do better than you think you can."

—BEVERLY SILLS

Bernstein was visually documented more than any other musician—more even than Herbert von Karajan, who set up a systematic video archive of his work in his later years. GREAT PERFORMANCES has taken advantage of this abundant material to show Bernstein conducting, rehearsing, lecturing at Harvard, teaching young conductors and players, scolding the Vienna Philharmonic (in fluent German) for its resistance to the music of Gustav Mahler, introducing a concert audience to the music of Charles Ives, telling an audience of children that the *William Tell* Overture "isn't about the Lone Ranger at all," and indulging in such philosophical pronouncements as "the twentieth century has been a badly written drama."

Bernstein was the first American-born conductor to serve as music director of the New York Philharmonic, holding the position from 1958 to 1969. After leaving the New York Philharmonic to devote more time to composing, he kept up a close relationship with the orchestra as its "conductor laureate." But his most memorable conducting on television came later with the Vienna Philharmonic, an orchestra in a class by itself and one with which he achieved an almost telepathic rapport. Sometimes during a concert with the Vienna Philharmonic, Bernstein would stop moving his baton and stand still, with his arms at his sides, allowing the orchestra to find its own way through the music, as if it were a gigantic chamber ensemble. This worked better, of course, in the music of Haydn, Mozart, and Beethoven—music that the orchestra's members knew as well as they did the alphabet—than in the less familiar and more complex works of Mahler. For much of Mahler's music, Bernstein had to be the orchestra's guide.

"If one is so lucky to have been gifted, then it seems to me that the greatest gift is being able to work at the thing you most love to do, twenty-four hours a day. I sing psalms and say 'hallelujah' every day for the gift of being both a performer and a creator."

—LEONARD BERNSTEIN

RIGHT: Bernstein conducts the Vienna Philharmonic Orchestra performing Mozart.

REDEFINING MAHLER FOR MODERNS

The maestro's affinity for Mahler was phenomenal; it dates back to the early days of his career, and it was a major factor—perhaps the single most important factor—in the growth of interest in Mahler's music that began in the 1960s, when the centennial of Mahler's birth was quickly followed by the fiftieth anniversary of his death. Mahler's emotional ambivalences, his combination of grandiose structures with subtle coloristic details, his inclination to make extreme musical gestures, is fatalism, his sense of irony, and his creative fascination with the rhythms and cadences of

folk music all struck a responsive chord in Leonard Bernstein's soul. Bernstein's interpretations of Mahler not only established the composer's reputation; for many music lovers they were the only way these works should be interpreted. This was particularly true of his televised performances with the Vienna Philharmonic—an orchestra for which Mahler himself had served as music director from 1898 to 1901. Mahler's tenure with the Vienna Philharmonic was brief and stormy, for the players, on the whole, never accepted either him or his music. More than half a century later Leonard Bernstein still had trouble, initially, convincing the orchestra of the value of some of this music. As time went on, though, the players, under Bernstein's passionate direction, became engrossed in Mahler's style (which often seems formed with this orchestra in mind), and the enthusiastic feedback received from their listeners helped to complete the orchestra's conversion.

Today, the Mahler symphonies are as much a Vienna Philharmonic specialty as the works of Beethoven or Johann Strauss, and the Bernstein interpretations with this orchestra, as seen on GREAT PERFORMANCES, have been for many people not only their first introduction to Mahler but also their definitive experience of his music. In the fourth season of GREAT PERFORMANCES, 1975–76, Bernstein kicked off this series of concerts with Mahler's Fourth, one of the easiest of his symphonies for a general audience to enjoy. The climactic finale of this symphony, like those of his Second and Third Symphonies, brings in the human voice, just as Beethoven did in his ninth, as if to say that there are worlds of music beyond what instruments alone can reveal. A soprano sings about the joys of children in heaven; the lyrics are those of a naive poem from a collection of folk poetry, *Des Knaben Wunderhorn* ("Youth's Magic Horn") from which Mahler took many song texts. It is punctuated, after its second, fourth, and seventh stanzas, with a tinkling motif that uses flute and sleigh bells to create an otherworldly sound. This sound, first heard at the beginning of the first movement, now returns at the end to pull the symphony together—or, rather, to show how tightly the composer has woven it. Between these two radiant sections, the second and third movements take a look at the absurdities of life and the terror and peace of death—yet the music begins and ends in affirmation.

Another highlight of the Bernstein-Mahler cycle, broadcast during the 1978–79 season, was Mahler's Symphony no. 8, nicknamed the "Symphony of a Thousand" because of the enormous performing forces it requires. Television helps to make the meaning of the nickname clear; on the small screen, the sheer numbers of instrumental and vocal performers are striking. In this symphony, too, Mahler's basic message is affirmative. There are only two enormous movements: the first an invocation of the creative spirit taken from the Roman Catholic liturgy; the second, a symposium on guilt, redemption, the joys of heaven, and the ennobling influence of women—particularly the Virgin Mary—on human life. It is set to music of a splendor that Bernstein has grasped and conveys to the audience with a power that is uniquely his own. In this, as in the other broadcasts, the GREAT PERFORMANCES series has captured Bernstein at his best.

In *The Well-Tempered Announcer: A Pronunciation Guide to Classical Music*, published in 1996 by Indiana University Press, linguist Robert A. Fradkin insists that Leonard Bernstein's name should be pronounced with a last syllable that rhymes with 'shine,' not with 'green.' In the seventh edition of Baker's *Biographical Dictionary of Musicians*, the meticulous musicologist Nicolas Slonimsky looks at other possibilities: "A debate rages as to the proper pronunciation of Bernstein's name; intimates used to refer to him as Bern*steen*, and he himself once said he preferred the 'democratic Yiddish' Bern*steen* to the 'aristocratic Germanic' Bern*styne*, but on his formal appearances on the radio or television, he reverted to the more universal 'Bern*styne*.' (Bern*styne* was always used in GREAT PERFORMANCES programs.)

In the same article, Slonimsky notes that in his youth Bernstein "did some work for publishers, arranging music for bands under the interlingual pseudonym Lenny Amber (Bernstein is the German word for 'amber'). The office established by Bernstein in 1959 to manage his professional life is called Amberson, Inc. It has continued to oversee the legacy of Leonard Bernstein since his death in 1990.

LEFT: Bernstein conducting the Vienna Philharmonic in Mahler's First Symphony.

Orchestral Music:

GREAT PERFORMANCES GOT ALONG WITH FEW GREAT ORCHESTRAL PERFORMANCES FOR its first two seasons. Then in 1974–75, it leaped into orchestral programming with three in a row: the Concertgebouw Orchestra of Amsterdam with Bernard Haitink conducting and Arthur Rubinstein as soloist in concertos of Beethoven and Brahms; Herbert von Karajan and the Berlin Philharmonic playing Bach and Beethoven; and Leonard Bernstein conducting the Boston Symphony in Tchaikovsky's Symphony no. 5.

The 1975–76 season made two things clear: that orchestral music would be a substantial part of programming in the still-new performing arts series (there were eleven orchestral performances in this season alone!) and that the great orchestras of America would be featured alongside those of Europe. Leonard Bernstein's presence increased significantly as he conducted two different orchestras in two composers' Fourth Symphonies: Beethoven's, with Bernstein's own New York Philharmonic, and Mahler's, with the orchestra that had once been Mahler's and was now becoming Bernstein's in a special way, the Vienna Philharmonic. This Mahler Fourth was the beginning of a series of Mahler performances conducted by Bernstein that remains, as the century ends, one of its most memorable and significant musical events.

AN AMERICAN ORCHESTRAL PRESENCE

The Cleveland Orchestra made its GREAT PERFORMANCES debut in that 1975–76 season, with Lorin Maazel conducting and Leonard Rose as cello soloist in Ernest Bloch's *Schelomo*. The Los Angeles Philharmonic was shown with Aaron Copland as conductor and Benny Goodman as soloist in Copland's Clarinet Concerto; André Previn conducted the New York Philharmonic with Van Cliburn as soloist in a program that included Grieg's Piano Concerto and Richard Strauss's *Ein Heldenleben*. Then GREAT PERFORMANCES went to London to present Bernstein, on tour with the New York Philharmonic, conducting an American program that included Gershwin's *Rhapsody in Blue* and Copland's *A Lincoln Portrait*.

The Chicago Symphony, conducted by its music director Sir Georg Solti in Mendelssohn's Symphony no. 4 and *Midsummer Night's Dream* music, made its GREAT PERFORMANCES debut in the 1976–77 season. This year, too, saw the series debut of the Academy of St. Martin-in-the-Fields (playing two Haydn cello concertos with Mstislav Rostropovich) and the Israel Philharmonic (conducted by Bernstein in Mahler's *Das Lied von der Erde*).

Most notably missing from the GREAT PERFORMANCES roster of American orchestras in these early seasons was the Philadelphia Orchestra under its music director Eugene Ormandy. This group made the first of its many appearances in the series during the 1977–78 season with a work particularly suited to the orchestra's sumptuous sound and virtuoso technique: Gustav Holst's *The Planets*. With this program, the series had presented at least one concert by all of the "Big Five" American orchestras (in alphabetical order: Boston, Chicago, Cleveland, New York, and Philadelphia), as well as Los Angeles, which vigorously claims a place on the traditionally East-oriented list.

THE HUNGARIAN PRODIGIES

No other conductor on television has had the kind of impact that Leonard Bernstein enjoyed. But the two leaders of American orchestras who came closest were both Hungarians, both natives of Budapest, and both graduates of that city's Royal Academy of Music, though it had changed its name to the Franz Liszt Academy between the time Philadelphia's Eugene Ormandy received his diploma in 1917 and Chicago's Georg Solti began his studies there in 1925. Both were prodigies; Ormandy began studying at the academy when he was five years old, Solti when he was thirteen.

Despite these similarities of background and the fact that they became the leaders of two of America's greatest orchestras, their musical personalities show striking contrasts. Ormandy was a violinist, Solti a pianist; Ormandy's experience was primarily orchestral, while Solti's included many operatic productions and recordings—among them, the first complete recording of Wagner's *Ring* cycle. It may be fanciful and it is certainly an oversimplification but it is also useful, in contrasting their styles, to think that Ormandy's approach to orchestral music was essentially that of a violinist, concerned with tonal beauty, smooth legato phrasing, and lyric grace, while Solti's was that of a pianist and opera conductor, intent on power and dramatic impact.

Both conductors made their orchestras notable exponents of Hungarian music, particularly the music of Béla Bartók, with whom they were personally acquainted. When Solti became the music director in Chicago, he acquired an orchestra that had perhaps already become, under Fritz Reiner's direction, the world's leading interpreter of Bartók. From Leopold Stokowski in Philadelphia, Ormandy acquired an orchestra eclectic in repertoire and technically prepared for any music it might be given to play.

The many appearances on GREAT PERFORMANCES of these conductors and their musicians have had numerous effects on the music world and American cultural life in general. Perhaps the most important of these accomplishments is that they have helped to define for a broad American public the remarkable quality of our country's best orchestras and have offered a glimpse of the variety of styles and emphases possible within the classical tradition.

"For those of us who grew up in the 1950s and '60s, Bernstein is something of a musical father. . . . He introduced a generation to classical music, gave us an insider's look at how it's put together, explained how and why composers write as they do, and suggested how we might all be better listeners."

—Richard Pontzious
SAN FRANCISCO EXAMINER

American Opera

IN THE 1940S, WHEN VIRGIL THOMSON WAS THE MUSIC CRITIC OF THE *NEW YORK HERALD Tribune,* he used to write about going to "hear" an opera. Today, for most newspaper critics writing about this odd mixture of music and drama, the operative verb would be "to see." That small but significant change reflects what has happened to opera in the half century between Thomson's heyday and the present. The most important development in that time was, in a word, television. In the United States, we need two words to do justice to what happened: GREAT PERFORMANCES.

The PBS television series has been around only since the 1972–73 season, and it did not show its first operatic production (*Pagliacci* from La Scala with Herbert von Karajan conducting) until 1974–75. There were two operas (*The Barber of Seville* and *The Ballad of Baby Doe*) in the next season, giving American opera a presence in the series from close to the beginning. The three in 1976–77 included GREAT PERFORMANCES' second *Barber of Seville,* this one from the New York City Opera, with Beverly Sills. The five in 1977–78 included two American operas, both by Gian Carlo Menotti: *The Consul* and *The Saint of Bleecker Street,* confirming a tradition of giving special attention to American opera that continues today.

In its first twenty-five years, ending in 1996–97 with *Emmeline* and *Madame Butterfly,* GREAT PERFORMANCES has shown nearly one hundred operatic productions, including more than a dozen by American composers, ranging in style from Kurt Weill's simple *Down in the Valley,* with its Appalachian folk melodies, to Samuel Barber's elaborately Shakespearean and grand-operatic *Antony and Cleopatra.* In the process, it has probably helped to make opera America's favorite form of classical music.

A BRIEF HISTORY OF AMERICAN OPERA

Opera was born in Italy around the year 1600 as an attempt by a group of Florentine poets and musicians to resurrect the glories of Greek tragedy. More than three centuries were to pass before American composers began to write operas of more than local and momentary interest, but in the twentieth century American opera has begun to take its place on the international scene.

There were American operas composed and produced before George Gershwin's *Porgy and Bess,* but today their names are known only to specialists. At first, most music critics refused to recognize *Porgy and Bess* as an opera. Its composer was, after all, a Tin Pan Alley tunesmith, and it was first produced not in an opera house but in a Broadway theater.

For decades, the Gershwin family refused all proposals for televising *Porgy and Bess.* By the

At the beginning of the twentieth century, it was not at all difficult to tell the difference between a Broadway musical and an opera; the two genres came from different worlds. But by the century's end, after *Porgy and Bess, The Consul,* and *The Saint of Bleecker Street* had enjoyed substantial runs on Broadway and opera-company productions on GREAT PERFORMANCES, the distinction has become blurred. Two more GREAT PERFORMANCES productions, Stephen Sondheim's blood-curdling *Sweeney Todd* and Leonard Bernstein's playfully philosophical *Candide* also straddle what once seemed an unbridgeable gap. These and other hard-to-classify works may give headaches to those whose job it is to define categories, but they have enormously enriched and enlarged American musical theater, and the best answer to the question "Is that an opera?" is to shrug, relax, and enjoy it.

LEFT: Gregg Baker as Crown and Cynthia Haymon as Bess in a scene from George and Ira Gershwin's *Porgy and Bess.*

time it was at last telecast—on GREAT PERFORMANCES in 1993—the original snobbish attitude toward this work had changed; it had been seen in nearly all the world's great opera houses, including the Metropolitan, which had been one of the last holdouts. The production shown on GREAT PERFORMANCES, in fact, originated at the Glyndebourne Festival in England, an opera company best known for its productions of Mozart.

GIAN CARLO MENOTTI'S *THE CONSUL*

The second American opera shown on GREAT PERFORMANCES, Menotti's *The Consul,* also began its life on Broadway. In 1950, it had a run of 269 performances in the Ethel Barrymore Theatre, but critics could not dismiss it for long as a mere Broadway show. In 1951, there were productions in the opera houses of Milan, London, Vienna, Berlin, and Zurich. The New York production won the Pulitzer Prize and the New York Drama Critics' Circle Award—a multidimensional triumph for Menotti, who was much more than just the composer. A complete man of the theater, he had composed two operas before reaching his teens; he wrote the libretto as well as the music for *The Consul* and other operas. He was also the stage director—a task that he still performs with painstaking perfectionism and lively imagination, not only for his own operas but for those of Verdi, Puccini, Tchaikovsky, and other composers.

The production shown on GREAT PERFORMANCES in 1978 was directed by Menotti and performed at the Festival of Two Worlds, known as Spoleto U.S.A., which he had founded in Charleston, South Carolina. In the early 1950s and even at its revival and television premiere in the late 1970s, *The Consul* was generally considered a Cold War drama, but Menotti is carefully nonspecific about the identity of the country where it takes place and the political orientation of the people involved. Today, with the Cold War fading into history, Menotti's story of people caught in the grinding, impersonal machinery of a bureaucracy is as powerful as ever. It will remain painfully relevant as long as people are persecuted for their beliefs and forced to leave their homes, as long as the powerless are shown no mercy and those who exercise power practice arrogance, bland evasions, and cold anonymity. It was a happy choice for presentation early in the history of GREAT PERFORMANCES, not only because it is easily accessible to people who are not hard-core opera fans but also because the composer's staging helped to establish the high standards of visual treatment and direction that the series has consistently provided.

The basic plot, thematically reinforced by many peripheral characters and incidents, concerns the story of Magda Sorel (soprano Marvellee Cariaga in the GREAT PERFORMANCES production), whose husband John (baritone David Clatworthy) is a leader of the armed resistance to an oppressive government. He is wounded by the secret police and flees to another country, telling Magda that she must get a visa and join him. For this purpose, she must visit a mysterious official, the Consul.

Like the title character in Samuel Beckett's play *Waiting for Godot,* the Consul is a central figure in the drama who never appears onstage. Instead, Magda has to deal with the Secretary (mezzo-soprano Sandra Walker), who puts her off with one evasion after another and smothers her hopes in

The libretto for Samuel Barber's opera *Antony and Cleopatra,* commissioned by the Metropolitan Opera to celebrate its move to Lincoln Center and shown in a production by the Lyric Opera of Chicago on GREAT PERFORMANCES during the 1991–92 season, was adapted from William Shakespeare's play.

RIGHT: Catherine Malfitano and Richard Cowan in the Chicago Lyric Opera's production of Samuel Barber's *Antony and Cleopatra.*

[*152*]

endless red tape. Magda's reaction, after a long, vain struggle, is the eloquent aria "To this we've come," protesting the dehumanization of society. She has wasted endless days in a large waiting room full of other people who are in a similar situation; notable among them is a Magician who can do tricks and hypnotize his fellow sufferers but who cannot help himself. At one point, the Secretary tells Magda that she can go in to see the Consul after the visitor currently in his office leaves. When the visitor comes out, she sees that he is a secret police agent who has been hounding her, and as the curtain comes down on the scene, Magda faints.

In the final scene, after many disappointments and frustrations, including the death of her baby, Magda puts her head in a gas oven and commits suicide amid hallucinatory visions. When she has died, her telephone rings. A message from her husband who has been captured? A notice that her visa has at last been approved? The opera ends in ambiguity. This ambiguity is also reflected in its music, which has the kind of limpid, powerful melodies always found in Menotti's compositions; here the score also includes passages of atonality that are particularly appropriate for the tensions of its plot.

THE SAINT OF BLEECKER STREET

In the same season, GREAT PERFORMANCES presented another Menotti opera that is American but, for most of us, as exotic as *The Consul*. Called *The Saint of Bleecker Street*, the opera looks at life in New York's Little Italy, focusing on the story of Annina, a devoutly religious young woman in fragile health who longs to become a nun, has mystic visions, and suffers the stigmata—inexplicable, mysteriously recurring wounds that replicate those of Jesus on the cross. In her neighbors' opinion, these wounds are a sign of sainthood and a source of healing power, but Annina has a troubled relationship with her brother Michele, who becomes a fugitive from justice; he murders his mistress because she has accused him (correctly) of incestuous feelings about his sister.

The Italian subject matter inspires a special flavor in the melodic writing and allows the composer-librettist to indulge in some local color that recalls such verismo classics as *Cavalleria rusticana*, including an outdoor religious procession and a traditional wedding reception.

IGOR STRAVINSKY'S *THE RAKE'S PROGRESS*

In *The Rake's Progress*, composed in 1951 and produced by GREAT PERFORMANCES for its 1995–96 season, Igor Stravinsky, the master of many musical styles, wrote in a brilliantly neoclassical style, notable for the lightness and clarity of its harmony and structures. Although the composer had a theory that music does not "express" anything, *The Rake's Progress* has remarkable expressive power, from the opening duet celebrating the joys of young love in the springtime to the final, harrowing monologue. Set in Bedlam, this final scene elaborates on the eighteenth- and nineteenth-century tradition of operatic mad scenes.

LEFT: Doug Fedderly as Tom Rakewell and Barbara Hendricks as Anne Trulove in Igor Stravinsky's *The Rake's Progress*.

In one sense, the central character Tom Rakewell (tenor Doug Fedderly in director Inger Aby's film adaptation shown on GREAT PERFORMANCES), who sells his soul to the devil, is a descendant of Faust. In another sense, at the opera's end, he is a descendant of Lucia di Lammermoor:

a victim of a situation that has gotten out of control and driven him insane. But above all, he traces his ancestry to a moralistic series of narrative paintings made in the 1730s by the English artist William Hogarth. In a sequence not unlike modern comic strips, Hogarth's cycle depicts the gradual deterioration of a young man whose life is destroyed by easy money and easy morals.

Stravinsky emigrated to the United States in 1939, became an American citizen in 1945, and was looking for a subject for an English-language opera, perhaps in part to celebrate his new identity, when he first saw Hogarth's paintings in 1947. The pictures, which do look like a series of operatic scenes, fired his imagination, and he began looking for a librettist to turn Hogarth's images into words. He could hardly have found a better writer for his purposes than the poet W. H. Auden, who brought in his friend Chester Kallmann as a collaborator.

The production shown on GREAT PERFORMANCES was not videotaped in an opera house; it was filmed on location, like the GREAT PERFORMANCES presentations of "Tosca from Rome," Benjamin Britten's *The Turn of the Screw*, and the most recent of the series' several *Madame Butterfly* productions. Shooting on location gives *The Rake's Progress* a fluidity of motion and a depth of background that may have helped its performers, including conductor Esa-Pekka Salonen, soprano Barbara Hendricks (as Tom's faithful fiancée Anne Trulove), and Håkan Hagegård (as the sinister Satan-figure Nick Shadow), to give one of the finest operatic performances seen in the series.

HISTORY ON THE OPERA STAGE: *NIXON IN CHINA*

Opera began to portray historical figures fairly early in its development, with Claudio Monteverdi's *L'Incoronazione di Poppea* ("The Coronation of Poppea"), a 1642 production that dealt with intrigues at the court of the Roman emperor Nero. In the past, the subjects of historical opera have usually been military leaders or heads of state, but in recent years American composers have written operas on other public figures whose lives have been considered glamorous and tragic, including Rudolph Valentino, Marilyn Monroe, and Jacqueline Kennedy Onassis.

The first American opera shown on GREAT PERFORMANCES Douglas Moore's *The Ballad of Baby Doe*, about the silver boom and bust in nineteenth-century Colorado, features several minor historic characters in leading roles as well as the legendary William Jennings Bryan in a cameo appearance. Carlisle Floyd's opera *Willie Stark*, based on Robert Penn Warren's novel *All the King's Men* and shown on GREAT PERFORMANCES in 1981–82, can be considered both historic and fictional. It tells the story of Huey Long, the demagogic depression-era governor of Louisiana, but the names and some historic details have been changed.

One historic figure who seemed an unlikely operatic subject, though he was a head of state and his life certainly had tragic elements, was Richard Milhous Nixon, president of the United States from 1969 to 1974, the central figure in the Watergate scandal and the only American president ever forced to resign under the shadow of a possible impeachment. A decade before Watergate, Nixon made a diplomatic gesture that was largely symbolic but still enormously meaningful, with implications and consequences that are still being worked out a quarter cen-

"[With Nixon in China, *John] Adams and his librettist, Alice Goodman . . . have created a deft theatrical cartoon, a fantasy in which world leaders sing and dance against a background of political events that are still fresh in the minds of many people. . . . It is a psychological study rather than a panoramic survey of events."*

—Daniel Webster
PHILADELPHIA INQUIRER

RIGHT: Thomas Hammons as Kissinger, Sanford Sylvan as Chou En-lai, and John Duykers as Mao Tse-tung in Peter Sellars's production of *Nixon In China* by John Adams.

tury later: from February 21 to 27, 1972, he visited China, a nation with which the United States had maintained a long-standing hostility, bringing his wife and his chief diplomatic adviser, Henry Kissinger. Nixon was able to begin the historically necessary rapprochement between the United States and China, which is still being uneasily and ambiguously pursued, precisely because his entire career had been dedicated to building a strong anti-Communist persona. Conservatives in Congress and the media would never have accepted such a gesture from a Democrat in the White House.

"Nixon in China . . . is a more moving experience on TV than on the stage, thanks to director Brian Large's probing camera work. He takes us up close, and shows us several sides of the characters simultaneously. The resulting emotional depth is crucial for leading the viewer through the opera's often confounding symbolism."

—David Patrick Stearns
USA TODAY

ABOVE: The opening scene from *Nixon in China.*

The production of *Nixon in China* that was shown on GREAT PERFORMANCES in the 1987–88 season began to be conceived in the luxuriant imagination of Peter Sellars in 1982. It took five years to bring together composer John Adams, librettist Alice Goodman, choreographer Mark Morris, designers Adrianne Lobel (sets) and Dunya Ramicova (costumes), and the cast that gave the premiere performance at the Houston Grand Opera on October 22, 1987.

Besides appearing on GREAT PERFORMANCES, *Nixon in China* was produced, after leaving Houston, at the Brooklyn Academy of Music, the John F. Kennedy Center for the Performing Arts in Washington, D.C., and the Netherlands Opera. It played before an unusually large number of people in four different opera houses. But this audience was dwarfed by the television audience who viewed it on GREAT PERFORMANCES, many of whom were seeing their first opera. What they saw was radically different from any other opera in the four-century history of the genre, beginning with the fact that several of the characters were still alive—able, if they could stand it, to turn on their television sets and see facsimiles of themselves singing in costume and makeup.

The most notable opera lover in the Nixon administration, Henry Kissinger, must have had the most serious problems with *Nixon in China*. He is caricatured moderately in the primary narrative and vehemently in the show-within-a-show, "The Red Detachment of Women." This is a ballet sequence, heavy with revolutionary and feminist propaganda, organized to entertain the Nixons by Chiang Ch'ing, Mao Tse-Tung's fourth wife. It presents Kissinger as the sadistic overseer of a sort of chain gang made up of enslaved women. The character who is treated most gently in the opera is Chinese Premier Chou En-Lai, portrayed (accurately) as an intelligent, honest, and conscientious man.

History usually waits a little longer than it did in this case before it accepts transformation into opera. Ordinary members of the audience were able to compare their personal impressions of several characters with their operatic counterparts. President and Mrs. Nixon and Henry Kissinger had all appeared frequently on television, and some of the events during Nixon's visit had also been televised. "It's prime time in the U.S.A. . . . . They watch us now," Nixon says as he lands in China. He is portrayed as intent on image and publicity, rather paranoid, totally political. Pat Nixon is warm-hearted, Chiang Ch'ing opportunistic and bloodthirsty. Mao, an old man who says, "Revolution is a boys' game," lives largely in the past.

There are no heroics, musical or theatrical, in *Nixon in China*—a characteristic that puts it outside the operatic mainstream. The most spectacular event in it, coming right at the beginning, is part of Sellars's staging: the landing of the aircraft *Spirit of '76* on the stage, looking remarkably like newsreel footage of the actual event.

Musically, John Adams's minimalist style consciously cultivates understatement, rarely calling attention to itself but supporting and enhancing the text and helping to define the characters. Nixon's familiar, choppy style of public speaking, for example, is clearly reflected in the music's rhythms. Goodman's libretto is notable for sharp characterizations and subtle ironies, but, true to the events it chronicles, *Nixon in China* deals largely with ceremonial functions and the participants' private reactions to public events. The final scene gives us their reflections on the various paths that have brought them to this encounter.

Essentially, *Nixon in China* is about the meeting of two worldviews. Mao's China is an ancient culture, deep and subtle in its awareness of history and psychology, with an overlay of revolutionary sentiment that is a temporary means of coping with present reality. Nixon's America, still relatively young and inexperienced, is too much inclined to believe its own slogans and is trying (with some success) to balance idealism and cynicism in its approach to the world. On the surface, *Nixon in China* looks like a topical treatment of a news event of passing interest. Studied at greater depth, it emerges as not only one of the most unusual but one of the most profoundly and permanently interesting operas ever shown on GREAT PERFORMANCES.

OPERA'S CHANGING IMAGE: *EINSTEIN ON THE BEACH*

Einstein on the Beach: The Changing Image of Opera, broadcast by GREAT PERFORMANCES during the

1985–86 season, was not a complete performance of the stage epic, which runs four and a half hours without intermission, but a performance documentary; it offers parts of the show along with commentary by choreographer-scenarist Robert Wilson, composer Philip Glass, and others. While many might challenge the assertion that this spectacle "changed forever the image of opera," there is a fine precision in the opening description in the program:

> "*Einstein on the Beach* is an opera like no other. There is no story, no hero or heroine, no obvious links between words, images, and music. A scene lasting thirty minutes may consist of a single image that changes at an almost glacial pace. The music may sustain a single note for minutes or explode in contagiously rhythmic combinations of voice, violin, and amplified instruments. It is an opera where dancers are the featured performers. . . . *Einstein on the Beach* falls somewhere between a spectacle and a meditation."

For most opera lovers, the image of opera remains essentially what it was before the American premiere of *Einstein on the Beach* in 1976, but unquestionably this post-Dada opus enlarged the possibilities of what some people are willing to call opera. Since *Einstein on the Beach* burst on the world, quite a few musical theater works have been composed and produced in this country that remain closer to the traditional definition of opera. Many have been shown on GREAT PERFORMANCES, including *The Gospel at Colonus, Willie Stark, Sweeney Todd, Candide, Goya, Nixon in China, The Aspern Papers, The Dangerous Liaisons,* and *Emmeline. The Real McTeague,* a new opera inspired by a silent film and directed by Robert Altman with some techniques borrowed from silent films, was the subject of an absorbing performance documentary in the 1992–93 season that (unlike *Einstein on the Beach*) made the viewer eager to see the whole opera.

CONRAD SUSA'S *THE DANGEROUS LIAISONS*

Like *The Rake's Progress,* Conrad Susa's opera *The Dangerous Liaisons,* which GREAT PERFORMANCES presented in its world premiere production in the 1994–95 season, is based on an eighteenth-century morality fable about the corruption of innocence and the horrible consequences of moral depravity. Like the paintings that were the inspiration for Stravinsky's masterpiece, Susa's source was a difficult one to transfer to the operatic stage: a collection of letters between fictional characters, arranged to make a novel.

One of the opera's minor triumphs is the way it weaves the motif of letter writing into its plot, from a love note stuck between the strings of a harp at the beginning to the discovery of a collection of letters near the end, leading to the downfall of the most wicked character in the story. Many scenes involve writing and receiving letters. Act One, Scene Two, titled "The Bedrooms," is a virtuoso exercise in split staging—or split screen on GREAT PERFORMANCES. It shows four people in four bedrooms writing or reading letters that advance and complicate the plot; one of them is using a prostitute's back as his writing desk.

The epistolary novel *Les Liaisons Dangereuses* by Pierre Choderlos de Laclos was published in 1782, almost on the brink of the French Revolution, chronicling and chastising the attitudes and activi-

"If ever a work was meant for television, it's Einstein on the Beach. *Glass's pulsating, gradated compositions have been described as 'trance music,' and television is, unrepentantly, the medium of trance."*

—Karrie Jacobs
VILLAGE VOICE

RIGHT: Tison Street (as Einstein) in backstage preparations for *Einstein on the Beach: The Changing Image of Opera.*

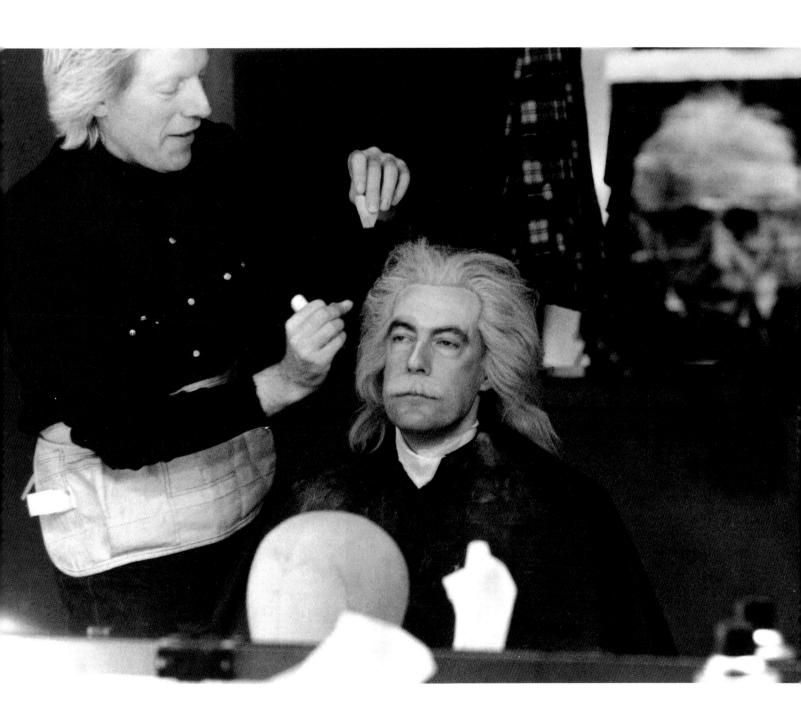

ties of amoral French aristocrats. The central characters are a capricious and malevolent widow, the Marquise de Merteuil (brilliantly portrayed in the GREAT PERFORMANCES production by Frederica von Stade) and her former lover, a notorious womanizer, the Vicomte de Valmont (baritone Thomas Hampson). Their letters discuss seduction as a subtle, complex, and slightly risky game.

The novel and the opera trace the step-by-step process through which Merteuil and Valmont work out and execute their plans for the seduction of two women: Madame de Tourvel (soprano Renee Fleming), the wife of a judge who is out of town, and Cécile de Volanges (soprano Mary Mills), an innocent fifteen-year-old who is betrothed to an elderly man, Monsieur de Gercourt, who never appears onstage. Merteuil has an intense grudge against Gercourt, a former lover. She wants Valmont to seduce Cécile because "that ass Gercourt/ Does not deserve a virgin bride." She will reward Valmont, who considers Cécile too easy to be interesting, with her own erotic favors. Valmont also intends to seduce Tourvel because she is "a real challenge . . . a very pious lady" and "all any lover needs/Is an obstacle."

Long accepted as a classic of French literature, *Les Liaisons Dangereuses* had only a small albeit highly dedicated following in the English-speaking world until the 1980s, when it was transformed into a hit play on Broadway by Christopher Hampton, followed quickly by two movies: *Dangerous Liaisons* and *Valmont*. Clearly, its time had come. The San Francisco Opera's commission for an opera by Susa and librettist Philip Littell, and the telecast of the opera on GREAT PERFORMANCES shortly after its premiere, completed the expropriation of this quintessentially French material for American audiences.

Susa's music is in a conservative modern idiom, sometimes (like Stravinsky's in *The Rake's Progress*) deliberately reminiscent of eighteenth-century styles in its arias and its marvelously effective ensemble numbers. It is particularly striking in the contrast between its two acts. Act One is a drawing-room comedy portraying the ups and downs of the erotic chase in a witty, deliciously wicked style. Act Two, starkly tragic, details the horrible effects of these games on the innocent and guilty alike. Madame de Tourvel, seduced and abandoned, goes insane and dies; Cécile, impregnated by Valmont, has a miscarriage and loses her reputation; Valmont is killed in a duel with Cécile's paramour. Merteuil, ravaged by smallpox and bankrupt, becomes a social outcast.

I was present, and deeply impressed, at the premiere of *The Dangerous Liaisons* in San Francisco, and I watched it again in the GREAT PERFORMANCES telecast. There is a lot to be said for the immediacy of being in the theater where an opera is being performed, but in many ways the television experience surpassed that of the opera house; close-up camera work provides perspectives on subtle details of body language and facial expression that are unavailable even from the best seats in a theater, and the television medium is particularly useful for clarifying the split-stage techniques that are used often and effectively in this opera.

LEFT: Thomas Hampson as the cynical Vicomte de Valmont and Frederica von Stade as his confederate, the Marquise de Merteuil, in the San Francisco Opera's production of *The Dangerous Liasons*.

For some time, it has been obvious that many novels are being written secondarily for circulation as books and primarily for possible development as movies. Similarly, perhaps we are on the brink of an age when operas will be composed with television as well as staged performance in mind. Or perhaps, as this book appears, that threshold has already been passed.

European Opera

WITH THE ARRIVAL OF TELEVISION AS A PRIMARY MEDIUM FOR OPERA, THE DIRECTOR, WHO decides how it should look and what the singers should do with their bodies, has become as important as the conductor, who decides how it should sound and what they should do with their voices. In the early twentieth century, the operatic stage director was little more than a traffic controller, responsible for the logistics of stage movement. Today, particularly on the video screen, he is often more of an auteur, a cocreator with the composer and librettist. A work of art that has been familiar for centuries can take on a new life when a Jean-Pierre Ponnelle finds in it hidden symbols and psychological subtleties, a Peter Sellars brings out contemporary resonances, or a Franco Zeffirelli gives it a new look, redefines the characters, and examines the scene from unfamiliar camera angles. GREAT PERFORMANCES has allowed a wide audience to experience the refreshing new visions of some of the world's greatest opera directors.

JEAN-PIERRE PONNELLE

Jean-Pierre Ponnelle, who died much too young in 1988, has had more opera productions shown on GREAT PERFORMANCES than any other director. His productions include Mozart's *The Marriage of Figaro* in 1977–78, *La Clemenza di Tito* in 1981–82, and *The Magic Flute* in 1983–84; Rossini's *La Cenerentola* in 1983–84; and Verdi's *Rigoletto* in 1984–85. But the most controversial and vividly remembered Ponnelle productions are undoubtedly the three surviving operas of Claudio Monteverdi (1567–1643), produced for Zurich Opera in collaboration with conductor Nikolaus Harnoncourt: *The Coronation of Poppea*, shown in 1980–81, and *The Return of Ulysses* and *Orfeo*, shown in 1981–82.

In harmony with Harnoncourt's period-instrument interpretation, Ponnelle's *Poppea* (about intrigue at the court of Nero) is staged in Renaissance costumes, as it might have been when it was new. The opera opens with a dialogue among three gods, Love, Fortune, and Virtue, about which has the most power in human affairs. Love and Fortune join forces against Virtue; she is no longer cultivated or even respected, they claim.

LEFT: Kiri Te Kanawa and Dietrich Fischer-Dieskau in Jean-Pierre Ponnelle's production of *The Marriage of Figaro*.

Most directors, emphasizing the opera's modernity, find this scene an embarrassment and omit it entirely or do all they can to deemphasize it. Ponnelle rightly sees it as a means of establishing the theme for the entire opera and a prime source of its special Renaissance flavor. He lavishes attention on its most minute details, placing even more emphasis on the acting and body language than the words, and later he keeps the gods on the scene, even when they have nothing to sing; whenever Love or Fortune is mentioned—as happens frequently—the god is there, sometimes not seen by the characters but always visible to the audience. In any production, Love must be visible in the crucial scene in which he intervenes to abort an attempted assassination of Poppea, but in Ponnelle's treatment, the god is a pervasive presence throughout the opera, exactly as the composer and librettist intended. This is one of the most brilliant opera productions ever to appear on television; one clear reason for its power is that Ponnelle has listened carefully to the music and thought intensely about the dynamics of the plot. One cannot say this of all operatic stage directors, and this is becoming a major problem in the age of the operatic auteur.

TWO DIRECTORS, TWO APPROACHES

Peter Sellars is another contemporary opera director who listens carefully, and other qualities put him clearly in the Ponnelle tradition: emphasis on symbols, psychological probing, and above all, a conscious effort to shake up traditional ideas about the operas. There is one significant difference: Sellars tries to be timely while Ponnelle tried to be timeless. Sellars relies extensively on visual shock and surprise, which can lose much of their power on repeated viewings. And Sellars, more than Ponnelle, tends to impose a rather detailed context and interpretation on his material that blots out other, equally valid possibilities. Sellars's concept for *The Marriage of Figaro*, for example, is piquant, fascinating, memorable; Ponnelle's, on the other hand, is completely faithful to the original conception of the work, reinforcing it with a thousand small details. It is, in this reviewer's opinion, simply the best *Marriage of Figaro* one could ever hope to see.

PETER SELLARS

Introducing an opera on GREAT PERFORMANCES, Peter Sellars goes for the hard sell: "There's a rape and a murder in the first ninety seconds of Mozart's *Don Giovanni*. . . . it's probably the greatest opera ever written." This is a slight exaggeration: although *Don Giovanni* is perhaps the greatest opera ever written, it actually opens with a five-minute overture and a witty two-minute aria by the Don's valet, Leporello, before we get to the rape—an action that Sellars clearly treats as completed, though most productions make it out to be an unsuccessful attempt.

Sellars uses overstatement not only in his introduction but in his staging in order to woo an audience for opera. What counts is that most of the time and for a substantial part of his audience, it works. Essentially, Sellars takes Mozart's operas out of eighteenth-century language, costumes, settings, and conventions, translates them into images, characterizations, and concepts familiar to a late twentieth-century movie audience, and highlights their relevance by showing the same passions at work in a modern setting.

Sellars does not actually change the words of *Don Giovanni*, but he does update the subtitles. In the first scene, for example, Giovanni tells Donna Anna, *"Donna folle! Indarno gridi!"* ("Foolish woman! Your screams are in vain.") This is translated as "Shut up, bitch!" The murder promised in his introduction is usually done with a sword, but Sellars has Don Giovanni pull out a gun, calmly shoot

"I asked the cameramen not to be objective, to stay in close-up most of the evening. Thus, you do not get the pall that comes over singers singing to nobody in particular."

—PETER SELLARS

RIGHT: Sanford Sylvan as Figaro and Jeanne Ommerlé as Susanna in Peter Sellars's production of *The Marriage of Figaro*.

his victim, then turn away to light a cigarette. At the end of the opera, the murder victim comes back to drag Giovanni down to hell. Usually, he comes back looking like a statue come to life. In this production, he looks like a corpse that has dug its way out of the grave.

With or without hype, this street-tough, modernized *Don Giovanni* is a compelling experience, not only adapted for a modern audience unfamiliar with opera but also made fresh for those who already know this work well. Brought up to the present and set in the devastated streets of the South Bronx, this *Don Giovanni* offers what Sellars calls "an evening in hell." The modernized staging gives a new impact to many scenes. For Giovanni's party in Act One, supplies are stolen from a neighborhood store. His solitary dinner in Act Two, usually staged as a lavish feast, is reduced to a hamburger and thick shake eaten on a sidewalk, out of a paper bag, while a boom box takes the place of the usual onstage wind ensemble.

Sellars has given equally provocative treatments to the two other operas Mozart composed with librettist Lorenzo Da Ponte; both were shown on GREAT PERFORMANCES during the 1991–92 season. *The Marriage of Figaro,* a study of class structures, sexual harassment, and the abuse of power, is set on the fifty-second floor of the luxurious Trump Tower in New York, where Figaro and his bride Susanna live in the laundry room. *Cosí Fan Tutte,* which is about the war between the sexes and the willingness of both sides to do some cheating, takes place in Despina's Diner, a seaside greasy spoon on Long Island. Don Alfonso, who starts the plot rolling and guides its course, is usually portrayed as a mellow old philosopher with theories about human frailty. Sellars makes him a Vietnam veteran, embittered and misogynistic, and it works remarkably well.

The Sellars versions of these three operas should not be the only ones you see; inevitably they neglect some of the original values in Da Ponte's words and Mozart's music. But they do bring the operas into sharp, fascinating focus and reveal valid dimensions that are usually ignored.

"Mr. Sellars is a gifted radical, and his theatrical insights do bring fresh vigor to works that may have become numbingly familiar. . . . Audiences will no doubt be startled, perhaps even incensed, by a Don Giovanni who mainlines dope and strips to his briefs for the famous 'Viva libertad' ensemble scene. But they won't forget him. And they'll never again be able to look at Mozart's Don Giovanni *in the same way."*

—John J. O'connor
NEW YORK TIMES

LEFT: Eugene Perry and Herbert Perry in Peter Sellars's production of *Don Giovanni*

ABOVE: Australian director Baz Luhrmann brings *La Bohème* to life by making his protagonists young, modern, and easy to identify with. This production, broadcast by GREAT PERFORMANCES in 1993–94 evoked a tremendous viewer response.

WAGNER'S RING CYCLE
MEETING THE CHALLENGES OF TELEVISED OPERA

For those who produce and perform opera, television has been both a challenge and an opportunity. What may look perfectly satisfactory from a good seat in a theater can quickly become static and remote—not to mention boring—when seen on a television screen. Nearly a century of cinematography has taught our eyes to expect constant changes of perspective: close-ups, distance shots, cutting from one performer to another, and pulling back to show the whole setting. In the theater, our eyes do some of this work without prompting. On the screen, we depend on the director and camera operators to do it for us.

With the more intimate approach provided by cameras, we also develop expectations. We expect the singers to look like the people they represent, and the costumes and sets to be convincing. This places burdens on the casting directors and designers that were much less pressing in an era when dim lighting could cover a multitude of shortcomings for audiences that were not visually demanding.

Most of the opera productions shown in the first quarter century of GREAT PERFORMANCES have been taped during live performances in opera houses, so the challenge of being unobtrusive has been added to the other challenges. When the opera production is filmed on location, as it was for *The Turn of the Screw* (1987–88), "*Tosca* from Rome" (1992–93), and *Madame Butterfly* (1996–97), there is more spaciousness, a greater sense of depth and solidity in the sets, and more freedom of movement for the performers. But the costs can be prohibitive. When the soundtrack is recorded separately from the visuals—a common practice in Europe—there can also be technical problems in synchronizing the sound with the singers' lips.

BRINGING THE *RING* TO THE SMALL SCREEN

Read a summary of Richard Wagner's four-opera cycle *Der Ring des Nibelungen* ("The Ring of the Nibelung"), with its magic spells, curses, gods, giants, shape-shifting dwarfs, water nymphs, and magic dragon, and you might think that Walt Disney would be its ideal interpreter. But under its comic-book surface, this massive epic conceals a moral message—so many moral messages, in fact, that Wagner himself, who wrote the words as well as the music, could not enumerate or explain them all. But the primary message, most experts would agree, is a warning against the abuse of power.

Its treatment of the power motif is one of the strongest elements in the 1976 Bayreuth production, conceived for the centennial of the *Ring* cycle's first performance. Conducted by Pierre Boulez, directed by Patrice Chereau, and designed by Richard Peduzzi and Jacques Schmidt, it was broadcast by GREAT PERFORMANCES during the 1982–83 season—and it provoked nearly as much controversy as the original *Ring* had a century earlier.

"In spite of much to criticize—the inadequate characterization of the gods, the ceaseless modulations and wearying chromaticism of the harmonies, the end result of leaving the listener totally exhausted—this music drama is the creation of a true giant in the history of art, comparable in his innovation only to Michelangelo. In music, there is nobody to approach Wagner."

—EDVARD GRIEG

LEFT: Donald McIntyre as Wotan in *Die Walküre*, Act III, the "Magic FIre Music" sequence from "A *Ring* for Television."

THE MYTH WAGNER MADE

The cycle is a myth, invented by Wagner partly from earlier Norse, Icelandic, and Germanic myths but largely derived from his own dark and steamy subconscious mind. It is full of symbols—gold, swords, spears, rings and caves, fire and dragon's blood, birds that talk and horseback-riding maidens who carry dead heroes off to Valhalla, home of the gods (built at terrible cost) and a kind of warrior's paradise. Along with the physical symbols, it is packed with musical symbols, little bits of melody called leitmotifs that Wagner identified with various elements in the story: the Rhine, fire, the curse, gold, Valhalla, and dozens more, in a wide variety of combinations and transformations.

The central symbol and motivating force is a horde of gold, hidden in the Rhine and guarded by three Rhine Maidens. Alberich, a Nibelung (dwarf), steals the gold, knowing that whoever manages to make a ring of it will rule the world, though to do so he must renounce all hope of love. With the help of his metal-working brother Mime, Alberich makes not only the ring but the Tarnhelm, a magic helmet that will allow him to take any shape he chooses.

He immediately begins to abuse his power, enslaves fellow Nibelungs (including his brother), and then loses the ring and helmet through trickery to Wotan, king of the gods, and Loge, the god of fire and the supreme trickster. But before losing the ring, Alberich places a curse on all who will own it after him.

From this point in this story, the ring passes from hand to hand, spreading destruction wherever it goes, through four evenings of opera that can total up to almost eighteen hours of music depending on the conductor's ideas of tempo. (Boulez, on GREAT PERFORMANCES, conducted one of the "quickest" *Ring* cycles of all time, coming in at about fourteen hours and fifteen minutes.) Finally, with the destruction of Valhalla and the death of Wotan's daughter Brunnhilde, the gold is returned to the Rhine and peace is restored.

Complementing its theme of power, the *Ring* cycle concerns a world without love—or almost without love. The only love in a tale that spans three generations is incestuous: that of Wotan's twin son and daughter Siegmund and Sieglinde for one another and of their son Siegfried for his aunt, Brunnhilde. Wotan, who has abused his power in contracting to have Valhalla built, abuses it again repeatedly in trying to correct his original error; he continues to make things worse until everything he has created is destroyed.

CONTINUING A TRADITION OF INNOVATION

The team that put together the centennial *Ring* for performance at Bayreuth in 1976 was French, brought in at the suggestion of conductor Boulez—much to the consternation of a substantial part of the hard-core Wagner fan club. This production was intensely controversial and greeted with loud protests, even during performances at Bayreuth, where the atmosphere is usually one of cathedral-like silence and reverence.

The controversy sprang not only from Chereau's modernized staging but also from Boulez's lightening, acceleration, and deemphasis of the orchestral textures. There were also complaints, not wholly unjustified, that the performers were selected more for their acting ability than the beauty of their voices. And indeed, this is the best-acted *Ring* in the history of the cycle—an appropriate distinction, since it was the first to be shown on television. Organized around a striking visual and thematic concept that makes the cycle a critique of the Industrial

"I think this 'Ring' will become compulsive viewing for millions—a sort of musical Forsyte Saga which will keep all viewers, not just opera buffs, glued to their screen . . . This is, quite simply, the most compelling and exciting opera I've ever seen on television. . . ."

—David Fingleton
DAILY EXPRESS

Revolution, the production's sets and costumes suggest the nineteenth century, and Wotan is portrayed as a kind of industrial tycoon.

The Chereau *Ring,* as it has come to be called, was not the first production to take liberties with the cycle's original staging concepts. Such variations were instigated at Bayreuth by the composer's grandson, Wieland Wagner, after World War II. The vehemence of the opposition is, in fact, a tribute to the power of this production. And in its own way, it is faithful to the cycle's original concepts. Wagner considered himself a revolutionary and spent years in exile for his revolutionary publications and activities. He believed that myths are "true for all time" and "eternally inexhaustible," which means that adaptations of them to new contexts—particularly his own modification of Norse myths to suit his artistic purposes—is right and even necessary.

As for Boulez's deemphasis on the orchestra, this falls squarely within the tradition started by Wagner himself. It was he who first decreed that the orchestra should be relegated to a pit under the stage to avoid distracting attention from the singers. And in his preparations for the first production, which were very carefully documented to serve as a guide to future generations, Wagner repeatedly stressed the importance of his dramatic text over his orchestral music, which, he suggested, should be "not noticed, but should grow with the drama organically into a whole."

It can be argued that the *Ring* that millions of Americans have seen on GREAT PERFORMANCES is, in some ways, a return to Wagner's original concepts. And without argument, it is a landmark in the performance history of this cycle.

"The days of the gods are over. The values of this world must be defined and invented anew. The people of today are standing on the brink of an abyss and listen intensely to the oracle coming up out of the depths of the earth. But they do not know what it means. . . . "

—PATRICE CHEREAU

A B O V E : Brunhilde and Sieglinde with the Valkyries in Act II of *Die Walküre,* from "A *Ring* for Television."

Jazz

⋇

JAZZ, AT ITS BEST, IS ESSENTIALLY AN EXPRESSION OF THE PERFORMER'S PERSONALITY. Unlike classical music, the inventor and the performer are frequently the same person, and sometimes the music is being born as the audience hears it. Many of the jazz programs shown on GREAT PERFORMANCES have originated in special occasions, organized as tributes to such giants as Duke Ellington, Miles Davis, and Dizzy Gillespie. These programs have offered the audience substantial looks at the subjects' lives as well as their music.

"ELLINGTON: THE MUSIC LIVES ON"

Early in the gala program "Ellington: The Music Lives On" (broadcast during GREAT PERFORMANCES' 1982–83 season), the quartet Sister Sledge takes just five minutes to give nine solid reasons for hailing Duke Ellington as one of America's greatest musicians. Singing "It Don't Mean a Thing If It Ain't Got That Swing," "I Let a Song Go Out of My Heart," "Don't Get Around Much Anymore," "Mood Indigo," "Do Nothin' Till You Hear from Me," "Just Squeeze Me," "In a Sentimental Mood," "I'm Beginning to See the Light," and "I've Got to Be a Rug-Cutter," the quartet makes the conclusion obvious—without even mentioning Ellington's orchestra and the numbers identified with it, numbers such as "Caravan" and "Take the A Train."

Hosted by Cicely Tyson, the program includes tributes to Ellington from a variety of sources. Bobby Short, who has sung Ellington's songs in many countries, says, "The public all around the world is aware of Duke Ellington's music." Yves Montand contributes, "He make you *meilleur* . . . he make you better. . . when you listen to Duke Ellington." Nat Hentoff points out "a deep, deep strain of unabashed romanticism" in Ellington's music and suggests that "he saw and heard all kinds of epiphanies . . . essences of American life." John Hammond pronounces Ellington "marvelously imaginative" and adds that he "loved the sound of the human voice, particularly the human voice without words"—and then Kathleen Battle demonstrates this point by singing the exquisite, wordless "Creole Love Call."

The program includes a lot more superb singing, along with some well-staged acting out of his great songs by such artists as Ken Page in "I'm Just a Lucky So-and-So," Treat Williams in "Satin Doll," Karen Akers in "In My Solitude," and Carly Simon in "I Got It Bad and That Ain't Good." An absorbing segment is devoted to his orchestra, an extraordinary collection of soloists that included some notable composers. Mercer Ellington, Duke's son, reflects on how the orchestra was "like family to me"; for years as he was growing up, he didn't realize that the pals who

"Duke Ellington's musical legacy is stunning. In addition to being a virtuoso at the piano, he composed jazz, theatrical works, Broadway shows, film scores, ballet, popular songs, symphonic suites, and sacred concerts that have rooted him in the American consciousness forever.

"Now, nine years after his death, public television is presenting a delightful celebration of his work in 'Ellington—The Music Lives On.' . . . This is irresistible television, a lively, entertaining, toe-tapping ninety minutes guaranteed to send you to bed whistling 'Mood Indigo,' 'Don't Get Around Much Anymore' or any of the three thousand or so other Ellington compositions."

— Jack Thomas
BOSTON GLOBE

LEFT: Miles Davis blowing hot and cool on "Miles Ahead: The Music Of Miles Davis."

took him to the beach or the movies were also great musicians.

Old film clips show Duke leading his orchestra and playing the piano—brilliantly—in the Cotton Club in the 1920s; they also offer glimpses of some of his early movie work. Featured soloists include Mae West in the movie *Belle of the Nineties* and Billie Holiday, whom he discovered and chose to sing the blues movement of his *Symphony in Black* when she was only nineteen. A clip from 1934 shows a segment of his *Ebony Rhapsody*, based very loosely on a Liszt Hungarian Rhapsody.

Cicely Tyson introduces one of the most distinctive segments with a little talk about music for dancing: "In the 1920s, '30s, and '40s, dancing styles changed as rapidly as they do today, but then, as now, Duke's music was always totally danceable." There follows a series of dance numbers to illustrate changing dance styles and the versatility of Ellington's music: a wildly comic twenties pas de deux to "East St. Louis Toodle-oo," a 1930s chorus line hoofing like a miniature Busby Berkeley routine to "Ring Dem Bells," and a very athletic 1940s jitterbug routine to "Perdido."

A segment on women in Ellington's music is introduced by a discussion of what Hentoff calls the composer-lyricist's "extra dimension of gentleness and verbal grace directed at women," who were, of course, the primary inspiration for his music. Most of the songs mentioned or performed to illustrate this point are now standards, such as "Satin Doll" and "Sophisticated Lady" (poignantly sung by Tammy Grimes). But the program also includes the first public performance of three songs from the musical *Queenie Pie*, which was left unfinished at his death in 1974.

From the familiar to the rare, this GREAT PERFORMANCES program confirms what Sister Sledge made clear from the start: Duke Ellington remains one of our national treasures.

"MILES AHEAD: THE MUSIC OF MILES DAVIS"

The last word on Miles Davis is spoken, by the musician himself, over the closing credits of "Miles Ahead: The Music of Miles Davis": "You can't do what you did six months ago." The voice-over commentary in this survey of his career, broadcast by GREAT PERFORMANCES during the 1986–87 season, says the same thing a little more ponderously: "His singular place in the history of American music is due to his insatiable appetite for change." And Bill Cosby says it with refreshing enthusiasm: "The great thing I love about Miles Davis is his ability to change and be ahead."

The primary interest of this program lies, as it should, in its abundant samples of the great jazz trumpeter's playing from the 1950s to the 1980s, featuring his "cool" style, the impressionism he cultivated with Gil Evans, his avant-garde treatment of pop material, and his acceptance of amplified instruments despite the agonized screams of purists. But almost equally important are the comments on this unique personality and his protean music making by Dizzy Gillespie, Herbie Hancock, Gil Evans, Keith Jarrett, Bill Cosby, and others— including Davis himself, whose comments are often as simple and straightforward as his music is elliptical and laden with overtones.

"I'm just a musician and I love music" is his one-sentence summary of what he is all about. Of the trumpet, he says merely, "It's my voice, that's what it is," a comment that harmonizes modestly with Evans's remark: "I can hardly think of anybody who can sing a song better than he can on an open trumpet." Sometimes Davis's remarks have a paradoxical profundity. On imitation and originality in jazz, he says, "Sometimes you have to play a long time to be able to play like yourself." And Dizzy Gillespie recalls Davis's early career, before he took his long time-out from 1975 to 1980: "He was shy . . . he never said anything on the stage. He never announced a number . . . he just played, and he probably figured that's enough, my music will speak for me."

Herbie Hancock recalls Davis's quest for something beyond perfection: "You want to be perfect in front of the people. That's not what Miles wants; Miles wants honesty." And George Benson associates him with a special kind of pride: he "made us realize that to be a jazz musician was a great honor and to be a black jazz musician was the ultimate honor."

"He said, 'Keith, you know why I don't play ballads anymore?' I said, 'No.' I said no because I wanted to hear the rest of it. If I did know the answer, I still would have said no. He said, 'Because I love playing ballads so much.' Now that's the sign of an artist . . . to be conscious enough to see that even what he loves has to move. Miles would rather have a bad band, I think, playing terrible music, than have a band that played what he'd played before. and that is against even his natural instincts, which makes it a creative act."

—KEITH JARRETT

"WOLF TRAP SALUTES DIZZY GILLESPIE"

In "Wolf Trap Salutes Dizzy Gillespie," shown on GREAT PERFORMANCES in the 1987–88 season, Carmen McRae sums it all up in just ten words: "He's the best progressive jazz trumpet player we have today." Wynton Marsalis also takes ten words to describe Gillespie from a trumpeter's point of view: "If you play trumpet in jazz, you're influenced by Dizzy."

The program, involving a stellar list of international jazz figures, marked the celebration of Gillespie's seventieth birthday, and it includes glimpses of him blowing out a formidable array of candles while an all-star band plays Lalo Schifrin's jazzy arrangement of "Happy Birthday." But most of the show is dedicated to music, particularly such Gillespie numbers as "A Night in Tunisia," "Salt Peanuts," and "Fiesta Mojo." There are also samples of his innovations in bebop and his integration of Afro-Cuban and Brazilian styles into the American jazz heritage. Between numbers, host Willis Conover provides highlights of Gillespie's five-decade career, including an archival film clip of the White House Jazz Festival when the trumpeter coaxed Jimmy Carter into doing a solo in "Salt Peanuts," then asked him, "Do you want to go on the road with us?"

Gillespie pays warm tribute to many of his colleagues and explains the unusual shape of his trumpet, with the bell tilted upward: it got bent by accident during a birthday party for his wife, and he liked the way that shape helped him to hear his own sound. "It was a revolution," he says.

Sadly missing from the celebration is the late Charlie Parker, Gillespie's partner in progressive jazz, but Gillespie insists that "his spirit permeated the whole performance." Among the colleagues who are present and with whom Gillespie performed memorably are saxophonists James Moody and Sonny Rollins; Jon Hendricks, who does some remarkable scat singing; and pianist Oscar Peterson.

LEFT: Dizzy Gillespie shows how he earned the tributes in "Wolf Trap Salutes Dizzy Gillespie: A Tribute to the Jazz Master."

"WYNTON MARSALIS: BLUES AND SWING"

From the beginning of "Wynton Marsalis: Blues and Swing," Marsalis makes it quite clear what he wants to accomplish: "What we're trying to do in the band is just pay as much homage as we

can to the nobility of our tradition." He is shown doing just that in words and, perhaps even more elo-
quently, in music, with performances of such numbers as "Caravan," "Do You Know What It Means to

Miss New Orleans," and "Cherokee." Playing with partners such as pianist Marcus Roberts,
Marsalis demonstrates the virtues of flexibility and innovation within the overriding virtue
of respect for a very special musical heritage. "The basis of jazz is blues and swing," he says,
and then shows us what he means. "Each generation of jazz musicians extends, elaborates,
and refines different aspects of the blues idiom."

The program begins with Marsalis explaining the inner dynamics of a small jazz
group to a class of Harvard students by comparing it to an automobile: "The bass is like the
wheels, the drums are like the motor, and the piano is like the body." In working sessions
with students, such as those at the Duke Ellington School of the Arts in Washington, D.C.,
Marsalis uses his crossover experience as both a jazz and a classical artist to show how the two traditions differ. He compares an Ellington composition to a Beethoven symphony, for example, and notes
that while players in a classical orchestra have to follow directions precisely, Ellington wrote "music
designed for people who are more individual thinkers."

Advising a student on phrasing in a classical trumpet concerto, he observes that classical
musicians "have brought onto themselves . . . a certain type of paranoia, a desire for perfection."
Classical music "wasn't meant to be played that way," he insists. He recommends Louis Armstrong as a
model, because "there's no fear in him when he's playing; he doesn't care if he misses some note. . . . It
doesn't make a difference."

But Marsalis's overriding message to young jazz musicians is to keep in touch with their tradition: "There has been very little respect for information. . . . This is so much the me generation, [but]
our time too will pass, and if you don't show respect for your elders and you don't show respect for
things that deserve respect, then you too will be . . . thrown out for the next new fad."

"CARNEGIE HALL SALUTES THE JAZZ MASTERS"

Andrew Carnegie, who gave the world Carnegie Hall more than a century ago, would not have under-
stood the concept of the Carnegie Hall Jazz Band, an excellent assemblage of New York musicians that
play in the GREAT PERFORMANCES program "Carnegie Hall Salutes the Jazz Masters" shown during the
1993–94 season. Jazz did not exist as a recognized form of musical activity until close to the end of
Andrew Carnegie's life, and the first notes of jazz played in Carnegie Hall were not heard
until 1938, eighteen years after his death.

RIGHT: Joe Henderson in "Carnegie Hall
Salutes The Jazz Masters."

That first Carnegie Hall jazz concert, featuring Benny Goodman, his band and quartet,
Count Basie, and members of the Basie and Ellington orchestras, was the beginning of a great tradition.
Since then—and particularly since it became the venue for Norman Granz's "Jazz at the Philharmonic"
concerts—most of the important figures on the jazz scene have performed at Carnegie Hall.

They are warmly and brilliantly remembered in the GREAT PERFORMANCES program.
Performed on April 6, 1994, and taped for telecast the following month, the concert commemorates

the fiftieth birthday of Granz's Verve record company. Hosted by Vanessa Williams (who sings "Tea for Two") and Herbie Hancock (who plays piano in many numbers, even leaning over once to reach inside and strum the strings), the program features film clips of such historic jazz figures as Art Tatum, Count Basie, Bill Evans, Ella Fitzgerald, Stan Getz, Miles Davis, Wes Montgomery, Billie Holiday, Dizzy Gillespie, and Lester Young—an eminent list of jazz performers, though there are some curious omissions, such as Louis Armstrong and Duke Ellington.

After being shown in a film clip and briefly, enthusiastically discussed by Williams or Hancock, the "Jazz Master" from an earlier generation receives a tribute, in the form of a performance, from a member of a younger generation. Most of the time, the tribute is given on the same kind of instrument played by the honoree, as when pianist Hank Jones honors Art Tatum by playing "Willow, Weep for Me" in a style about as close to Tatum's as anyone could hope for, or when Betty Carter does the same for Ella Fitzgerald, scat-singing through "How High the Moon."

In some cases, however—perhaps because the original was considered even more inimitable than Tatum or Fitzgerald—musicians associated with the master offer their tribute on a different instrument. Thus, guitarist Wes Montgomery is commemorated by organist Jimmy Smith playing "Walk on the Wild Side" with the Carnegie Hall Jazz Band, and Miles Davis is recalled by Herbie Hancock on piano and John McLaughlin (who might have tried to do a Wes Montgomery tribute) on guitar in "It's About That Time."

BELOW: Antonio Carlos Jobim in one of his final concert apparances with jazz guitarist Pat Metheny in "Carnegie Hall Salutes The Jazz Masters."

Among the outstanding numbers in a program with many notable performances are Antonio Carlos Jobim's "Desafinado," Dee Dee Bridgewater in "It Was Just One of Those Things," trombonist J. J. Johnson in several numbers, Abbey Lincoln's "I Must Have That Man," and trumpeter Roy Hargrove's "Manteca." The "Manteca" arrangement includes the most unusual solo on the program: Steve Turre playing a table full of seashells on which he performs as though they were valveless trumpets or saxophones. The image is a great summary of the individualism and iconoclasm of American jazz.

"LENA HORNE: THE LADY AND HER MUSIC"

If ever there was a one-woman show in America, it was Lena Horne, who was featured in a 1984–85 Great Performances extravaganza entitled "Lena Horne: The Lady and Her Music." Hardly stopping for breath, she sings, as only she can, a variety of songs that range from a comic Calypso-style number on automated living, "Push de Button," to "The Lady Is a Tramp." But her speaking voice has as much impact as her singing—for instance, in a hilarious interaction with an offstage voice that instructs her to "think thin" and try to make her mouth "pretty, like Jeanette MacDonald," or in stories of the old days at the Cotton Club and imitations of such colleagues as Tina Turner. She is at her best, of course, in definitive performances of such classics as "But Not for Me," "Can't Help Lovin' That Man of Mine," and "Stormy Weather."

"Mysteriously Lena Horne, manages to transform pretty tunes and banal lyrics into something that is both erotic and political, a fretting of raw edges."

—John Leonard
NEW YORK *MAGAZINE*

ABOVE: "Lena Horne: The Lady and Her Music"

Great Vocal Performances

THE SPLENDORS OF THE HUMAN VOICE

———————————— ✺ ————————————

IN ADDITION TO ITS BROADCASTS OF EIGHTY-FIVE FULL OPERAS DURING ITS FIRST TWENTY-five years, GREAT PERFORMANCES has offered a wide range of programs that focus on the voice alone. From opera recitals celebrating the splendid technique and glorious sounds of such stars as Plácido Domingo, Marilyn Horne, Luciano Pavarotti, Beverly Sills, and Dame Joan Sutherland, among others, to the rich new sonorities of Paul McCartney's *Liverpool Oratorio,* Andrew Lloyd Webber's *Requiem,* and Boublil and Schönberg's *Les Misérables*, these programs demonstrate the potential for passion and power contained in the human voice. Of the various opera documentaries, Luciano Pavarotti's is particularly entertaining.

LUCIANO PAVAROTTI: MY WORLD

Luciano Pavarotti: My World, which was shown in the 1995–96 season of GREAT PERFORMANCES, may be the best video documentation ever made of the great and ultra-popular tenor's art. The performances are carefully selected from an abundance of material, taped literally all around the world (Paris, Rome, New York, Beijing, and Miami Beach are a few examples), and Pavarotti is shown constantly in top form.

The twenty-three selections offer a thorough survey of the most popular tenor classics, including some that are not Pavarotti specialties, such as Lehar's "Dein ist mein ganzes Herz" ("Yours is my heart alone") sung in Italian, "Granada" sung in Spanish, and "Panis Angelicus" sung in Latin. Pavarotti's vocal quality comes across in powerful contrast when he sings a duet with another popular idol, Sting.

A highlight of the show is the moment that ranks as one of the funniest in Pavarotti's career: during the "Three Tenors" concert in Rome, Pavarotti shows off with a long-held note in "O Sole Mio," and fellow tenors Plácido Domingo and José Carreras go into a huddle; then they do a hilarious and exact imitation of him, complete with vocal acrobatics and hand gestures. Pavarotti, caught by surprise, cracks up.

LEFT: Plácido Domingo, here singing Gian Carlo Menotti's *Goya,* also performed a number of operatic recitals and concerts on GREAT PERFORMANCES

The program provides pleasant bits of commentary and travelogue, such as the sight of Pavarotti riding a bicycle in Beijing, but what stands out is the singing: Pavarotti at his best.

"BAROQUE DUET"

One advantage of television over the concert hall as a venue for music is its ability to put the experience in context, to observe the performers outside the formalities of the recital stage. This dimension of television performance is particularly well used in GREAT PERFORMANCES' 1991–92 program "Baroque Duet: Kathleen Battle and Wynton Marsalis."

A soprano who has sung on most of the world's great opera stages and a jazz trumpeter who also plays impressively in eighteenth-century concertos—what brought them together was a highly specialized kind of baroque music: duets for soprano and high-pitched trumpet. The program features three works that use this combination with special brilliance: Alessandro Scarlatti's cantata "Su le sponde del Tebro" ("On the Tiber's Strands"), Handel's aria "Let the Bright Seraphim," and Bach's cantata "Jauchzet Gott in allen Landen" ("Praise God in All Nations"). But the show also provides an inside look at the route the artists must take to the final performance, and this journey proves as fascinating as the music itself.

As he prepares for the first rehearsal, Marsalis confides that early jazz musicians tried to imitate the voices of women singing in church: "We instrumentalists try to get to that level of clarity." And he intends to turn to Battle as a similar model: "I want to stand close so I can hear the way she's phrasing it."

The two performers ease into their rehearsals gradually, coordinating and polishing; in between, the camera follows each of them home, allowing us to meet their families. Battle is shown singing in the Alan Chapel A.M.E. Church in Portsmouth, Ohio, where she grew up, and reminiscing about her schoolteachers; because her teachers lived in her neighborhood and knew her parents, she says, "you couldn't get away with anything; they challenged you and they expected the best of you." Marsalis is shown in New Orleans, visiting with his family, working out, developing new techniques, and playing in concert with his father and two brothers. By the time Marsalis and Battle stand together, formally clad, in front of an orchestra and an audience, the GREAT PERFORMANCES viewer has shared in an experience that is not merely musical but also richly human.

"PAUL MCCARTNEY'S *LIVERPOOL ORATORIO*"

Genius at work—two geniuses, really. Paul McCartney hums or whistles a tune while his collaborator, composer-conductor Carl Davis, sits at a piano picking out motifs, working with them in tandem with

"When I first heard the choir in rehearsals, 140 voices singing the chorale at the end of the first movement, it was a very lip-biting moment. I was fighting back the tears. It sort of takes you by surprise. When you've written something, you don't expect anybody to explain it back to you better than you wrote it."

—PAUL MCCARTNEY

RIGHT: Kathleen Battle and Wynton Marsalis recaptured a rarely performed but charming repertoire on "Baroque Duet."

McCartney, and writing them down. The *Liverpool Oratorio,* a musical reminiscence of McCartney's childhood, is taking shape before the eyes of the GREAT PERFORMANCES audience in the documentary that preceded the music's first telecast. The audience—following McCartney and Davis as they prepare the music, travel around Liverpool, and rehearse with Kiri Te Kanawa, other soloists, and the choir—have a chance to get acquainted with the composer and the music itself.

The broadcast was carefully titled "Paul McCartney's *Liverpool Oratorio,*" not to distinguish it from any other "Liverpool Oratorios" currently before the public but to get the two most important words up front. It is safe to assume that at least ten times as many people—perhaps one hundred times as many—will tune in to an oratorio if they see McCartney's name on it, than if it were by some little-known musician of an earlier era.

By any name, the *Liverpool Oratorio,* which GREAT PERFORMANCES broadcast in 1991–92, is a crossover classic by a pop composer who has been too busy turning out music to take time to learn to read and write it. "I sort of write music without being able to write it down," as he explains to a group of admirers. That's where Davis comes in: amanuensis, orchestrator, expert on musical forms and on what can be expected of a soprano or tenor voice, he takes McCartney's ideas and translates them into standard forms and notation.

This does not mean that it is really Carl Davis's *Liverpool Oratorio.* McCartney has an incred-

ible melodic gift and a good sense of larger musical structures; he also knows English oratorio style intimately, having been a member of a boys' choir in Liverpool. "We looked like little angels," he confides, "but believe me, we weren't."

"THE ANDREW LLOYD WEBBER *REQUIEM*"

GREAT PERFORMANCES broadcast another blockbuster pop-to-classical crossover work during its 1984–85 season: "The Andrew Lloyd Webber *Requiem*." Andrew Lloyd Webber is, certainly financially but also artistically, England's most successful writer of musical theater works since Sir Arthur Sullivan. His first work in this form, *Joseph and the Amazing Technicolor Dreamcoat,* is still produced regularly in many parts of the world, and his subsequent creations, including *Jesus Christ Superstar, Evita, Cats,* and *The Phantom of the Opera,* are always in production somewhere. He has had as many as five shows playing simultaneously on Broadway.

Unlike McCartney, Webber comes from a musical family; his father was a choir director and composer, and his brother is a classical cellist for whom Andrew has composed a set of variations on the same Paganini theme that inspired Brahms, Rachmaninoff, and more than a dozen other composers. Webber's *Requiem* stands comfortably in the same tradition as Fauré's, and one segment of it, the "Pie Jesu," became simultaneously a staple of classical recitals and a popular best-seller.

"*LES MISÉRABLES* IN CONCERT"

Les Misérables, which originated as a fairly modest French musical by Alain Boublil and Claude-Michel Schönberg, was transformed into one of the century's most spectacular theatrical phenomena when Cameron MacIntosh brought it to London for extensive revisions. Among the additions was state-of-the-art staging that includes a battle on the barricades during a student uprising in Paris, a trip through the city's legendary sewer system, and a suicide onstage when Inspector Javert jumps off a bridge. To celebrate the tenth anniversary of the show, which had by then been produced all around the world, a concert performance was given in London's Royal Albert Hall using singers from various productions, in costumes but without scenery. That program, "*Les Misérables* in Concert," which was broadcast in the 1995–96 season of GREAT PERFORMANCES, is regarded by many as the best-sung performance of the musical ever heard. Heading the cast is Colm Wilkinson, the definitive Jean Valjean, supported by a superb group of actor-singers that includes Philip Quast as Javert; Ruthie Henshaw as Fantine; Alan Armstrong as a definitive Thenardier; Jennie Galloway, superbly vulgar as his wife; and Lea Salonga as Eponine.

This concert version lacks the spectacular sets, but the staging is suggested by the use of still photos and film clips, sometimes cleverly synchronized with the sound. Beyond the technical razzle-dazzle, the enduring value of *Les Misérables* lies where it should: in the words and music. The sight of people in period costume singing into microphones and the

LEFT: Alan Armstrong as Thenardier and Jenny Galloway as Madame Thenardier hold forth in the wildly popular "*Les Misérables* in Concert."

often obtrusive presence of spotlights detracts a bit from the theatrical illusion, but the microphones and cameras also offer substantial advantages. On television, the words come through with a clarity seldom attained through a theater's amplification, and the camera's close-ups give the acting a subtlety and impact that can only be experienced from the most expensive seats of an auditorium.

A Cappella

———————————— ✌ ————————————

AS GREAT PERFORMANCES MOVES INTO ITS SECOND QUARTER CENTURY, CHAMBER MUSIC offers significant potential for the series' growth. Chamber music made its first appearance in the series during the sixth season, 1977–78, when the Juilliard String Quartet played two of Beethoven's quartets. Since then, chamber music programs have been rare but distinguished, featuring such groups as the Chamber Music Society of Lincoln Center and the Tokyo String Quartet.

Several programs have consisted of true chamber music that has exploded the rather stodgy and elitist impression this term creates in the mind of the average television viewer. One of these was the 1983–84 season's telecast of Stravinsky's *A Soldier's Tale* with its witty animation by R. O. Blechman. Another was a fresh, iconoclastic interpretation of Bach's Brandenburg Concertos, televised in 1984–85 with Nikolaus Harnoncourt conducting the Concentus Musicus of Vienna.

But the most revolutionary chamber music telecast on GREAT PERFORMANCES was one that few observers would have put in that category until it was defined as such by an unimpeachable authority: the official publication of Chamber Music America. "*Spike & Co.: Do It A Cappella,* the title of a television special and recording project sponsored by Spike Lee in 1990, showcased six chamber vocal ensembles performing repertoire ranging from doo-wop to African to Gospel, all without any instrumental accompaniment," said *Chamber Music* magazine in its August 1997 issue. "As if by divine decree, the phrase 'Do it a cappella' has become the battle cry of thousands of singers who have formed small ensembles on college campuses, street corners, and in living rooms across the country. Their mission is as simple as it is passionate—to perform any style of music [in small ensembles] using only the human voice."

GREAT PERFORMANCES, which has helped to build a nationwide audience for American opera, has done the same for vocal chamber music. The six groups featured on *Do It A Cappella* range in style from the South African ethnic flavor of Ladysmith Black Mombazo to the urban sophistication of the Mint Juleps, the Persuasions, and Rockapella. One of this style's attractions is captured by a member of Rockapella: "The thing about a cappella music is, you don't have to drag around equipment, you don't have to practice piano, maybe you vocalize half an hour a day, but that's it. You travel light. You work light."

LEFT: The Persuasions perform their classic "Looking for an Echo" in an echo-friendly deserted room on *Spike & Co.: Do It A Cappella.*

The a cappella genre has been around ever since people began to sing, and it has been used in every musical style from Renaissance madrigals to rock and the blues. *Do It A Cappella* explores some of its most striking possibilities—and reveals them to a large, mainstream American audience.

Celebrations of American Song

A LEGACY OF STYLES AND STYLISTS

⸺✑⸺

FROM THE BEGINNING, GREAT PERFORMANCES HAS HONORED AMERICAN SONGWRITERS with tributes that have informed and delighted television audiences. Here we sample some of the programs that have brought a wide range of styles, as well as some of our most famous song stylists, into American homes.

GEORGE GERSHWIN AND THE JAZZ AGE STYLE

One of the most elaborate nonoperatic music programs ever shown on GREAT PERFORMANCES was the celebration of George Gershwin given in two parts, "The Jazz Age" and "'S Wonderful!," during the 1987–88 season. These shows, originating jointly in London and New York, were under the musical direction of Michael Tilson Thomas, who serves as host and narrator, plays the piano, and conducts the London Symphony Orchestra and the New York–based Orchestra of Saint Luke's—sometimes, as in *Rhapsody in Blue,* leading the musicians from the keyboard.

The value of these programs is not only documentary and musical but musicological, for they offer quite a bit of music (and often very good music) that had never been performed before or that had been forgotten for a half century or more. Cynthia Haymon and Ruby Hinds give the first performance of "Lonely Boy," a powerful duet that was dropped from *Porgy and Bess,* and Mikhail Baryshnikov dances *Nocturnes,* a ballet that uses, as Tilson Thomas describes it, "unpublished and newly discovered versions of pieces spanning Gershwin's entire life, reflecting his haunted and elusive moods." Much of the music in this work is unfamiliar but has a distinctive Gershwin flavor.

A few pieces are *almost* familiar, such as a "Promenade" whose melodies are well known but that is presented in an unfamiliar orchestration. On the other hand, many of the dance numbers scattered through the two programs are performed with their original orchestrations, period costumes, and choreography, beginning with the original 1919 wind band arrangement of "Swanee," which includes a chorus, dancing, and a solo by Larry Kert that calls Al Jolson to mind.

A nice touch, early in the show, is the inclusion of Anton Rubinstein's old-fashioned, sentimental Melody in F, performed by Tilson Thomas, who describes Gershwin's affection for the tune and analyzes the ways in which it may have affected the composer's style. Leonard Bernstein's moody performance of Prelude no. 2 and violinist Nigel Kennedy's interpretation of Prelude no. 1, in the Heifetz arrangement, are other memorable moments.

"Hosted by conductor Michael Tilson Thomas, who sits behind a piano talking softly to the audience, this ambitious, star-studded salute appears to have emptied out Gershwin's trunks, including all the memorable numbers along with the lesser compositions. . . . This is one of those musical potpourris that offer something for everybody."

—Kay Gardella
NEW YORK DAILY NEWS

LEFT: Natalie Cole superbly and touchingly honors her father in "Unforgettable, with Love: Natalie Cole Sings the Songs of Nat King Cole."

[*193*]

And in two programs full of great singing, some of the vocal performances that stand out include "Somebody Loves Me" sung by Cleo Laine, "But Not for Me" interpreted by Maureen McGovern, and a trio treatment of "Someone to Watch over Me" by McGovern, Madeline Kahn, and Julia Migenes.

IRA GERSHWIN AND THE ART OF THE LYRIC

Ira Gershwin is usually remembered for the dazzling songs he wrote with his brother George—such immortal tunes as "I Got Rhythm," "'S Wonderful," "Embraceable You," and "But Not for Me"—and these are the first four numbers in "Ira Gershwin at 100: A Celebration at Carnegie Hall," part of GREAT PERFORMANCES' 1996–97 season. But Ira composed more than seven hundred songs in his long career, and his collaborators included Jerome Kern ("Long Ago and Far Away"), Kurt Weill ("The Saga of Jenny"; "My Ship"), Harold Arlen ("The Man That Got Away"), Vernon Duke ("I Can't Get Started"), and even Aaron Copland.

Ira Gershwin's lyrics were good enough to be published in book form—a distinction he shares with Noël Coward, Cole Porter, and Alan Jay Lerner but with few other pop lyricists. His range of styles and subjects speaks for itself, as does the consistently high quality of his workmanship.

"Ira Gershwin at 100" provides some good visuals from old photos and newsreels showing the environment in which George and Ira grew up; it also serves up delightful anecdotes about his shyness, his deficiencies as a poker player, and his schoolteacherish insistence that his friends speak grammatically.

Highlights are numerous, including Karen Akers in "But Not for Me"; David Garrison's fancy footwork and good singing in "Stairway to Paradise"; Ruth Brown's intense treatment of "The Man That Got Away"; Karen Ziemba and Scott Wise's singing, dancing, and exchange of fast patter in "My One and Only Highland Fling"; Dawn Upshaw's wistful "My Ship"; and Christine Ebersole's hilarious "Saga of Jenny." Every performer handles the words with special care and affection, as is only appropriate, since this time a wordsmith, rather than a tunesmith, is in the spotlight.

SOPRANOS AND SPIRITUALS

"Spirituals as show pieces are the subject of 'Kathleen Battle and Jessye Norman Sing Spirituals.' The two stars leave the viewer with no doubts about their personal connection to their material. . . . They are both supremely expressive of other-worldly ecstasies. Vocally, Norman and Battle are in peak form. . . . They take risks in making the music immediate in utterly compelling, vivid performances."

—John Henken
LOS ANGELES TIMES

RIGHT: Michael Feinstein and Liza Minnelli, quintessential stylists each, join a star-studded cast in "Celebrating Gershwin."

The torch is quite consciously passed from an older to a younger generation at the beginning of "Kathleen Battle and Jessye Norman Sing Spirituals," shown on GREAT PERFORMANCES in the 1990–91 season. At the beginning of the program, the late Marian Anderson, the singer most closely associated with this music, discusses the meaning of the spiritual and tells the audience it is "privileged to hear these two persons," because they have "a knowledge of and a love for the spirituals that you don't hear every day."

Battle and Norman also bring the two greatest voices recorded in this music since Anderson's own, which is heard in several film clips, and they offer an operatic awareness of the music's inherent drama, a brilliant sense of humor in "Scandalize My Name," and, although they had never before worked together, a fine sense of partnership.

The music of "Deep River," "He's Got the Whole World in His Hands," "Balm in

Gilead," "Swing Low, Sweet Chariot," and other spirituals can be marvelously effective without such superstar voices and the highly professional orchestral and choral arrangements conducted by James Levine. But this simple, richly communicative music takes on added attractions in the deluxe treatment given it for this program.

I HEAR AMERICA SINGING

All the experts will tell you that the song recital is a dying format for classical music, at least in the United States, and songs by American composers are even more neglected than those by Europeans. But this is not happening because of a shortage of outstanding young singers or worthwhile musical material, as is brilliantly demonstrated in the program entitled *Thomas Hampson: I Hear America Singing*, hosted by baritone Thomas Hampson and broadcast during the 1996–97 season of GREAT PERFORMANCES.

The program begins with Stephen Foster and spirituals and songs of the nineteenth century; includes such early twentieth-century composers as Edward MacDowell, Charles Tomlinson Griffes, and Charles Ives; and ends with the living composers Ned Rorem and William Bolcom. Hampson's collaborators in presenting this cornucopia of American song are a Who's Who of recitalists: sopranos Dawn Upshaw and Harolynn Blackwell, mezzo-sopranos Frederica von Stade and Marilyn Horne, and tenor Jerry Hadley. Hampson gives moving performances of "Beautiful Dreamer" and "Deep River," as well as a rambunctious "General William Booth Enters into Heaven" by the undeservedly neglected Sidney Homer (1864–1953). Upshaw is very funny in Aaron Copland's "Why Do They Shut Me Out of Heaven?" and von Stade is even funnier in a pseudo-sexy treatment of Bolcom's "Amor." Hadley catches precisely the small-boy spirit of Ives's "The Circus Band" as well as the world-weariness in John Duke's "Richard Cory." The well-chosen visuals include newsreel film clips, views of Walden Pond, and touching glimpses of African-American family life used to illustrate Blackwell's singing of "My People," a lovely song by Ricky Ian Gordon and Langston Hughes.

"In his poem, Walt Whitman wrote, 'I hear America singing, the varied carols I hear . . . Singing with open mouths their strong melodious songs.' That diversity of life, experience and imagination is reflected in American song."

—THOMAS HAMPSON

LEFT: Thomas Hampson revives great American art songs on *Thomas Hampson: I Hear America Singing.*

JUDY GARLAND: HER LIFE AND ART ON FILM

Even if we leave out the movies, from *The Wizard of Oz* to *A Star Is Born*, no singer has been more fully documented on film than Judy Garland, and none has more richly deserved such documentation. She is only seven years old in the first film clip included in the documentary *Judy Garland: The Concert Years*, which GREAT PERFORMANCES broadcast during its 1984–85 season. The documentary is narrated primarily by her daughter Lorna, for whom she had a song written specially by Johnny Mercer to match the songs she sang for her two other children: "Liza" and "Happiness Is Just a Thing Called Joe." Narration of her life and analysis of her art are a significant part of the documentary, but its vitality comes from the dozens of songs she interprets as only Garland could, with beautiful tone, sensitive phrasing, and total emotional identification.

The program includes most of the songs associated with her, from "Over the Rainbow" and

"Clang, Clang, Clang Went the Trolley" to "The Man That Got Away," but there are also many unique moments: a tour de force when she sings "Old Man River," which few fans would consider her kind of song; a moment from history when, over the objections of network executives, she sings "The Battle Hymn of the Republic" for President John F. Kennedy after his assassination; and comic duets with Ethel Merman and Barbra Streisand. There is even a hilarious skit with Bob Newhart in which they play a couple watching the *Judy Garland Show* and she says, "She hasn't sung a note in years; she just moves her lips to old records." It takes a very special kind of personality to be able to make fun of herself, and Garland's personality is exactly what comes through in these old black-and-white films.

NATALIE AND NAT KING COLE: A DYNASTY OF AMERICAN SONG STYLISTS

American popular music has not been around long enough to engender the kind of dynasties that classical music has seen, with the cantata- and concerto-writing Bachs or the waltz-writing Strausses, but it is beginning to happen as Liza Minnelli, Nancy Sinatra, and Natalie Cole attest. In "Unforgettable, with Love: Natalie Cole Sings the Songs of Nat King Cole," broadcast during GREAT PERFORMANCES' 1991–92 season, we see a great talent successfully bridging the generation gap. This program is a deeply touching, musically versatile, and sensitive tribute to a father who was an extraordinary musical stylist, endowed with a voice of unique tonal quality and expressive power.

Predictably, considering all the changes in popular music between his generation and hers, Natalie Cole's personal style is somewhat different from her father's, but she has a keen appreciation of traditional jazz and ballad styles, and she adapts beautifully to the requirements of her father's material. The most magic moment in this program comes near the end, when she sings "Unforgettable" in a duet with a film clip of her father. The two voices are completely compatible, not only because of a family resemblance but much more because Natalie has intensively and lovingly studied his phrasing, tone production, and verbal emphases.

Natalie's own choice of styles ranges from a swinging "Route 66" and a consciously old-fashioned "Straighten Up and Fly Right" to hauntingly sentimental treatments of "Tenderly" and "Autumn Leaves." And her performance of a song called "This Will Make You Laugh," composed by her father, leaves one wondering whether our deep respect for Nat King Cole as a performer may have kept us from appreciating fully his gifts as a composer.

LINDA RONSTADT AND THE SONGS OF HER FATHER

A different kind of paternal tribute is offered in "Linda Ronstadt: Canciones de Mi Padre." "Mexico is the land of magic," Ronstadt says as she introduces this lavishly produced, fast-moving, and intensely colorful program of mariachi music and dancing, shown during GREAT PERFORMANCES' 1988–89 season. Then she proceeds to demonstrate what she means in an hourlong show that we wish had been two or three times as long.

Mariachi is Mexico's folk music, and although it varies from one region to another, it is recog-

nizable everywhere for its instrumental color, vitality, vivid dance rhythms, close harmonies, and

intense passions. For Ronstadt, it is a family heritage: her grandfather, father, and aunt were all mari-

achi musicians. She absorbed the mariachi tradition by living in it from early childhood,

and with the aid of two first-class ensembles—the Mariachi Vargas and Ballet Folklorico de

la Fonda—she pours her love of it into one of the most colorful music programs ever shown

on GREAT PERFORMANCES.

ABOVE: Linda Ronstadt celebrates her heritage in "Linda Ronstadt: Canciones de Mi Padre."

When her father sang her the *corridos, rancheras,* and *huapangas* that are collectively called

mariachi, Ronstadt admits, "I didn't always understand the language, but it never mattered because the

music told me what I needed to know." She takes care, however, to let viewers know what is in the

words as well as the music, sometimes through a spoken explanation of the song, sometimes through

subtitles or a written-out summary of the text. The songs illustrate her assertion that they "may be

about sad things, but the music is triumphant, strong, proud, and full of life."

Besides her solos, some of the finest moments in the program come in the distinctive vocal

harmonies of her duets with Danny Valdez and in the dance numbers, particularly the two best

known to Norteamericanos: "La Bamba" and "El Jarabe Tapatio," which we usually call "The Mexican

Hat Dance."

Music of America and the World

IN THE LAST QUARTER CENTURY, GREAT PERFORMANCES' MUSICAL PROGRAMMING HAS brought into American homes a varied and superbly performed sample of the world's musical treasures: from Wagner's *Ring* cycle performed at the Wagner shrine in Bayreuth with cosmic symbolic overtones to the jaunty dance rhythms and soulful melodies of mariachi; from a cappella musicians singing in a subway because they love the echo to Leonard Bernstein talking, conducting, playing the piano, and exploring the anguish and joy of Gustav Mahler's symphonies or the sober splendors of Brahms.

These programs have brought American audiences face to face with the unique creative spirits of our musical culture: such jazz giants as Miles Davis and Dizzy Gillespie; such innovative spirits as Peter Sellars and Philip Glass; such theatrical geniuses as Stephen Sondheim and George and Ira Gershwin; and such outstanding performers as Lena Horne, Kathleen Battle, Judy Garland, and Wynton Marsalis.

GREAT PERFORMANCES has been particularly influential as a medium for opera. It has brought us landmark productions from the great opera houses and festivals of Europe. It has gone beyond the opera house with a *Tosca* filmed on location in Rome and a *Turn of the Screw* filmed in Czechoslovakia with English singers supplying the voices for Czech actors. But even more important, it has shown America the variety and vitality of its own operatic culture, from traditional classics such as *The Consul* and *The Ballad of Baby Doe* to experiments like *Einstein on the Beach*. It has aided incalculably in developing an American audience for our own opera and has thus helped enable the production of such new operas as *The Aspern Papers*, *The Dangerous Liaisons*, and *Emmeline*. And the television cameras of GREAT PERFORMANCES have allowed close encounters with such operatic personalities as Luciano Pavarotti and Marilyn Horne.

America's greatest orchestras—from Boston, Chicago, Cleveland, Los Angeles, New York, and Philadelphia—have been shown on GREAT PERFORMANCES with the same kind of meticulous production that has been lavished on their European counterparts in Vienna, Berlin, Amsterdam, and London.

Over its quarter century of existence, GREAT PERFORMANCES has made many implicit statements about music. Most notably, its programming has insisted that music, in all its forms and flavors, is a vital element in our lives. And it has demonstrated that the United States is a culture where all forms of music are welcomed, assimilated, and raised to new heights of artistic achievement.

LEFT: Two superb sopranos lift their voices and their viewers' spirits in "Kathleen Battle and Jessye Norman Sing Spirituals"; FOLLOWING PAGE: Bob Dylan playing "Soon" in "Celebrating Gershwin."

GREAT PERFORMANCES
Music Programs

The following has been used to describe the music programs:

LFLC = LIVE FROM LINCOLN CENTER

TITLE
Works (Composer), Conductor
Performing Ensemble, Season
AWARDS

AARON COPLAND'S 85TH BIRTHDAY, LFLC
Mehta, Bernstein
New York Philharmonic, 1985–1986

ABBADO IN BERLIN: THE FIRST YEAR
Abbado
Berlin Philharmonic, 1991–1992

THE ABDUCTION FROM THE SERAGLIO
(Mozart), Stein
Salzburg Festival, 1989–1990

AIDA
(Verdi), Tchakarov
Houston Grand Opera, 1987–1988

ALL RICHARD STRAUSS PROGRAM
*Death and Transfiguration, Four Last Songs,
Till Eulenspiegel* (R. Strauss), Solti
Chicago Symphony, 1977–1978

AMAZING GRACE: AMERICA IN SONG
The Music Project Inc., 1976–1977

AN AMERICAN CHRISTMAS: WORDS AND MUSIC
1983–1984

ANDRÉ WATTS AND THE PHILHARMONIC, LFLC
*Celebrating Watts' 25th year with
the New York Philharmonic,* Mehta
New York Philharmonic, 1987–1988

ANDRÉ WATTS IN RECITAL, LFLC
1984–1985

THE ANDREW LLOYD WEBBER *REQUIEM*
Maazel, Orchestra of St. Luke's,
St. Thomas Choir, 1984–1985

ANTONY AND CLEOPATRA
(Barber), Buckley
Lyric Opera of Chicago, 1991–1992

**THE ART OF SINGING:
GOLDEN VOICES, SILVER SCREEN**
Documentary featuring Maria Callas, Enrico
Caruso, Kirsten Flagstad, and more
1997–1998

ASINAMALI!
(Ngema)
1987–1988

THE ASPERN PAPERS
(Argento), Rescigno
Dallas Opera, 1988–1989

BACH *CHRISTMAS ORATORIO,*
in 2 parts:
THE NATIVITY, THE EPIPHANY,
Harnoncourt, Concentus Musicus of Vienna,
Tolz Boys Choir, 1984–1985

BACH TO BACH, LFLC
Hogwood, Academy of Ancient Music
and Chamber Music
Society of Lincoln Center, 1984–1985

THE BALLAD OF BABY DOE, LFLC
(Moore), Somogi
New York City Opera, 1975–1976

THE BARBER OF SEVILLE
(Rossini), Abbado
La Scala, 1975–1976

THE BARBER OF SEVILLE, LFLC
(Rossini), Caldwell
New York City Opera, 1976–1977

**BAROQUE DUET: KATHLEEN BATTLE
AND WYNTON MARSALIS**
(Scarlatti, Handel, Bach)
1991–1992

BERLIN PHILHARMONIC
Don Quichotte (R. Strauss), *Overture* (Weber)
von Karajan
Berlin Philharmonic, 1978–1979

BERLIN PHILHARMONIC
Suite #2 in D minor (Bach), *Symphony #5*
(Beethoven), von Karajan
Berlin Philharmonic, 1974–1975

BERLIN PHILHARMONIC
Symphony #9 (Beethoven), von Karajan
Berlin Philharmonic, 1975–1976

BERLIN PHILHARMONIC
Symphony #2 (Brahms), *Coriolan Overture*
(Beethoven), von Karajan
Berlin Philharmonic, 1976–1977

BERLIN PHILHARMONIC
Symphony #4 (Brahms), von Karajan
Berlin Philharmonic, 1975–1976

BERNSTEIN AT 70
Bernstein, Ozawa, Tilson Thomas, Williams
Boston Symphony and Tanglewood Institute
1988–1989
EMMY

BERNSTEIN: CONDUCTOR, SOLOIST, TEACHER
Symphony #39, Piano Concerto #17 (Mozart)
Vienna Philharmonic, 1983–1984

**BERNSTEIN CONDUCTS HAYDN'S MASS
IN TIME OF WAR**
Bavarian Radio Orchestra, 1985–1986

BERNSTEIN CONDUCTS MAHLER
Symphony #1
Vienna Philharmonic, 1984–1985

BERNSTEIN CONDUCTS MAHLER
Symphony #2
London Symphony, 1980–1981

BERNSTEIN CONDUCTS MAHLER
Symphony #5
Vienna Philharmonic, 1981–1982

BERNSTEIN CONDUCTS MAHLER
Symphony #6
Vienna Philharmonic, 1983–1984

BERNSTEIN CONDUCTS MAHLER
Symphony #8
Vienna Philharmonic, 1978–1979

BERNSTEIN CONDUCTS MAHLER
Symphony #9
Vienna Philharmonic, 1979–1980

BERNSTEIN CONDUCTS *WEST SIDE STORY*
rehearsals and recording sessions, (Bernstein)
1984–1985

BERNSTEIN IN TANGLEWOOD
Symphony #5 (Tchaikovsky), Bernstein
Boston Symphony Orchestra, 1974–1975

BERNSTEIN ON BRAHMS
Parts 4 and 5, *Symphony #2, Piano Concerto #1*
(Brahms), Bernstein
Vienna Philharmonic, 1986–1987

BERNSTEIN ON BRAHMS
Part 6, *Symphony #3* (Brahms), Bernstein
Vienna Philharmonic, 1987–1988

BERNSTEIN ON BRAHMS
—REFLECTIONS AND PERFORMANCE
Parts 1-3, *Academic Festival Overture, Serenade in A, Violin Concerto, Symphony #1* (Brahms), Bernstein
Vienna Philharmonic, 1985–1986

BERNSTEIN'S MASS
(Bernstein), Mauceri
Yale University, 1973–1974

BEST OF BROADWAY
Star-filled Gala, 1984–1985

BEVERLY! HER FAREWELL PERFORMANCE, LFLC
Act 2 of Die Fledermaus (J. Strauss), Rudel
New York City Opera Orchestra, 1980–1981

BLACK AND BLUE
1992–1993
(*A scene from* Black and Blue)

BOBBY MCFERRIN: LOOSELY MOZART—
THE NEW INNOVATORS OF CLASSICAL MUSIC
1996–1997

A BRAHMS LIEDER RECITAL
(Brahms)
1978–1979

BRANDENBURG CONCERTI
in 2 parts, (Bach), Harnoncourt
Concentus Musicus of Vienna, 1984–1985

BROADWAY SINGS: THE MUSIC OF JULE STYNE
Pippen
1986–1987
EMMY

BURT BACHARACH: THIS IS NOW
Documentary featuring clips of Marlene Dietrich, Dusty Springfield, Tom Jones, Aretha Franklin, and Dionne Warwick
1996–1997

THE CABINET OF DR. RAMIREZ
Adapted from the silent film
The Cabinet of Dr. Caligari, (Adams)
1992–1993

CANDIDE, LFLC
(Bernstein), Bernstein
New York City Opera, 1986–1987

CAPRICCIO
(R. Strauss), Stein
Salzburg Festival, Vienna Philharmonic
1991–1992

CARLOS KLEIBER CONDUCTS BEETHOVEN
Symphonies #4, #7 (Beethoven), Kleiber
Concertgebouw Orchestra, 1986–1987

CARMEN, LFLC
(Bizet), Keene
New York City Opera, 1984–1985

CARMEN
(Bizet), Kleiber
Vienna State Opera, 1979–1980

A CARNEGIE HALL CHRISTMAS CONCERT
Previn
Orchestra of St. Luke's, American Boychoir
1991–1992

CARNEGIE HALL OPENING NIGHT 1994
(Mozart, Berlioz, Rossini, Bellini), Marriner
Academy of St. Martin-in-the-Fields, 1994–1995

CARNEGIE HALL OPENING NIGHT 1995
(Tchaikovsky), Ozawa
Boston Symphony Orchestra, 1995–1996

CARNEGIE HALL OPENING NIGHT 1996
(Brahms), Abbado
Berlin Philharmonic Orchestra, 1996–1997

CARNEGIE HALL OPENING NIGHT 1997
(Elgar, Tchaikovsky), Barenboim
Chicago Symphony Orchestra, 1997–1998

CARNEGIE HALL SALUTES THE JAZZ MASTERS
1993–1994

CAVALLERIA RUSTICANA
(Mascagni), Prêtre
La Scala, 1985–1986
EMMY

CAVALLERIA RUSTICANA
(Mascagni), von Karajan
La Scala, 1977–1978

CELEBRATING GERSHWIN
2-part series:
THE JAZZ AGE, 'S WONDERFUL!
(Gershwin), Tilson Thomas
1987–1988
EMMY

CHAMBER MUSIC SOCIETY
OF LINCOLN CENTER, LFLC
(Bach, Beethoven, Tchaikovsky)
Chamber Music Society of Lincoln Center
1980–1981

CHAMBER MUSIC SOCIETY
OF LINCOLN CENTER, LFLC
(Beethoven, Brahms, Mendelssohn)
Chamber Music Society of Lincoln Center
1978–1979

CHAMBER MUSIC SOCIETY
OF LINCOLN CENTER, LFLC
Chamber Music Society of Lincoln Center
1982–1983

CHAMBER MUSIC SOCIETY
OF LINCOLN CENTER, LFLC
Chamber Music Society of Lincoln Center
1985–1986

CHRISTMAS WITH FLICKA
Frederica von Stade Sings
Christmas Music from Austria, Rudel
1987–1988

CINDERELLA
(Rossini), Chailly
Salzburg Festival, Vienna Philharmonic
1988–1989

CINDERELLA, LFLC
(Rossini), Salesky
New York City Opera, 1980–1981

CONCERTGEBOUW ORCHESTRA
Piano Concerto #3 (Beethoven),
Piano Concerto #1 (Brahms), Haitink
Concertgebouw Orchestra, 1974–1975

THE CONSUL
(Menotti), Keene
Spoleto Festival U.S.A., 1977–1978

COPLAND CONDUCTS COPLAND
Clarinet Concerto (Copland), Copland
Los Angeles Philharmonic, 1975–1976

THE CORONATION OF POPPEA
(Monteverdi), Harnoncourt
Zurich Opera, 1980–1981

THE COTTON CLUB REMEMBERED
Cab Calloway and friends, Cohen
1985–1986

CREATING RAGTIME
Documentary
1997–1998

THE CUNNING LITTLE VIXEN, LFLC
(Janacek), Bergeson
New York City Opera, 1983–1984

THE DANGEROUS LIAISONS
(Susa), Runnicles
San Francisco Opera, 1994–1995

DAS LIED VON DER ERDE
(Mahler), Bernstein
Israel Philharmonic, 1976–1977

DER ROSENKAVALIER
(R. Strauss), Kleiber
Bavarian State Opera, 1980–1981

DIDO AND AENEAS
Film adaptation, (Purcell)
1995–1996

DIE FLEDERMAUS
(J. Strauss), Boehm
Vienna Philharmonic, 1981–1982

DIE ZAUBERFLÖTE, LFLC
(Mozart), Comissiona
New York City Opera, 1987–1988

DIVAS
Documentary featuring clips of Maria Callas,
Joan Sutherland, Jessye Norman, Montserrat
Caballe, and others
1995–1996

DON GIOVANNI
(Mozart), von Karajan
Salzburg Festival, 1987–1988

DOWN IN THE VALLEY
(Weill), Davis
1983–1984

EINSTEIN ON THE BEACH:
THE CHANGING IMAGE OF OPERA
Documentary, (Glass)
BAM/Next Wave Festival, 1985–1986

EL GATO MONTES
FROM THE LOS ANGELES OPERA
Penella
Los Angeles Opera, 1994–1995

ELEKTRA
(R. Strauss), Boehm
Vienna Philharmonic, 1985–1986

THE ELIXIR OF LOVE
(Donizetti)
Lyon National Opera, 1997–1998

ELLINGTON: THE MUSIC LIVES ON
1982–1983

EMMELINE FROM THE SANTA FE OPERA
(Picker), Manahan
Santa Fe Opera, 1996–1997

AN EVENING WITH ALAN JAY LERNER
1989–1990

AN EVENING WITH DANNY KAYE, LFLC
New York Philharmonic, 1981–1982

AN EVENING WITH ITZHAK PERLMAN, LFLC
Violin Concerto in D major (Brahms),
Violin Concerto in E minor (Mendelssohn),
(Vivaldi), Zinman
New York Philharmonic, 1981–1982

AN EVENING WITH PLÁCIDO DOMINGO, LFLC
deMain
New York City Opera Orchestra, 1986–1987

FALSTAFF
(Verdi), Solti
Vienna Philharmonic, Deutsche Oper Berlin,
1985–1986

FAUST
(Gounod), Prêtre
Lyric Opera of Chicago, 1979–1980

A FAUST SYMPHONY
(Liszt), Bernstein
Boston Symphony, 1976–1977

FESTIVAL! SPOLETO, U.S.A.
1982–1983

FIDELIO
(Beethoven), Bernstein
Vienna State Opera, 1978–1979

FOLLIES IN CONCERT
(Sondheim)
1985–1986

THE FOUR SEASONS
(Vivaldi)
English Chamber Orchestra, 1983–1984

THE FRED ASTAIRE SONGBOOK
Documentary
1990–1991

FROM VIENNA:
THE NEW YEAR'S CELEBRATION 1995
Mehta
Vienna Philharmonic, 1994–1995

FROM VIENNA:
THE NEW YEAR'S CELEBRATION 1996
Maazel
Vienna Philharmonic, 1995–1996

FROM VIENNA:
THE NEW YEAR'S CELEBRATION 1997
Muti
Vienna Philharmonic, 1996–1997

FROM VIENNA:
THE NEW YEAR'S CELEBRATION 1998
Mehta
Vienna Philharmonic, Vienna Choir Boys,
1997–1998

THE GERSHWINS' PORGY AND BESS
(Gershwin)
Glyndebourne Festival, 1993–1994

GIAN CARLO MENOTTI: THE MUSICAL MAGICIAN
1986–1987

THE GIRL OF THE GOLDEN WEST
(Puccini), Slatkin
Metropolitan Opera, 1991–1992

THE GOSPEL AT COLONUS
(Telson)
Brooklyn Academy of Music, 1985–1986
INTERNATIONAL FILM & TV FESTIVAL
OF NEW YORK

GOYA
(Menotti), de Burgos
Washington Opera, 1986–1987
EMMY

GREAT RUSSIAN THEATER MUSIC, LFLC
Mehta
New York Philharmonic, 1984–1985

GUYS AND DOLLS OFF THE RECORD
Documentary on original cast recording session
1992–1993

HANSEL AND GRETEL
(Humperdinck), Solti
Vienna Philharmonic, 1986–1987

HARRY CONNICK, JR. & HIS ORCHESTRA:
SWINGING OUT WITH HARRY
1990–1991

THE HUMAN VOICE, LA VOIX HUMAINE
double-bill of play and opera
(Poulenc)
1979–1980

AN IMMIGRANT'S AMERICA: SCHELOMO
(Bloch), Maazel
Cleveland Orchestra, 1975–1976

IN CONCERT: NEW JERSEY CHAMBER MUSIC
SOCIETY AND TOKYO STRING QUARTET
1987–1988

IRA GERSHWIN AT 100:
A CELEBRATION AT CARNEGIE HALL
1996–1997

IRVING BERLIN'S AMERICA—A SALUTE TO THE
COMPOSER OF AMERICA'S FAVORITE SONGS
1985–1986

ITZHAK PERLMAN: IN THE FIDDLER'S HOUSE
1995–1996
EMMY, GOLDEN ROSE INTERNATIONAL
COMPETITION-MONTREAUX

JAMES GALWAY AND MOSTLY MOZART, LFLC
Schwarz
Mostly Mozart Festival Orchestra, 1981–1982

JERRY HERMAN'S BROADWAY AT THE BOWL
1993–1994

JOAN SUTHERLAND AND LUCIANO PAVAROTTI, LFLC
Bonynge
New York Philharmonic, 1978–1979

JOAN SUTHERLAND AND MARILYN HORNE
IN CONCERT, LFLC
Bonynge
New York Philharmonic, 1979–1980

JOHN BARRY'S MOVIOLA
Documentary
1992–1993

JOSE CARRERAS, DIANA ROSS,
PLÁCIDO DOMINGO: CHRISTMAS IN VIENNA
Sutej
Vienna Symphony, Gumpoldskirchner
Children's Choir, 1992–1993

JUDY GARLAND: THE CONCERT YEARS
Documentary
1984–1985

JUILLIARD AT 80, LFLC
Mester and Falletta
Juilliard Orchestras/Music School/Dance
Ensemble/Theater Center, 1985–1986

JUILLIARD STRING QUARTET PLAYS BEETHOVEN
Quartets: Op. 18, #4, Op. 59, #1 (Beethoven)
Juilliard String Quartet, 1977–1978

JULIE ANDREWS: BACK ON BROADWAY
Documentary
1995–1996

JULIE ANDREWS IN CONCERT
Fraser
1989–1990
EMMY

**KATHLEEN BATTLE AND JESSYE NORMAN
SING SPIRITUALS**
Levine
1990–1991

KOYAANISQATSI
Film with Philip Glass score, (Glass)
1984–1985

L'AFRICAINE
(Meyerbeer), Mansouri
San Francisco Opera, 1989–1990

LA BOHÈME FROM AUSTRALIAN OPERA
(Puccini), Smith
Australian Opera, 1993–1994

LA CENERENTOLA
(Rossini), Abbado
La Scala, 1983–1984

LA CENERENTOLA FROM HOUSTON
(Rossini), Campanella
Houston Grand Opera, 1995–1996

LA CLEMENZA DI TITO
(Mozart), Levine
Vienna Philharmonic, 1981–1982

LA RONDINE, LFLC
(Puccini), Siciliani
New York City Opera, 1985–1986

LEAN BY JARRE
Chicago Symphony Orchestra, 1992–1993

**LEGENDARY MAESTROS:
THE ART OF CONDUCTING**
1994–1995

LENA HORNE: THE LADY AND HER MUSIC
1984–1985

LEONARD BERNSTEIN: THE GIFT OF MUSIC
Documentary
1993–1994

LES MISÉRABLES IN CONCERT
(Boublil and Schönberg)
1995–1996
*(Colm Wilkinson as Jean Valjean and Philip Quast
as Javert in* Les Misérables)

THE LIFE OF VERDI
6-part series
1983-1984

**LINCOLN CENTER FANFARE—
25TH ANNIVERSARY,** LFLC
1984–1985

LINDA RONSTADT: CANCIONES DE MI PADRE
Ballet Folklorico de la Fonda, 1988–1989
EMMY

LOS ANGELES PHILHARMONIC
Bassoon Concerto (Mozart), *Concerto for Orchestra*
(Bartok), Mehta
Los Angeles Philharmonic, 1977–1978

LUCIA DI LAMMERMOOR, LFLC
(Donizetti), Somogi
New York City Opera, 1981–1982

LUCIANO PAVAROTTI IN CONCERT, LFLC
Metropolitan Opera Orchestra, 1977–1978

LUCIANO PAVAROTTI: MY WORLD
Documentary
1995–1996

MACBETH
(Verdi), Stapleton
London Symphony Orchestra, 1978–1979

MADAMA BUTTERFLY
(Puccini), Gomez-Martinez
Lyric Opera of Chicago, 1988–1989

MADAMA BUTTERFLY
(Puccini), Jean-Pierre Ponnelle film, von Karajan
Vienna Philharmonic, 1976–1977

MADAMA BUTTERFLY, LFLC
(Puccini), Keene
New York City Opera, 1982–1983

MADAME BUTTERFLY
Film adaptation
1996–1997

THE MAESTROS OF PHILADELPHIA
Documentary featuring Stokowski, Ormandy,
Muti, and Sawallisch
1992–1993

THE MAGIC FLUTE
(Mozart), Levine
Salzburg Festival, Vienna State Opera
Orchestra, 1983–1984

MANON, LFLC
(Massenet), Rudel
New York City Opera, 1977–1978

**MARIA CALLAS:
AN INTERNATIONAL CELEBRATION**
1983–1984

**MARIA CALLAS: AN OPERATIC BIOGRAPHY—
THE WOMAN BEHIND THE DIVA**
1988–1989

MARILYN HORNE IN CONCERT, LFLC
Slatkin
American Symphony Orchestra, 1983–1984

THE MARRIAGE OF FIGARO
(Mozart), Boehm
Vienna State Opera, 1977–1978

A MASKED BALL
(Verdi), Levine
Metropolitan Opera, 1990–1991

MASS IN B MINOR
(Bach), Richter
Munich Bach Orchestra, 1973–1974

MEFISTOFELE
(Boito), Arena
San Francisco Opera, 1990–1991

MELBA
4-part film
1988–1989

**THE METROPOLITAN OPERA SILVER
ANNIVERSARY GALA**
Levine
1991–1992

MIAMI'S NEW WORLD SYMPHONY
(Mahler), *Piano Concerto* (Tchaikovsky)
Tilson Thomas
New World Symphony, 1989–1990

THE MIKADO
(Gilbert and Sullivan), Robinson
English National Opera, 1988–1989

MILES AHEAD: THE MUSIC OF MILES DAVIS
1986–1987

MILES DAVIS: A TRIBUTE
1992–1993

THE MOST HAPPY FELLA
(Loesser)
1979–1980

MOSTLY MOZART FESTIVAL, LFLC
Schwarz
Mostly Mozart Orchestra, 1986–1987

MOSTLY MOZART MEETS SALIERI, LFLC
Schwarz
Mostly Mozart Orchestra, 1984–1985

MOZART IN SALZBURG
Levine
Vienna Philharmonic, 1989–1990

MOZART *REQUIEM*
(Mozart), Boehm
Vienna Symphony, 1974–1975

MUSIC BY RICHARD RODGERS
1989–1990

MUSIC FOR THE MOVIES:
THE HOLLYWOOD SOUND
Documentary
1995–1996

MUSIC FROM AMERICA:
NEW YORK PHILHARMONIC
Rhapsody in Blue (Gershwin), *Lincoln Portrait*
(Copland), Bernstein
New York Philharmonic, 1975–1976

THE MUSIC MAKERS:
AN ASCAP CELEBRATION OF AMERICAN MUSIC
1987–1988

THE MUSIC OF ALAN MENKEN:
A WHOLE NEW WORLD
1997–1998

THE MUSIC OF KANDER AND EBB:
RAZZLE DAZZLE
1997–1998

THE MUSIC OF KURT WEILL: SEPTEMBER SONGS
1994–1995

MUSICALS GREAT MUSICALS:
THE ARTHUR FREED UNIT AT MGM
1996–1997

NATALIE COLE'S UNTRADITIONAL
TRADITIONAL CHRISTMAS
New York Restoration Choir, 1995–1996

THE NEW JERSEY PERFORMING ARTS CENTER
OPENING NIGHT GALA
1997–1998

THE NEW MOON
(Romberg), Coleman
New York City Opera, 1988–1989

NEW YEAR'S EVE AT THE PHILHARMONIC, LFLC
Mehta
New York Philharmonic, 1987–1988

NEW YEAR'S EVE GALA, LFLC
Mehta
New York Philharmonic, 1984–1985

NEW YORK PHILHARMONIC, LFLC
(Brahms, Beethoven), Davis
New York Philharmonic, 1987–1988

NEW YORK PHILHARMONIC, LFLC
Egmont Overture, Piano Concerto #3 (Beethoven),
New World Symphony (Dvorak), Kubelik
New York Philharmonic, 1976–1977

NEW YORK PHILHARMONIC, LFLC
(Mozart, Verdi, Strauss), Mehta
New York Philharmonic, 1982–1983
EMMY

NEW YORK PHILHARMONIC, LFLC
(Mozart, Wagner, Stravinsky), Mehta
New York Philharmonic, 1977–1978

NEW YORK PHILHARMONIC, LFLC
Piano Concerto #1 (Grieg), *Ein Heldenleben*
(R. Strauss), Previn
New York Philharmonic, 1975–1976

NEW YORK PHILHARMONIC, LFLC
Piano Concerto #1 (Tchaikovsky), (Beethoven,
Bartok), Mehta
New York Philharmonic, 1979–1980

NEW YORK PHILHARMONIC, LFLC
Piano Concerto #2 (Brahms), *Also Sprach
Zarathustra* (R. Strauss), Leinsdorf
New York Philharmonic, 1977–1978

NEW YORK PHILHARMONIC, LFLC
Piano Concerto #4 (Beethoven), *Ein Heldenleben*
(R. Strauss), Mehta
New York Philharmonic, 1980–1981

NEW YORK PHILHARMONIC, LFLC
Piano Concerto #5 (Beethoven), (Wagner,
Prokofiev), Mehta
New York Philharmonic, 1978–1979

NEW YORK PHILHARMONIC, LFLC
(Strauss, Mozart), Mehta
New York Philharmonic, 1983–1984

NEW YORK PHILHARMONIC
Symphony #4 (Tchaikovsky), Bernstein
New York Philharmonic, 1975–1976
EMMY

NEW YORK PHILHARMONIC, LFLC
Symphony #9 (Beethoven), Mehta
New York Philharmonic, 1982–1983

NEW YORK PHILHARMONIC, LFLC
Violin Concerto (Tchaikovsky), (Stravinsky,
Moussorgsky), Mehta
New York Philharmonic, 1978–1979

NEW YORK PHILHARMONIC, LFLC
(Vivaldi, Telemann, Hindemith, Wagner), Mehta
New York Philharmonic, 1984–1985

NEW YORK PHILHARMONIC GALA, LFLC
Mehta
New York Philharmonic, 1985–1986

NEW YORK PHILHARMONIC
60TH BIRTHDAY CONCERT, LFLC
(Bach, Mozart, Vivaldi, Brahms), Mehta
New York Philharmonic, 1980–1981

THE NIGHT OF MUSIC: A GLOBAL CELEBRATION
1986–1987

NIXON IN CHINA
(Adams), de Main
Houston Grand Opera, 1987–1988
EMMY

OEDIPUS REX
(Stravinsky), Ozawa
1992–1993
EMMY

ON THE TOWN **IN CONCERT**
(Bernstein), Tilson Thomas
London Symphony Orchestra, 1993–1994

THE ORCHESTRA
Zbigniew Rybzynski's film interpretation
of six musical scores
1989–1990
EMMY, PRIX ITALIA

ORFEO
(Monteverdi), Harnoncourt
Zurich Opera, 1981–1982

ORMANDY AT 80
Symphony #2 (Rachmaninov), Ormandy
Philadelphia Orchestra, 1979–1980

ORMANDY CONDUCTS TCHAIKOVSKY
Violin Concerto (Tchaikovsky), Ormandy
Philadelphia Orchestra, 1980–1981

ORMANDY CONDUCTS
THE PHILADELPHIA ORCHESTRA
(Strauss, Wolf-Ferrari), Ormandy
Philadelphia Orchestra, 1981–1982

OTELLO
(Verdi), von Karajan
Deutsche Oper Berlin, 1986–1987

OZAWA
*Profile of the Japanese Conductor,
His Life and His Career*
Boston Symphony Orchestra, 1986–1987

PAGLIACCI
(Leoncavallo), Prêtre
La Scala, 1984–1985

PAGLIACCI
(Leoncavallo), von Karajan
La Scala, 1974–1975

PASSING THE BATON
*Solti and Barenboim
at the Chicago Symphony Orchestra*
1993–1994

PAUL MCCARTNEY'S *LIVERPOOL ORATORIO*
(McCartney), Davis
Royal Liverpool Philharmonic and Chorus
1991–1992

PAVAROTTI AND CHORAL ARTISTS
MEN'S CHORUS, LFLC
Mehta
New York Philharmonic, 1982–1983

PAVAROTTI AND THE ITALIAN TENOR
Documentary
1992–1993

PAVAROTTI IN CONCERT, LFLC
(Respighi, Paganini, Verdi, Donizetti, Puccini),
Mehta
New York Philharmonic, 1979–1980
EMMY

PAVAROTTI PLUS!, LFLC
Buckley
New York City Opera Orchestra, 1985–1986

PAVAROTTI RETURNS TO NAPLES
Documentary
1987–1988

PETE TOWNSHEND'S *PSYCHODERELICT*
(Townshend)
1993–1994

PETER SELLARS DIRECTS *COSÍ FAN TUTTE*
(Mozart), Smith
Vienna Symphony, 1990–1991

PETER SELLARS DIRECTS *DON GIOVANNI*
(Mozart), Smith
Vienna Symphony, 1990–1991

PETER SELLARS DIRECTS
THE MARRIAGE OF FIGARO
(Mozart), Smith
Vienna Symphony, 1990–1991

PETER, PAUL & MARY: LIFELINES
1995–1996

PHILADELPHIA ORCHESTRA
La Mer (Debussy), *Firebird* (Stravinsky)
Ormandy
Philadelphia Orchestra, 1978–1979

THE PHILADELPHIA ORCHESTRA AT WOLF TRAP
(Rachmaninov, Shostakovich, Britten),
Temirkanov
Philadelphia Orchestra, 1988–1989

PIANO RECITAL BY ANDRÉ WATTS, LFLC
(Liszt, Rachmaninov, Schubert, Gershwin)
1976–1977

PLÁCIDO DOMINGO CELEBRATES SEVILLE
Levine
Vienna Symphony, 1983–1984
EMMY

PLÁCIDO DOMINGO:
THE CONCERT FOR PLANET EARTH
1992–1993

THE PLANETS
(Holst), Ormandy
Philadelphia Orchestra, 1977–1978

PORGY AND BESS: AN AMERICAN VOICE
Documentary
1997–1998

PURLIE
Gary Geld, Ossie Davis, Philip Rose
1983–1984

QUARTET
Documentary featuring Kronos Quartet,
Modern Jazz Quartet, Gospel Elites, and others
1993–1994

THE QUEEN OF SPADES
(Tchaikovsky), Nelsson
Opera Company of Philadelphia, 1983–1984

THE RAKE'S PROGRESS
Film adaptation, (Stravinsky), Salonen
1995–1996

THE REAL MCTEAGUE
Documentary
(Bolcom)
Chicago Lyric Opera, 1992–1993

THE RETURN OF ULYSSES
(Monteverdi), Harnoncourt
Zurich Opera, 1981–1982

RICHARD TUCKER OPERA GALA
Conlon
Metropolitan Opera Orchestra, 1990–1991

RIGOLETTO
(Verdi), Chailly
Vienna Philharmonic, 1984–1985
EMMY

A *RING* **FOR TELEVISION**
8-part series:
DER RING DES NIBELUNGEN: DAS RHEINGOLD,
DIE WALKÜRE, SIEGFRIED, GÖTTERDÄMMERUNG
(Wagner), Boulez
Bayreuth Festival, 1982–1983

ROBERT ALTMAN'S JAZZ '34
1996–1997

ROSSINI IN VERSAILLES
(Rossini), Abbado
Chamber Orchestra of Europe, 1985–1986

ROSTROPOVICH PLAYS HAYDN
Cello Concerti #1, #2 (Haydn)
Academy of St. Martin-in-the-Fields Orchestra
1976–1977

RUBINSTEIN AT 90
Piano Concerto (Grieg), *Piano Concerto #2*
(Saint-Saëns), Previn
London Symphony, 1976–1977

RUBINSTEIN PLAYS CHOPIN
(Chopin), Previn
London Symphony, 1975–1976

THE SAINT OF BLEECKER STREET, LFLC
(Menotti), Kellogg
New York City Opera, 1977–1978

SALOME
(R. Strauss), Goetz Friedrich film, Boehm
Vienna State Opera Orchestra, 1976–1977

SAMSON ET DALILA
(Saint-Saëns), Rudel
San Francisco Opera, 1981–1982

THE SAN FRANCISCO OPERA
75TH ANNIVERSARY GALA
1997–1998

SCHUBERT MASS #6 IN E-FLAT MAJOR
(Schubert), Boehm
Vienna Boys Choir, Vienna Hofmusikkappelle
Orchestra, 1981–1982

SHE LOVES ME
(Bock)
1979–1980

SHOW BOAT
(Kern, Hammerstein II)
Paper Mill Playhouse, 1989–1990

A SOLDIER'S TALE
(Stravinsky), with animation, Schwarz
Los Angeles Chamber Orchestra, 1983–1984
(animation by R. O. Blechman)

SOLTI CONDUCTS MENDELSSOHN
Symphony #3, Violin Concerto (Mendelssohn)
Solti
Chicago Symphony, 1980–1981

SOLTI CONDUCTS MENDELSSOHN
Symphony #4, Midsummer Night's Dream
(Mendelssohn), Solti
Chicago Symphony, 1976–1977

SOLTI CONDUCTS ROSSINI
Overtures (Rossini), Solti
Chicago Symphony, 1982–1983

SOLTI CONDUCTS SCHUBERT
Symphonies #6, #8 (Schubert), Solti
Chicago Symphony, 1979–1980

SOLTI ON TOUR
Symphony #7 (Bruckner), Solti
Chicago Symphony, 1978–1979

SOLTI'S BEETHOVEN SYMPHONY #5 REVISITED
Symphony #5 (Beethoven), Solti
Chicago Symphony, 1989–1990

SOME ENCHANTED EVENING:
CELEBRATING OSCAR HAMMERSTEIN II
1994–1995

SONDHEIM: A CELEBRATION AT CARNEGIE HALL
American Theatre Orchestra, 1992–1993

THE SONGS OF SIX FAMILIES
Documentary
1993–1994

THE SORCERESS: KIRI TE KANAWA
(Handel)
1993–1994

SPIKE & CO.: DO IT A CAPPELLA
Documentary
1990–1991

ST. JOHN PASSION
(Bach), Richter
Munich Bach Orchestra, 1979–1980

ST. MATTHEW PASSION
in 2 parts
(Bach), Richter
Munich Bach Orchestra, 1975–1976

STEVE REICH: A NEW MUSICAL LANGUAGE
Tilson Thomas
Brooklyn Philharmonic, 1986–1987

THE STORY OF GOSPEL MUSIC
Documentary featuring Mahalia Jackson,
Aretha Franklin, and others
1996–1997

STREET SCENE, LFLC
(Weill), Mauceri
New York City Opera, 1979–1980

SUTHERLAND, HORNE, PAVAROTTI
IN CONCERT, LFLC
Bonynge
New York City Opera Orchestra, 1980–1981

SUTHERLAND IN *ANNA BOLENA,* LFLC
(Donizetti), Bonynge,
New York City Opera Orchestra, 1985–1986

SWEENEY TODD:
THE DEMON BARBER OF FLEET STREET
(Sondheim)
1984–1985
EMMYS

SYLVIA FINE KAYE'S
MUSICAL COMEDY TONIGHT
(Kern)
1985–1986
EMMYS

THE SYMPHONY OF RHYTHM:
SOLTI CONDUCTS BEETHOVEN'S SEVENTH
Symphony #7 (Beethoven), Solti
Chicago Symphony Orchestra, 1992–1993

TANNHÄUSER
(Wagner), Davis
Bayreuth Festival, 1979–1980

TESTIMONY
Tony Palmer film portrait of Dmitri
Shostakovich, Barshai
London Philharmonic, 1988–1989

THIRTY-TWO SHORT FILMS ABOUT GLENN GOULD
1995–1996

THOMAS HAMPSON: I HEAR AMERICA SINGING
Performance documentary featuring Marilyn
Horne, Frederica von Stade, Dawn Upshaw, and
others, performing music of Foster, Copland,
Bernstein, and others
1996–1997

TOSCA
(Puccini), Bartoletti
New York Philharmonic, 1978–1979

TOSCA FROM ROME
(Puccini)
1992–1993
EMMYS

TOSCANINI: THE MAESTRO
1987–1988

TURANDOT FROM THE SAN FRANCISCO OPERA
San Francisco Opera, 1993–1994

THE TURK IN ITALY, LFLC
(Rossini), Rudel
New York City Opera, 1978–1979

THE TURN OF THE SCREW
Czech film, (Britten), Davis
Covent Garden Chamber Ensemble, 1987–1988
(*Britten's* The Turn of the Screw)

TWO PHILHARMONIC ORCHESTRAS, LFLC
(Tchaikovsky, Bartok, Berlioz), Mehta
New York Philharmonic, Israel Philharmonic
1981–1982

UNFORGETTABLE, WITH LOVE: NATALIE COLE
SINGS THE SONGS OF NAT KING COLE
1991–1992
EMMY, NAACP IMAGE AWARD

VANESSA
(Barber), Keene
Spoleto Festival U.S.A., 1978–1979

VERDI *REQUIEM,* LFLC
(Verdi), Mehta
New York Philharmonic, 1980–1981

VERDI *REQUIEM*
(Verdi), von Karajan
La Scala Orchestra, 1977–1978

VIENNA PHILHARMONIC
Piano Concerto #2 (Brahms), Abbado
Vienna Philharmonic, 1981–1982

VIENNA PHILHARMONIC
Symphony #4 (Mahler), Bernstein
Vienna Philharmonic, 1975–1976

VIENNA PHILHARMONIC
Symphonies #34, #40, Minuet (Mozart), Boehm
Vienna Philharmonic, 1975–1976

VLADIMIR HOROWITZ: A REMINISCENCE
Documentary
1993–1994

VLADIMIR HOROWITZ: THE LAST ROMANTIC
1986–1987, EMMY

VON KARAJAN CONDUCTS BRUCKNER
Symphony #9 (Bruckner), von Karajan
Vienna Philharmonic, 1979–1980

VON KARAJAN IN SALZBURG
von Karajan
Vienna Philharmonic, 1987–1988

WAGNER
in 4 parts, Tony Palmer film, Solti
1986–1987

WILLIE STARK
(Floyd), de Main
Houston Grand Opera, 1981–1982

WOLF TRAP SALUTES DIZZY GILLESPIE:
A TRIBUTE TO THE JAZZ MASTER
1987–1988

WYNTON MARSALIS: BLUES AND SWING
Marsalis Quartet
1988–1989

ZUBIN MEHTA
AND THE NEW YORK PHILHARMONIC, LFLC
Tzigane (Ravel), *Symphony #5* (Tchaikovsky)
Mehta, New York Philharmonic, 1986–1987

FOLLOWING PAGE: *The Coronation of Poppea.*

GREAT PERFORMANCES

1972-1997

A THIRTEEN/WNET SERIES ON PBS

JAC VENZA
Executive Producer

STAFF EXECUTIVES, PRODUCERS, AND DIRECTORS:

EMILE ARDOLINO
ANN BLUMENTHAL
MERRILL BROCKWAY
KEN CAVENDER
GARY CLARE
GLENN DUBOSE
RHODA GRAUER
DAVID GRIFFITHS
JAN GURA

DAVID HORN
GLENN JORDAN
VIRGINIA KASSEL
JUDY KINBERG
SUSAN LACY
LINDSAY LAW
DAVID LOXTON
RON MAXWELL
BILL MURPHY

KIMBERLY MYERS
BILL O'DONNELL
MITCH OWGANG
SAM PAUL
KIM POWERS
MARGARET SELBY
JOHN WALKER
PETER WEINBERG

SERIES FUNDERS:

The National Endowment for the Arts

The Corporation for Public Broadcasting

Public Television Viewers

Public Broadcasting Service (PBS)

Dorothy and Lewis Cullman

The Aaron Diamond Foundation

*The Ira and Leonore Gershwin
Philanthropic Fund*

*The LuEsther T. Mertz
Charitable Trust*

Murray and Belle Nathan

Exxon 1973 - 1988

Martin Marietta 1987 - 1991

Texaco 1990 - 1992

Duracell Inc. 1992 - 1994

Deluxe Corporation 1994 - 1996

The Chase Manhattan Corporation 1997 -

The Chase Manhattan Private Bank 1997 -

GREAT PERFORMANCES
Repertory List

This repertory listing is in alphabetical order within season, without repeat dates. The following abbreviations and symbols have been used:

DIA = DANCE IN AMERICA
LFLC = LIVE FROM LINCOLN CENTER
* = Videocassette available

TITLE
Author/(Composer)/Choreographer
Performing Ensemble

1972–1973

HOGAN'S GOAT
William Alfred

THE RIMERS OF ELDRITCH
Lanford Wilson
Circle Repertory Company

TO BE YOUNG, GIFTED AND BLACK *
adapted from Lorraine Hansberry

1973–1974

ANTIGONE
Jean Anouilh

BERNSTEIN'S MASS
(Bernstein)
Yale University

THE CEREMONY OF INNOCENCE
Ronald Ribman
American Place Theatre

THE CONTRACTOR
David Storey
Chelsea Theater Center

CYRANO DE BERGERAC
Edmond Rostand
American Conservatory Theatre

ENEMIES
Maxim Gorky
Repertory Theater of Lincoln Center

FEASTING WITH PANTHERS
Richard Cumming and Adrian Hall
Trinity Square Repertory

IN FASHION
adapted from Georges Feydeau
Actors Theatre of Louisville

JUNE MOON
George S. Kaufman and Ring Lardner

KING LEAR
William Shakespeare
New York Shakespeare Festival

MASS IN B MINOR
(Bach)
Munich Bach Orchestra

A MEMORY OF TWO MONDAYS
Arthur Miller

MONKEY, MONKEY, BOTTLE OF BEER
Martha Sheiness
Cincinnati Playhouse in the Park

PARADISE LOST
Clifford Odets

A TOUCH OF THE POET
Eugene O'Neill

THE WIDOWING OF MRS. HOLROYD
adapted from D.H. Lawrence
Long Wharf Theater

1974–1975

BERLIN PHILHARMONIC
(Bach, Beethoven)
Berlin Philharmonic

BERNSTEIN IN TANGLEWOOD
(Tchaikovsky)
Boston Symphony Orchestra

BROTHER TO DRAGONS
adapted from Robert Penn Warren
Trinity Square Repertory Co.

CONCERTGEBOUW ORCHESTRA
(Beethoven, Brahms)
Concertgebouw Orchestra

FORGET-ME-NOT LANE
Peter Nichols
Long Wharf Theatre

MOZART REQUIEM
(Mozart)
Vienna Symphony

PAGLIACCI
(Leoncavallo)
La Scala

RULES OF THE GAME
Luigi Pirandello
APA-Phoenix Theatre

THE SCHOOL FOR SCANDAL
Richard Sheridan
The Guthrie Theater

THE SEAGULL
Anton Chekhov
Williamstown Theatre Festival
(photo: Kevin McCarthy and Blythe Danner)

WHO'S HAPPY NOW?
Oliver Hailey
Mark Taper Forum

THE YEAR OF THE DRAGON
Frank Chin
American Place Theatre

ZALMEN OR THE MADNESS OF GOD
Elie Wiesel
Arena Stage

1975–1976

ALL OVER
Edward Albee
Hartford Stage Co.

AMERICAN BALLET THEATRE, LFLC *
American Ballet Theatre

THE BALLAD OF BABY DOE, LFLC
(Moore)
New York City Opera

THE BARBER OF SEVILLE
(Rossini)
La Scala

BERLIN PHILHARMONIC
(Beethoven)
Berlin Philharmonic

BERLIN PHILHARMONIC
(Brahms)
Berlin Philharmonic

BEYOND THE HORIZON
Eugene O'Neill
McCarter Theater Co.

CITY CENTER JOFFREY BALLET, DIA
Joffrey Ballet

COPLAND CONDUCTS COPLAND
(Copland)
Los Angeles Philharmonic

ECCENTRICITIES OF A NIGHTINGALE
Tennessee Williams
Old Globe Theater

THE FIRST BREEZE OF SUMMER
Leslie Lee
Negro Ensemble Co.

AN IMMIGRANT'S AMERICA: SCHELOMO
(Bloch)
Cleveland Orchestra

JENNIE: LADY RANDOLPH CHURCHILL
Julian Mitchell

MARTHA GRAHAM DANCE COMPANY, DIA *
Martha Graham Dance Co.

THE MOUND BUILDERS
Lanford Wilson
Circle Repertory Theater

MUSIC FROM AMERICA:
NEW YORK PHILHARMONIC
(Gershwin, Copland)
New York Philharmonic

NEW YORK PHILHARMONIC, LFLC
(Grieg, R. Srauss)
New York Philharmonic

NEW YORK PHILHARMONIC, LFLC
(Tchaikovsky)
New York Philharmonic

THE PATRIOTS
Sidney Kingsley
Asolo State Theater

PENNSYLVANIA BALLET, DIA
Pennsylvania Ballet

RUBINSTEIN PLAYS CHOPIN
(Chopin)
London Symphony

SEA MARKS
Gardner McKay
Manhattan Theatre Club

ST. MATTHEW PASSION
in 2 parts
(Bach)
Munich Bach Orchestra

SUE'S LEG/REMEMBERING THE THIRTIES, DIA
Twyla Tharp
Twyla Tharp Dance Co.

THE TIME OF YOUR LIFE
William Saroyan
The Acting Company

VIENNA PHILHARMONIC
(Mahler)
Vienna Philharmonic

VIENNA PHILHARMONIC
(Mozart)
Vienna Philharmonic

1976–1977

AH, WILDERNESS!
Eugene O'Neill
Long Wharf Theater

AMAZING GRACE: AMERICA IN SONG
The Music Project Inc.

AMERICAN BALLET THEATRE, DIA
American Ballet Theatre

AMERICAN BALLET THEATRE, LFLC
American Ballet Theatre

THE BARBER OF SEVILLE, LFLC*
(Rossini)
New York City Opera

BERLIN PHILHARMONIC
(Brahms, Beethoven)
Berlin Philharmonic

CHILDHOOD
5-part series:
BAA BAA BLACKSHEEP
adapted from Rudyard Kipling;
A GREAT DAY FOR BONZO
adapted from H.E. Bates;
EASTER TELLS SUCH DREADFUL LIES
adapted from Barbara Waring;
POSSESSIONS
adapted from George Ewart Evans;
AN ONLY CHILD
adapted from Frank O'Connor

THE CHRISTMAS CHESTER MYSTERY PLAYS

DANCE THEATRE OF HARLEM, DIA*
Dance Theatre of Harlem

DAS LIED VON DER ERDE
(Mahler)
Israel Philharmonic

THE EASTER CHESTER MYSTERY PLAYS
END OF SUMMER *
S.N. Behrman
Asolo State Theatre

A FAUST SYMPHONY
(Liszt)
Boston Symphony

HARD TIMES
4-part series
adapted from Charles Dickens

MADAMA BUTTERFLY
Jean-Pierre Ponnelle film
(Puccini)
Vienna Philharmonic

MERCE CUNNINGHAM DANCE COMPANY:
AN EVENT FOR TELEVISION, DIA
Merce Cunningham
Merce Cunningham Co.

NEW YORK PHILHARMONIC, LFLC
(Beethoven, Dvorak)
New York Philharmonic

PIANO RECITAL BY ANDRÉ WATTS, LFLC
(Liszt, Rachmaninov, Schubert, Gershwin)

PILOBOLUS DANCE THEATRE, DIA
Pilobolus Dance Theatre

THE PRINCE OF HOMBURG
Heinrich Von Kleist
Chelsea Theater Center

ROSTROPOVICH PLAYS HAYDN
(Haydn)
Academy of St. Martin-in-the-Fields

RUBINSTEIN AT 90
(Grieg, Saint-Saëns)
London Symphony

SALOME *
Goetz Friedrich film
(R. Strauss)
Vienna State Opera Orchestra

SECRET SERVICE
William Gillette
APA-Phoenix Theatre
(Photo: John Lithgow and Meryl Streep)

SOLTI CONDUCTS MENDELSSOHN
(Mendelssohn)
Chicago Symphony

THE TAMING OF THE SHREW ∗
William Shakespeare
American Conservatory Theatre

TRAILBLAZERS OF MODERN DANCE, DIA

WAITING FOR GODOT
Samuel Beckett
Los Angeles Actors Theatre

1977–1978

ABIDE WITH ME
J. Mitchell

ALL RICHARD STRAUSS PROGRAM
(R. Strauss)
Chicago Symphony

AMERICAN BALLET THEATRE, LFLC
American Ballet Theatre

THE ARCATA PROMISE
David Mercer

CAVALLERIA RUSTICANA
(Mascagni)
La Scala

CHOREOGRAPHY BY BALANCHINE—
PART 1 WITH THE NEW YORK CITY BALLET, DIA ∗
George Balanchine
New York City Ballet

CHOREOGRAPHY BY BALANCHINE
—PART 2 WITH THE NEW YORK CITY BALLET, DIA ∗
George Balanchine
New York City Ballet

THE CONSUL
(Menotti)
Spoleto Festival U.S.A.

COPPELIA, LFLC
George Balanchine
New York City Ballet

COUNT DRACULA
adapted from Bram Stoker
(photo: Louis Jourdan)

JUILLIARD STRING QUARTET
PLAYS BEETHOVEN
(Beethoven)
Juilliard String Quartet

LOS ANGELES PHILHARMONIC
(Mozart, Bartok)
Los Angeles Philharmonic

LUCIANO PAVAROTTI IN CONCERT, LFLC
Metropolitan Opera Orchestra

MANON, LFLC ∗
(Massenet)
New York City Opera

THE MARRIAGE OF FIGARO ∗
(Mozart)
Vienna State Opera

NEW YORK PHILHARMONIC, LFLC
(Brahms, R. Strauss)
New York Philharmonic

NEW YORK PHILHARMONIC, LFLC
(Mozart, Wagner, Stravinsky)
New York Philharmonic

THE NORMAN CONQUESTS
3-part series
Alan Ayckbourn

OUT OF OUR FATHER'S HOUSE
adapted from Eve Merriam

PAUL TAYLOR DANCE COMPANY, DIA ∗
Paul Taylor
Paul Taylor Dance Co.

THE PLANETS
(Holst)
Philadelphia Orchestra

PROFESSIONAL FOUL
Tom Stoppard

THE ROYAL FAMILY
Edna Ferber and George S. Kaufman
APA-Phoenix Theater

THE SAINT OF BLEECKER STREET, LFLC
(Menotti)
New York City Opera

SAN FRANCISCO BALLET: ROMEO AND JULIET, DIA
Michael Smuin
San Francisco Ballet

SARAH
Profile of Sarah Bernhardt
Suzanne Grossman

SHOOTING THE CHANDELIER
David Mercer

TARTUFFE
Molière
Circle in the Square

THE TRIAL OF THE MOKE
Daniel Stein
Milwaukee Repertory Theater

UNCOMMON WOMEN AND OTHERS ∗
Wendy Wasserstein
APA-Phoenix Theater

VERDI REQUIEM, LFLC ∗
Giuseppe Verdi
La Scala Orchestra

VERNA, USO GIRL
adapted from Paul Gallico

1978–1979

AMERICAN BALLET THEATRE, LFLC
American Ballet Theatre

BERLIN PHILHARMONIC
(R. Strauss, Weber)
Berlin Philharmonic

BERNSTEIN CONDUCTS MAHLER
(Mahler)
Vienna Philharmonic

A BRAHMS LIEDER RECITAL
(Brahms)

CHAMBER MUSIC SOCIETY OF LINCOLN CENTER,
LFLC
(Beethoven, Brahms, Mendelssohn)
Chamber Music Society of Lincoln Center

CHOREOGRAPHY BY BALANCHINE—
PART 3 WITH THE NEW YORK CITY BALLET, DIA ∗
George Balanchine
New York City Ballet

CHOREOGRAPHY BY BALANCHINE—
PART 4 WITH THE NEW YORK CITY BALLET, DIA ∗
George Balanchine
New York City Ballet

THE COLLECTION
Harold Pinter

THE FELD BALLET, DIA
Elliot Feld
Feld Ballet

FIDELIO
(Beethoven)
Vienna State Opera

THE GOOD DOCTOR
Neil Simon

JOAN SUTHERLAND AND LUCIANO PAVAROTTI, LFLC
New York Philharmonic

MACBETH
(Verdi)
London Symphony Orchestra

MARTHA GRAHAM DANCE COMPANY:
CLYTEMNESTRA, DIA*
Martha Graham
Martha Graham Dance Co.

A MONTH IN THE COUNTRY
Frederick Ashton
Royal Ballet Co.

MOURNING BECOMES ELECTRA
5-part series
Eugene O'Neill

NEW YORK PHILHARMONIC, LFLC
(Beethoven, Wagner, Prokofiev)
New York Philharmonic

NEW YORK PHILHARMONIC, LFLC
(Tchaikovsky, Stravinsky, Mussorgsky)
New York Philharmonic

PHILADELPHIA ORCHESTRA
(Debussy, Stravinsky)
Philadelphia Orchestra

SOLTI ON TOUR
(Bruckner)
Chicago Symphony

THANK YOU, COMRADES
James Hawkins

TOSCA
(Puccini)
New York Philharmonic

THE TURK IN ITALY, LFLC
(Rossini)
New York City Opera

VANESSA
(Barber)
Spoleto Festival U.S.A.

WHEN HELL FREEZES OVER I'LL SKATE
Vinnette Carroll

1979–1980

AMERICAN BALLET THEATRE, DIA
American Ballet Theatre

BERNSTEIN CONDUCTS MAHLER
(Mahler)
Vienna Philharmonic

BEYOND THE MAINSTREAM, DIA

CARMEN
(Bizet)
Vienna State Opera

DIVINE DRUMBEATS:
KATHERINE DUNHAM AND HER PEOPLE, DIA
Katherine Dunham

THE DREAM
Frederick Ashton
Royal Ballet Co.

FAUST
(Gounod)
Lyric Opera of Chicago

HAPPY DAYS
Samuel Beckett
New York Shakespeare Festival

THE HUMAN VOICE, *LA VOIX HUMAINE*
double-bill of play and opera
(Poulenc)

JOAN SUTHERLAND
AND MARILYN HORNE IN CONCERT, LFLC
New York Philharmonic

A LIFE IN THE THEATRE
David Mamet

MOLIÈRE
Ariane Mnouchkine

THE MOST HAPPY FELLA
(Loesser)

NEW YORK PHILHARMONIC, LFLC
(Tchaikovsky, Beethoven, Bartok)
New York Philharmonic

ON GIANT'S SHOULDERS
Michael Robson and Marjorie Wallace

ORMANDY AT 80
(Rachmaninov)
Philadelphia Orchestra

PAVAROTTI IN CONCERT, LFLC
(Respighi, Paganini, Verdi, Donizetti, Puccini)
New York Philharmonic

SHE LOVES ME *
(Bock)

SOLTI CONDUCTS SCHUBERT
(Schubert)
Chicago Symphony

ST. JOHN PASSION
(Bach)
Munich Bach Orchestra

STREET SCENE, LFLC
(Weill)
New York City Opera

TANNHÄUSER
(Wagner)
Bayreuth Festival

THREE JOHN CHEEVER STORIES:
THE SORROWS OF GIN, O YOUTH AND BEAUTY!,
THE FIVE FORTY-EIGHT *
adapted from John Cheever

A TRIBUTE TO JOHN HUSTON
Film Society of Lincoln Center

TWO DUETS: CHOREOGRAPHY BY
JEROME ROBBINS AND PETER MARTINS, DIA
New York City Ballet

VON KARAJAN CONDUCTS BRUCKNER
(Bruckner)
Vienna Philharmonic

1980–1981

AMERICAN DANCE FESTIVAL: PILOBOLUS, DIA
Pilobolus Dance Theatre

BERNSTEIN CONDUCTS MAHLER
(Mahler)
London Symphony

BEVERLY! HER FAREWELL PERFORMANCE, LFLC
(J. Strauss)
New York City Opera Orchestra

BIG BLONDE
adapted from Dorothy Parker
(photo: John Lithgow)

CHAMBER MUSIC SOCIETY OF LINCOLN CENTER,
LFLC
(Bach, Beethoven, Tchaikovsky)
Chamber Music Society of Lincoln Center

CINDERELLA, LFLC
(Rossini)
New York City Opera

THE CORONATION OF POPPEA
(Monteverdi)
Zurich Opera

DER ROSENKAVALIER
(R. Strauss)
Bavarian State Opera

AN EVENING WITH AMERICAN BALLET THEATRE,
LFLC
American Ballet Theatre

GIRLS IN THEIR SUMMER DRESSES **AND OTHER**
STORIES: *GIRLS IN THEIR SUMMER DRESSES,*
THE MONUMENT, THE MAN WHO MARRIED
A FRENCH WIFE
adapted from Irwin Shaw
GUESTS OF THE NATION
adapted from Frank O'Connor
Colonnades Theater Lab

LIFE ON THE MISSISSIPPI*
adapted from Mark Twain

NEW YORK PHILHARMONIC, LFLC
(Beethoven, R. Strauss)
New York Philharmonic

**NEW YORK PHILHARMONIC
60TH BIRTHDAY CONCERT,** LFLC
(Bach, Mozart, Vivaldi, Brahms)
New York Philharmonic

**NUREYEV AND THE JOFFREY BALLET:
IN TRIBUTE TO NIJINSKY,** DIA*
Joffrey Ballet

ORMANDY CONDUCTS TCHAIKOVSKY
(Tchaikovsky)
Philadelphia Orchestra

**THE PRIVATE HISTORY
OF A CAMPAIGN THAT FAILED**
adapted from Mark Twain

SOLTI CONDUCTS MENDELSSOHN
(Mendelssohn)
Chicago Symphony

THE SPELLBOUND CHILD WITH
THE NEW YORK CITY BALLET, DIA
George Balanchine
New York City Ballet

STAYING ON

SUTHERLAND, HORNE, PAVAROTTI IN CONCERT,
LFLC
New York City Opera Orchestra

THE TEMPEST: LIVE WITH
THE SAN FRANCISCO BALLET, DIA
Michael Smuin
San Francisco Ballet

TINKER, TAILOR, SOLDIER, SPY*
7-part series
adapted from John le Carré

VERDI REQUIEM, LFLC
(Verdi)
New York Philharmonic

1981-1982

BERNSTEIN CONDUCTS MAHLER
(Mahler)
Vienna Philharmonic

BOURNONVILLE DANCES, DIA
Auguste Bournonville
New York City Ballet

BRIDESHEAD REVISITED*
11-part series
adapted from Evelyn Waugh

DIE FLEDERMAUS
(J. Strauss)
Vienna Philharmonic

EDITH WHARTON
3-part series:
THE HOUSE OF MIRTH, SUMMER, LOOKING BACK
adapted from Edith Wharton

AN EVENING WITH DANNY KAYE, LFLC*
New York Philharmonic

AN EVENING WITH ITZHAK PERLMAN, LFLC
(Brahms, Mendelssohn, Vivaldi)
New York Philharmonic

JAMES GALWAY AND MOSTLY MOZART, LFLC*
Mostly Mozart Festival Orchestra

LA CLEMENZA DI TITO
(Mozart)
Vienna Philharmonic

LUCIA DI LAMMERMOOR, LFLC
(Donizetti)
New York City Opera

MRS. REINHARDT*
Edna O'Brien

ORFEO
(Monteverdi)
Zurich Opera

**ORMANDY CONDUCTS
THE PHILADELPHIA ORCHESTRA**
Philadelphia Orchestra

PAUL TAYLOR: THREE MODERN CLASSICS, DIA
Paul Taylor
Paul Taylor Dance Co.

PAUL TAYLOR: TWO LANDMARK DANCES, DIA
Paul Taylor
Paul Taylor Dance Co.

THE RETURN OF ULYSSES
(Monteverdi)
Zurich Opera

SAMSON ET DALILA*
(Saint-Saëns)
San Francisco Opera

SCHUBERT MASS #6 IN E-FLAT MAJOR
(Schubert)
*Vienna Boys Choir, Vienna Hofmusikkappelle
Orchestra*

A TRIBUTE TO BILLY WILDER
Film Society of Lincoln Center

TWO PHILHARMONIC ORCHESTRAS, LFLC
(Tchaikovsky, Bartok, Berlioz)
New York Philharmonic, Israel Philharmonic

VIENNA PHILHARMONIC
(Brahms)
Vienna Philharmonic

WILLIE STARK
(Floyd)
Houston Grand Opera

1982–1983

BALANCHINE CELEBRATES STRAVINSKY, DIA
George Balanchine
New York City Ballet

THE CATHERINE WHEEL, DIA*
Twyla Tharp
Twyla Tharp Dance Co.

CHAMBER MUSIC SOCIETY OF LINCOLN CENTER,
LFLC
Chamber Music Society of Lincoln Center

THE CHARTERHOUSE OF PARMA
adapted from Marie-Henri Stendhal

ELLINGTON: THE MUSIC LIVES ON

FESTIVAL! SPOLETO, U.S.A.

**THE GREAT PERFORMANCES
10TH ANNIVERSARY SPECIAL**

THE GREEN TABLE WITH THE JOFFREY BALLET,
DIA
Kurt Jooss
Joffrey Ballet Co.

THE INNOCENTS ABROAD
adapted from Mark Twain

MADAMA BUTTERFLY, LFLC
(Puccini)
New York City Opera

THE MAGIC FLUTE WITH
THE NEW YORK CITY BALLET, DIA
Peter Martins
New York City Ballet

THE MYSTERIOUS STRANGER
adapted from Mark Twain

NEW YORK PHILHARMONIC, LFLC
(Beethoven)
New York Philharmonic

NEW YORK PHILHARMONIC, LFLC*
(Mozart, Verdi, R. Strauss)
New York Philharmonic

**PAVAROTTI AND CHORAL ARTISTS
MEN'S CHORUS,** LFLC
New York Philharmonic

THE REGARD OF FLIGHT
Bill Irwin
American Place Theatre

A RING FOR TELEVISION*
8-part series:
**DER RING DES NIBELUNGEN: DAS RHEINGOLD,
DIE WALKÜRE, SIEGFRIED, GÖTTERDÄMMERUNG**
(Wagner), *Bayreuth Festival*

SOLTI CONDUCTS ROSSINI
(Rossini)
Chicago Symphony

STRAVINSKY AND BALANCHINE:
GENIUS HAS A BIRTHDAY, LFLC
George Balanchine
New York City Ballet

1983–1984

ALICE IN WONDERLAND *
adapted from Lewis Carroll

AMERICAN BALLET THEATRE:
DON QUIXOTE, DIA*
American Ballet Theatre

AN AMERICAN CHRISTMAS: WORDS AND MUSIC

BALANCHINE, PARTS I AND II, DIA
Documentary

BERNSTEIN: CONDUCTOR, SOLOIST, TEACHER
(Mozart)
Vienna Philharmonic

BERNSTEIN CONDUCTS MAHLER
(Mahler)
Vienna Philharmonic

BUDDENBROOKS
9-part series
adapted from Thomas Mann

A CHOREOGRAPHER'S NOTEBOOK: STRAVINSKY
PIANO BALLETS BY PETER MARTINS, DIA
Peter Martins
New York City Ballet

THE CUNNING LITTLE VIXEN, LFLC
(Janacek)
New York City Opera

DOWN IN THE VALLEY
Kurt Weill

THE FOUR SEASONS
(Vivaldi)
English Chamber Orchestra

LA CENERENTOLA *
(Rossini)
La Scala

THE LIFE OF VERDI
6-part series

THE MAGIC FLUTE
(Mozart)
Salzburg Festival, Vienna State Opera Orchestra

MARIA CALLAS:
AN INTERNATIONAL CELEBRATION

MARILYN HORNE IN CONCERT, LFLC
American Symphony Orchestra

NEW YORK PHILHARMONIC, LFLC
(R. Strauss, Mozart)
New York Philharmonic

PLÁCIDO DOMINGO CELEBRATES SEVILLE
Vienna Symphony

PRINCESS GRACE REMEMBERED
Nancy Reagan, narrator

PURLIE
Gary Geld, Ossie Davis, Philip Rose

THE QUEEN OF SPADES
(Tchaikovsky)
Opera Company of Philadelphia

SAN FRANCISCO BALLET:
A SONG FOR DEAD WARRIORS, DIA
Michael Smuin
San Francisco Ballet

A SOLDIER'S TALE *
(Stravinsky), with animation
Los Angeles Chamber Orchestra

A TRIBUTE TO BALANCHINE, LFLC
George Balanchine
New York City Ballet

1984–1985

AMERICAN BALLET THEATRE AT THE MET, DIA*
American Ballet Theatre

ANDRÉ WATTS IN RECITAL, LFLC*

THE ANDREW LLOYD WEBBER *REQUIEM* *
(Webber)
Orchestra of St. Luke's, St. Thomas Choir

BACH *CHRISTMAS ORATORIO*
in 2 parts:
THE NATIVITY, THE EPIPHANY
(Bach)
Concentus Musicus of Vienna, Tolz Boys Choir

BACH TO BACH, LFLC
(Bach)
*Academy of Ancient Music and Chamber Music
Society of Lincoln Center*

BARYSHNIKOV BY THARP
WITH AMERICAN BALLET THEATRE, DIA*
Twyla Tharp
American Ballet Theatre

BERNSTEIN CONDUCTS MAHLER
(Mahler)
Vienna Philharmonic

BERNSTEIN CONDUCTS *WEST SIDE STORY* *
(Bernstein), rehearsals and recording sessions

BEST OF BROADWAY
Star-filled Gala

BRANDENBURG CONCERTI
in 2 parts
(Bach)
Concentus Musicus of Vienna

CARMEN, LFLC
(Bizet)
New York City Opera

DANCE BLACK AMERICA
Alvin Ailey American Dance Theatre

THE DINING ROOM *
A.R. Gurney
Astor Place Theatre

AN ENGLISHMAN ABROAD *
Alan Bennett

AN EVENING OF DANCE AND CONVERSATION
WITH MARTHA GRAHAM, DIA
Martha Graham
Martha Graham Dance Co.

GREAT RUSSIAN THEATER MUSIC, LFLC
New York Philharmonic

JUDY GARLAND: THE CONCERT YEARS

KOYAANISQATSI
(Glass), film with Philip Glass score

LENA HORNE: THE LADY AND HER MUSIC *

LINCOLN CENTER FANFARE—
25TH ANNIVERSARY, LFLC

MAN FROM MOSCOW
3-part series, Greville Wynne

MOSTLY MOZART MEETS SALIERI, LFLC
Mostly Mozart Orchestra

NEW YEAR'S EVE GALA, LFLC
New York Philharmonic

NEW YORK PHILHARMONIC, LFLC
(Vivaldi, Telemann, Hindemith, Wagner)
New York Philharmonic

PAGLIACCI *
(Leoncavallo)
La Scala

RIGOLETTO
(Verdi)
Vienna Philharmonic

SWEENEY TODD:
THE DEMON BARBER OF FLEET STREET *
(Sondheim)

TAKING MY TURN
Will Holt

THE TAYLOR COMPANY: RECENT DANCES, DIA
Paul Taylor
Paul Taylor Dance Co.

TO THE LIGHTHOUSE
adapted from Virginia Woolf

YOU CAN'T TAKE IT WITH YOU
George S. Kaufman and Moss Hart

1985–1986

AARON COPLAND'S 85TH BIRTHDAY, LFLC
New York Philharmonic

**ALVIN AILEY AMERICAN DANCE THEATER:
THREE BY THREE,** DIA
Alvin Ailey American Dance Theater

**BERNSTEIN CONDUCTS HAYDN'S MASS
IN TIME OF WAR**
(Haydn)
Bavarian Radio Orchestra

**BERNSTEIN ON BRAHMS—
REFLECTIONS AND PERFORMANCE**
Parts 1-3
(Brahms)
Vienna Philharmonic

BOXES
Sydney (Aus.) Dance Co.

CAVALLERIA RUSTICANA
(Mascagni)
La Scala

**CHAMBER MUSIC SOCIETY OF LINCOLN
CENTER,** LFLC
Chamber Music Society of Lincoln Center

**CHOREOGRAPHY BY JEROME ROBBINS
WITH THE NEW YORK CITY BALLET,** DIA
Jerome Robbins
New York City Ballet

THE COTTON CLUB REMEMBERED

**DANCE THEATRE OF HARLEM IN
A STREETCAR NAMED DESIRE, DIA***
Dance Theatre of Harlem

DR. FISCHER OF GENEVA
adapted from Graham Greene

EARLY DAYS
David Storey

**EINSTEIN ON THE BEACH:
THE CHANGING IMAGE OF OPERA***
Documentary, (Glass)
BAM/Next Wave Festival

ELEKTRA
Goetz Friedrich film
(R. Strauss)
Vienna Philharmonic

FALSTAFF
(Verdi)
Vienna Philharmonic, Deutsche Oper Berlin

FOLLIES IN CONCERT*
(Sondheim)

THE GOSPEL AT COLONUS*
Bob Telson
Brooklyn Academy of Music

GROWN UPS
Jules Feiffer

HEARTBREAK HOUSE*
George Bernard Shaw

THE IMPORTANCE OF BEING EARNEST
Oscar Wilde

**IRVING BERLIN'S AMERICA: A SALUTE TO THE
COMPOSER OF AMERICA'S FAVORITE SONGS**

JUILLIARD AT 80, LFLC
*Juilliard Orchestras/Music School/Dance
Ensemble/Theater Center*

LA RONDINE, LFLC
(Puccini)
New York City Opera

LAURENCE OLIVIER: A LIFE
Documentary

MASTER HAROLD . . . AND THE BOYS*
Athol Fugard

A MIDSUMMER NIGHT'S DREAM, LFLC
George Balanchine
New York City Ballet

NEW YORK PHILHARMONIC GALA, LFLC
New York Philharmonic

ON THE RAZZLE
adapted from Johann Nestroy

PAVAROTTI PLUS!, LFLC
New York City Opera Orchestra

ROSSINI IN VERSAILLES
(Rossini)
Chamber Orchestra of Europe

SAN FRANCISCO BALLET IN *CINDERELLA,* DIA
Michael Smuin
San Francisco Ballet

SUTHERLAND IN *ANNA BOLENA,* LFLC
(Donizetti)
New York City Opera Orchestra

SYLVIA FINE KAYE'S MUSICAL COMEDY TONIGHT
(Kern)

1986–1987

AGNES, THE INDOMITABLE DE MILLE, DIA
Documentary

BARYSHNIKOV ON BROADWAY
with *A Chorus Line* cast

BERNSTEIN ON BRAHMS
Parts 4 and 5
(Brahms)
Vienna Philharmonic

BROADWAY SINGS: THE MUSIC OF JULE STYNE
(Styne), A star-studded Gala

CANDIDE, LFLC
(Bernstein)
New York City Opera

CARLOS KLEIBER CONDUCTS BEETHOVEN
(Beethoven)
Concertgebouw Orchestra

COMEDY OF ERRORS, LFLC
William Shakespeare
Flying Karamazov Brothers

AN EVENING WITH PLÁCIDO DOMINGO, LFLC
New York City Opera Orchestra

GIAN CARLO MENOTTI: THE MUSICAL MAGICIAN

THE GOLDEN YEARS
3-part series:
THE EBONY TOWER
adapted from John Fowles;
MONSIGNOR QUIXOTE
adapted from Graham Greene;
DECEMBER FLOWER
adapted from Judy Allen

GOYA
(Menotti)
Washington Opera

HANSEL AND GRETEL
(Humperdinck)
Vienna Philharmonic

**IN MEMORY OF . . .
A BALLET BY JEROME ROBBINS,** DIA
Jerome Robbins
New York City Ballet

JAMES STEWART: A WONDERFUL LIFE

MARK MORRIS, DIA
Mark Morris
Mark Morris Dance Co.

MILES AHEAD: THE MUSIC OF MILES DAVIS*

MOSTLY MOZART FESTIVAL, LFLC
Mostly Mozart Orchestra

THE NIGHT OF MUSIC: A GLOBAL CELEBRATION

OTELLO
(Verdi)
Deutsche Oper Berlin

OZAWA
Boston Symphony Orchestra

QUARTERMAINE'S TERMS
Simon Gray

SEIZE THE DAY*
adapted from Saul Bellow

THE SILENTS (1): *THE THIEF OF BAGDAD*
restored film

STEVE REICH: A NEW MUSICAL LANGUAGE
(Reich)
Brooklyn Philharmonic

VLADIMIR HOROWITZ: THE LAST ROMANTIC *

WAGNER *
in 4 parts
Tony Palmer film

**ZUBIN MEHTA AND THE NEW YORK
PHILHARMONIC,** LFLC
(Ravel, Tchaikovsky)
New York Philharmonic

1987–1988

AIDA
(Verdi)
Houston Grand Opera

AMERICAN BALLET THEATRE, LFLC
American Ballet Theatre

ANDRÉ WATTS AND THE PHILHARMONIC, LFLC
New York Philharmonic

ASINAMALI!
(Ngema)

BACALL ON BOGART *
Documentary

**BALANCHINE AND CUNNINGHAM: AN EVENING
AT AMERICAN BALLET THEATRE,** DIA
American Ballet Theatre

BERNSTEIN ON BRAHMS
Part 6
(Brahms)
Vienna Philharmonic

CELEBRATING GERSHWIN
2-part series:
THE JAZZ AGE, 'S WONDERFUL!
(Gershwin)

CHRISTMAS WITH FLICKA *
*Frederica von Stade Sings Christmas Music
from Austria*

DAVID GORDON'S MADE IN U.S.A., DIA
David Gordon
American Ballet Theatre, D. Gordon Pick-Up Co.

DIE ZAUBERFLÖTE, LFLC
(Mozart)
New York City Opera

DON GIOVANNI *
(Mozart)
Salzburg Festival

**IN CONCERT: NEW JERSEY CHAMBER MUSIC
SOCIETY AND TOKYO STRING QUARTET**
*New Jersey Chamber Music Society,
Tokyo String Quartet*

THE MISER
Molière

**THE MUSIC MAKERS:
AN ASCAP CELEBRATION OF AMERICAN MUSIC**

NEW YEAR'S EVE AT THE PHILHARMONIC, LFLC
New York Philharmonic

NEW YORK PHILHARMONIC, LFLC
(Brahms, Beethoven)
New York Philharmonic

NIXON IN CHINA
(Adams)
Houston Grand Opera

ON THE MOVE: THE CENTRAL BALLET OF CHINA
Documentary

ONCE IN A LIFETIME
George S. Kaufman and Moss Hart
Royal Shakespeare Festival

PAUL TAYLOR: *ROSES* **and** *LAST LOOK,* DIA
Paul Taylor
Paul Taylor Dance Co.

PAVAROTTI RETURNS TO NAPLES
Documentary

THE SILENTS (2): *OUR HOSPITALITY*
reconstructed film

TALES FROM THE HOLLYWOOD HILLS
(3 teleplays from American short stories):
NATICA JACKSON
adapted from John O'Hara;
A TABLE AT CIRO'S
adapted from Budd Schulberg;
PAT HOBBY TEAMED WITH GENIUS
adapted from F. Scott Fitzgerald

TOSCANINI: THE MAESTRO

THE TURN OF THE SCREW
(Britten)
Covent Garden Chamber Ensemble

VON KARAJAN IN SALZBURG
Vienna Philharmonic

WOLF TRAP PRESENTS THE KIROV BALLET
Kirov Ballet

**WOLF TRAP SALUTES DIZZY GILLESPIE: A
TRIBUTE TO THE JAZZ MASTER** *

1988–1989

THE ASPERN PAPERS
(Argento)
Dallas Opera

BARYSHNIKOV DANCES BALANCHINE, DIA
George Balanchine
American Ballet Theatre

BERNSTEIN AT 70
Boston Symphony and Tanglewood Institute

CINDERELLA
(Rossini)
Salzburg Festival, Vienna Philharmonic

GREGORY HINES: TAP DANCE IN AMERICA, DIA

JOHN GIELGUD: AN ACTOR'S LIFE
Documentary

LA SYLPHIDE **WITH THE PENNSYLVANIA/
MILWAUKEE BALLET,** DIA
Pennsylvania & Milwaukee Ballet Cos.

LINDA RONSTADT: CANCIONES DE MI PADRE *
Ballet Folklorico de la Fonda

MADAMA BUTTERFLY
(Puccini)
Lyric Opera of Chicago

**MARIA CALLAS: AN OPERATIC BIOGRAPHY—
THE WOMAN BEHIND THE DIVA**

MELBA
4-part film

THE MIKADO *
(Gilbert and Sullivan)
English National Opera

THE NEW MOON
(Romberg)
New York City Opera

A NIGHT AT THE JOFFREY, DIA
Joffrey Ballet

NUREYEV'S *CINDERELLA*
Rudolf Nureyev
Paris Opera Ballet

THE PHILADELPHIA ORCHESTRA AT WOLF TRAP
(Rachmaninov, Shostakovich, Britten)
Philadelphia Orchestra

THE SILENTS (3): *THE EAGLE* *
restored film

TALES FROM THE HOLLYWOOD HILLS
(3 more teleplays from American short stories):
THE OLD RELIABLE
adapted from P.G. Wodehouse;
GOLDEN LAND
adapted from William Faulkner;
THE CLOSED SET
adapted from Gavin Lambert

TESTIMONY
Tony Palmer film portrait of Dmitri Shostakovich
London Philharmonic

WYNTON MARSALIS: BLUES AND SWING *
Marsalis Quartet